DOG ONLY KNOWS

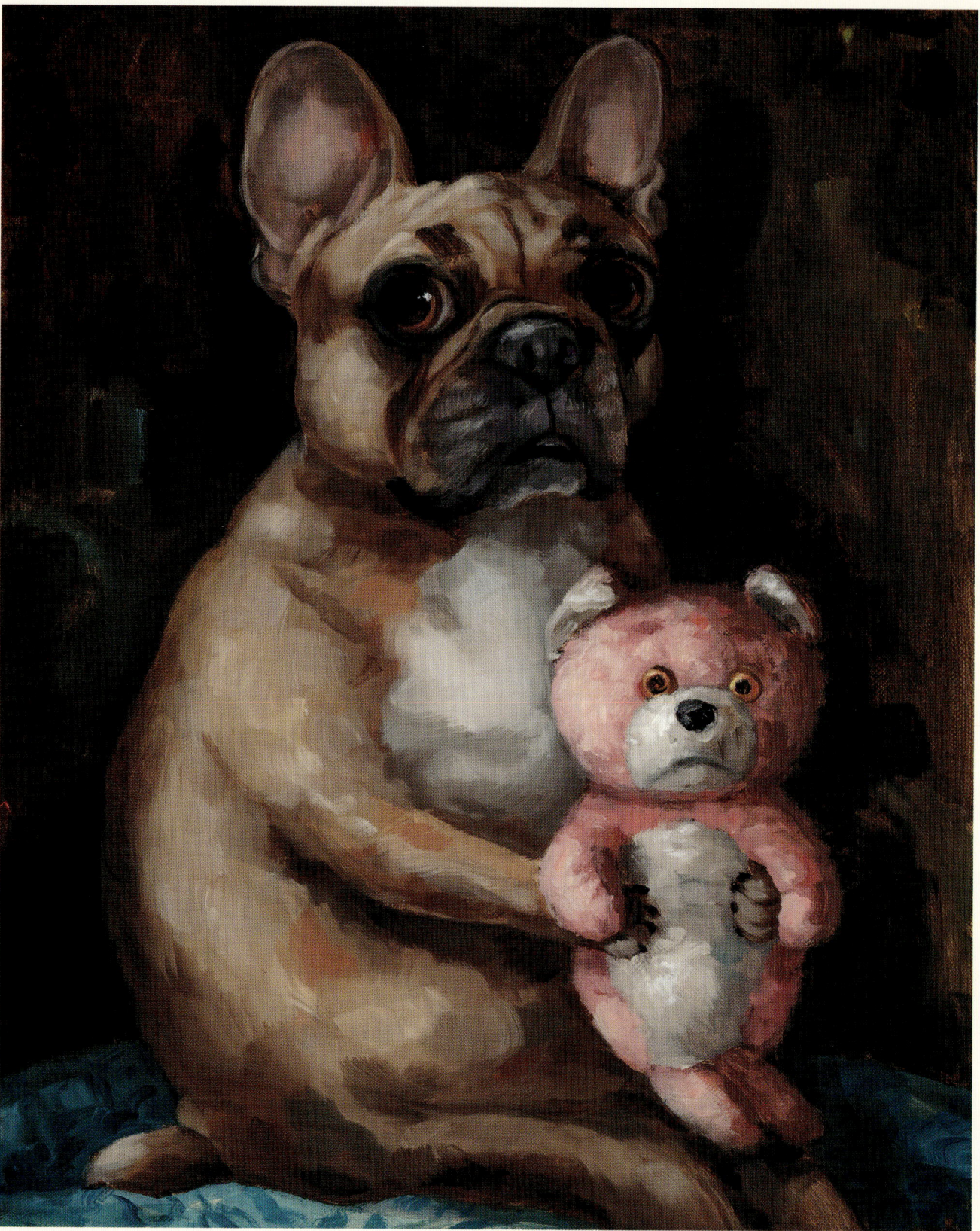

DOG ONLY KNOWS

THE DOG PORTRAITS OF
Alison Friend

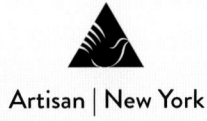

Artisan | New York

Library of Congress Cataloging-in-Publication Data is on file.
ISBN 978-1-64829-478-5

Design by Jane Treuhaft

Artisan books may be purchased in bulk for business, educational, or promotional use. For information, please contact your local bookseller or the Hachette Book Group Special Markets Department at special.markets@hbgusa.com.

The publisher is not responsible for websites (or their content) that are not owned by the publisher.

The Hachette Speakers Bureau provides a wide range of authors for speaking events. To find out more, go to hachettespeakersbureau.com or email HachetteSpeakers@hbgusa.com.

Published by Artisan,
an imprint of Workman Publishing,
a division of Hachette Book Group, Inc.
1290 Avenue of the Americas
New York, NY 10104
artisanbooks.com

The Artisan name and logo are registered trademarks of Hachette Book Group, Inc.

Printed in China (APO) on responsibly sourced paper

Jacket © 2025 Hachette Book Group, Inc.

10 9 8 7 6 5 4 3 2

Frontispiece: *Resting Face*

For all the dogs I have loved

FOREWORD

The front door closes.

Outside, the car starts up and slowly pulls out of the driveway.

A moment passes and a quick sniff of the air confirms . . . the Second-Best Part of the Day has begun!

What is the Second-Best Part of the Day, you ask?

It can be a time for shenanigans, like when your terrier breaks out the poker cards, pours a couple fingers of whiskey, and lights a cigar. Perhaps it's a time for relaxation, like when your dachshund applies a cucumber eye mask for a spa day. Or maybe it's a time for guilty pleasures, like when your retriever cracks open their favorite romance novel.

You probably know the old adage: *When the cat is away, the mice will play.*

But what does the cat—or dog—do when the humans are away? This is the question Alison Friend answers in her charming series of anthropomorphic paintings, reminiscent of classical portraiture and lovingly rendered in oil on gesso.

When I first encountered Alison's work, I immediately fell in love with her ability to imagine the secret lives of pets—painting them beautifully, capturing their personalities, and evoking our own pets, current and past.

The titles, the stories, and the little details will tug at your heartstrings. It's rare for someone to experience Alison's work for the first time without laughing or smiling. I saw this firsthand as I exhibited and lived with Alison's work for the past couple of years.

But it eventually dawned on me that perhaps what I love even more are the things Alison doesn't paint.

She has created a world where our pets are never scared, never lonely. They don't grow old, their vision doesn't dim, their muzzles don't gray. They don't whine or cry. They don't sit by the door, anxiously waiting for us to come home.

And when we do return? When the car pulls back into the driveway, when the keys jingle in the door? That's when the Second-Best Part of the Day ends and the Very Best Part of the Day begins . . . when we're reunited again.

After all, there's another old adage that every pet knows by heart: *When my human returns, there are no concerns.*

—KEN HASHIMOTO HARMAN,
Gallery Owner and Curator
NY, SF, LA

INTRODUCTION

I have drawn and painted animals for as long as I can remember.

My dad was an artist, and I always wanted to be just like him. I wanted to play cricket like he did. I wanted to wear the same shoes he did (I don't know why I remember that, but I do). Mostly I wanted to paint like he did. He loved animals, and he painted a lot of horses and birds and, occasionally, dogs. He used to paint in his shed at the bottom of the garden, and I remember vividly the smell of sawdust and linseed oil. When I began painting in oils a few years ago, the smell of the linseed oil took me right back. This might be part of the reason I love using oil paints so much.

He passed away when I was eight years old. His gifts to me were a love of painting and drawing and, dare I say, his talent for it. As a child I would spend hours copying animals from encyclopaedias and drawing funny comic strips about the neighbour's cats. It's a superpower to be able to make people laugh, and humour has remained a huge part of my work.

Before the pandemic, I had been working full-time as a children's book illustrator, but when the world shut down, I moved away from digital work and began painting in oils. Character creation was my favourite part of illustrating books, so it felt natural to paint portraits of imagined animal characters.

I found I loved returning to a traditional medium—and it was this, along with generous responses to the new work on social media, that spurred me to paint more.

Nostalgia has always been a big part of my work, especially in these portraits. Interiors with recurring features from my childhood. A wallpaper pattern and a particular colour palette. Memories of visiting aunts and uncles and their dogs. (I looked forward to seeing the dogs more than anything.) The snacks and treats we ate. All these things evoke such a strong sense of comfort and belonging.

By the time I've finished each piece, the character feels like a friend. I rarely begin with a firm idea of what the character will look like. One brushstroke can change their expression. I go with it, and they make themselves known.

Since I began painting these portraits, people have started to send me photos and stories about their dogs. These lovely connections have made this journey so much more rewarding.

So here we are! This is the book, and I really hope you enjoy it.

There are moments when I pinch myself and ask, *How did I get here?*

Dog only knows!

—ALISON FRIEND

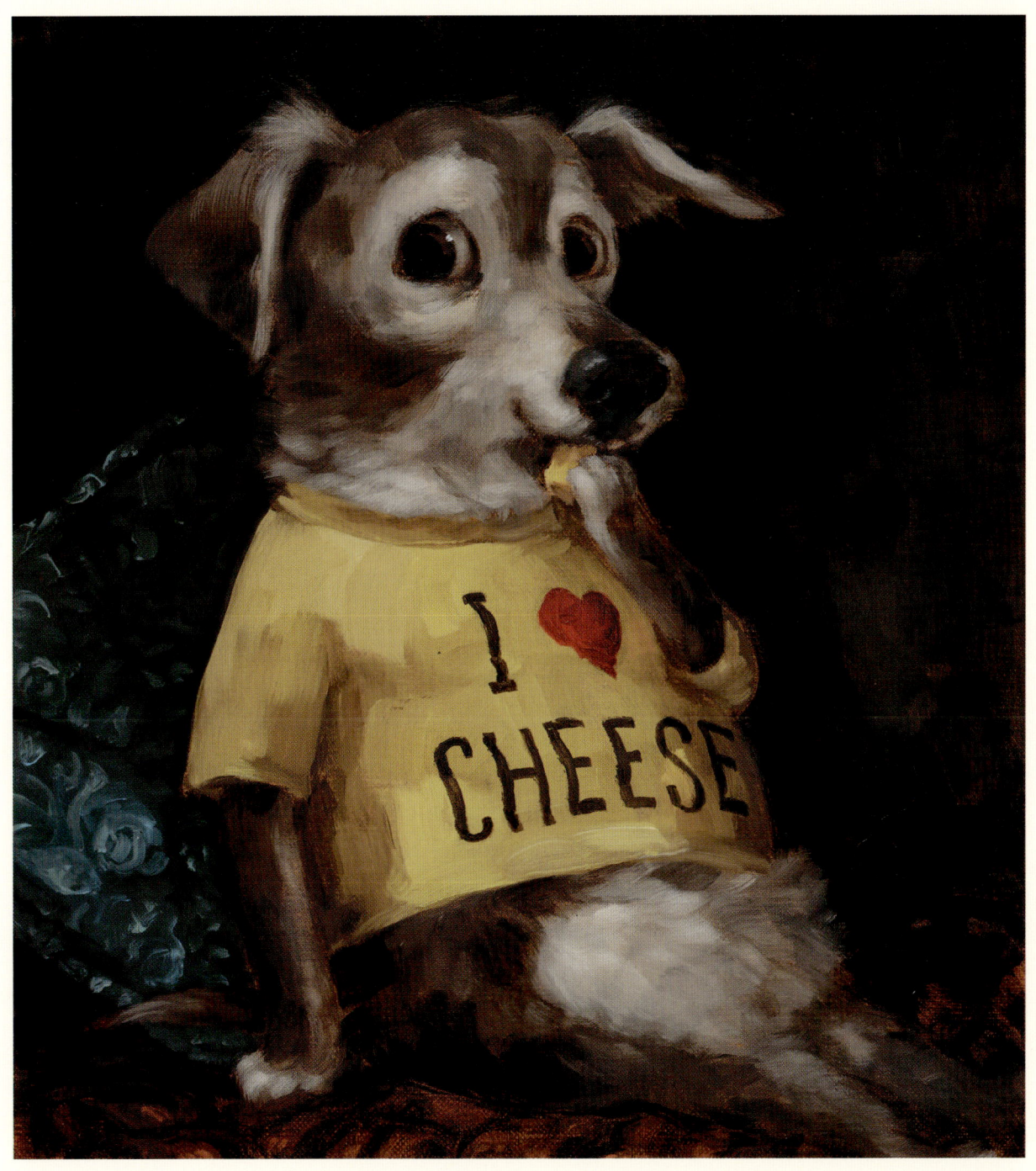

I HEART CHEESE | When life gives you cheese, make it extra cheesy!

RUPERT

Not your standard poodle

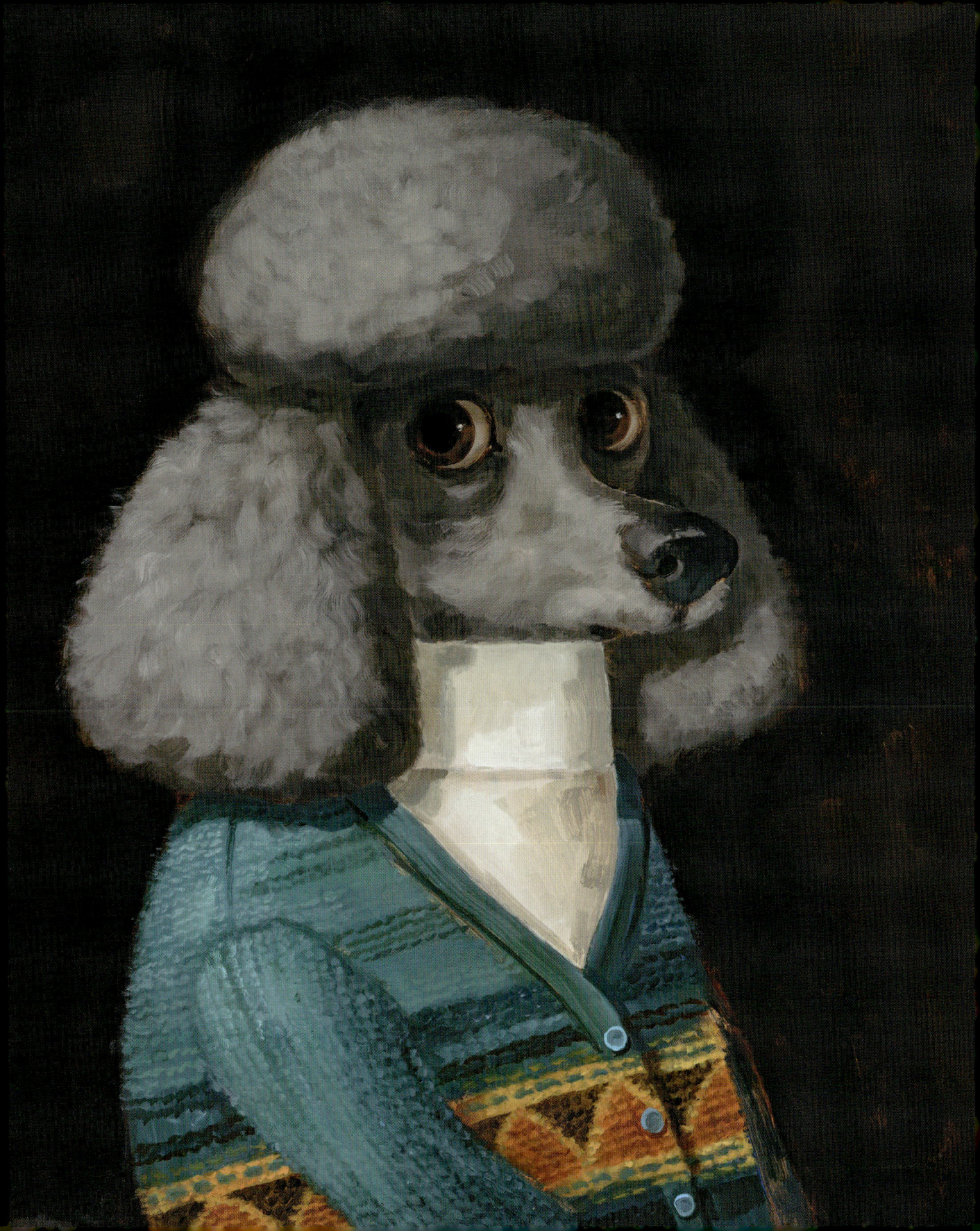

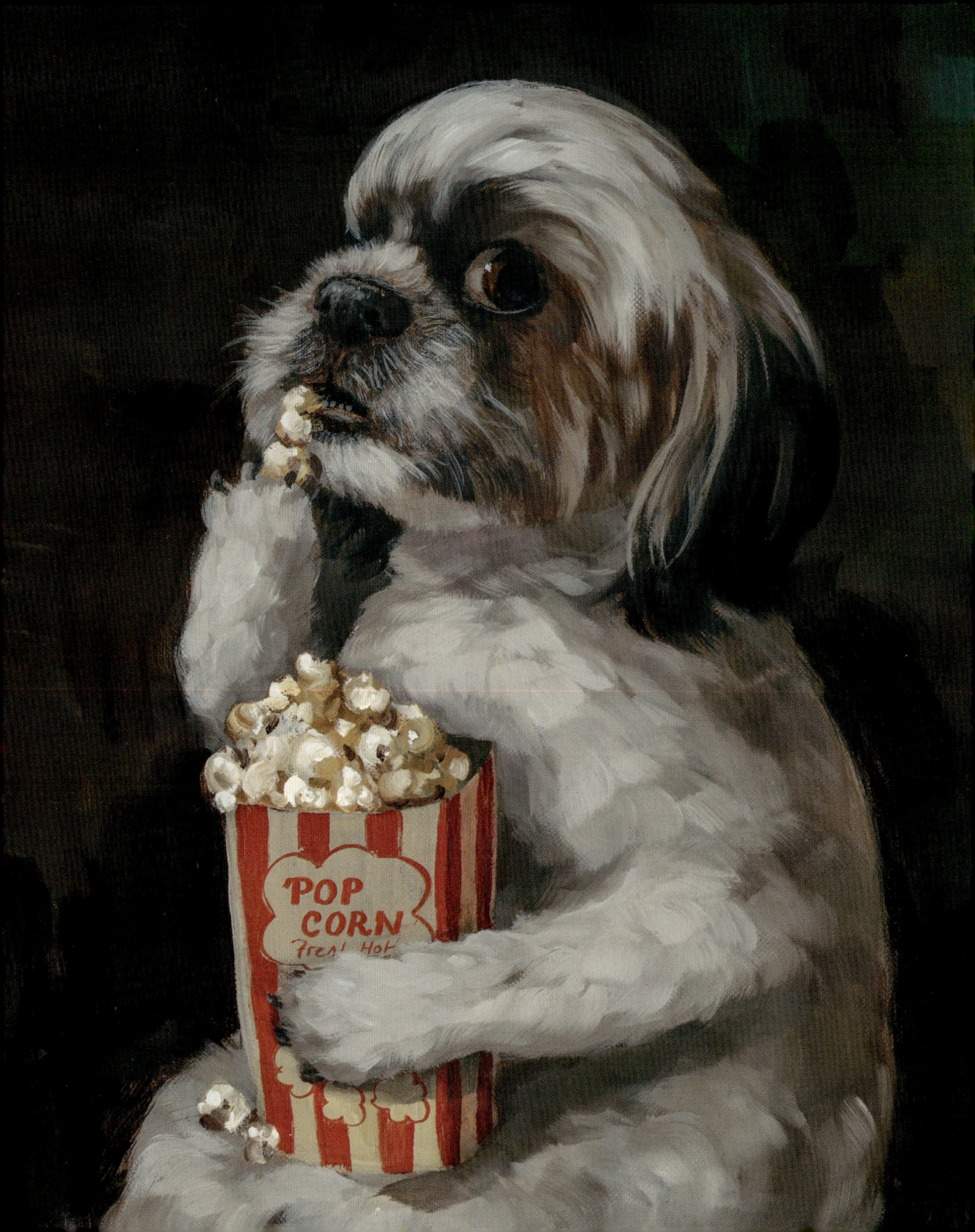

MAGGIE

When it comes to popcorn . . .
she isn't good at sharing

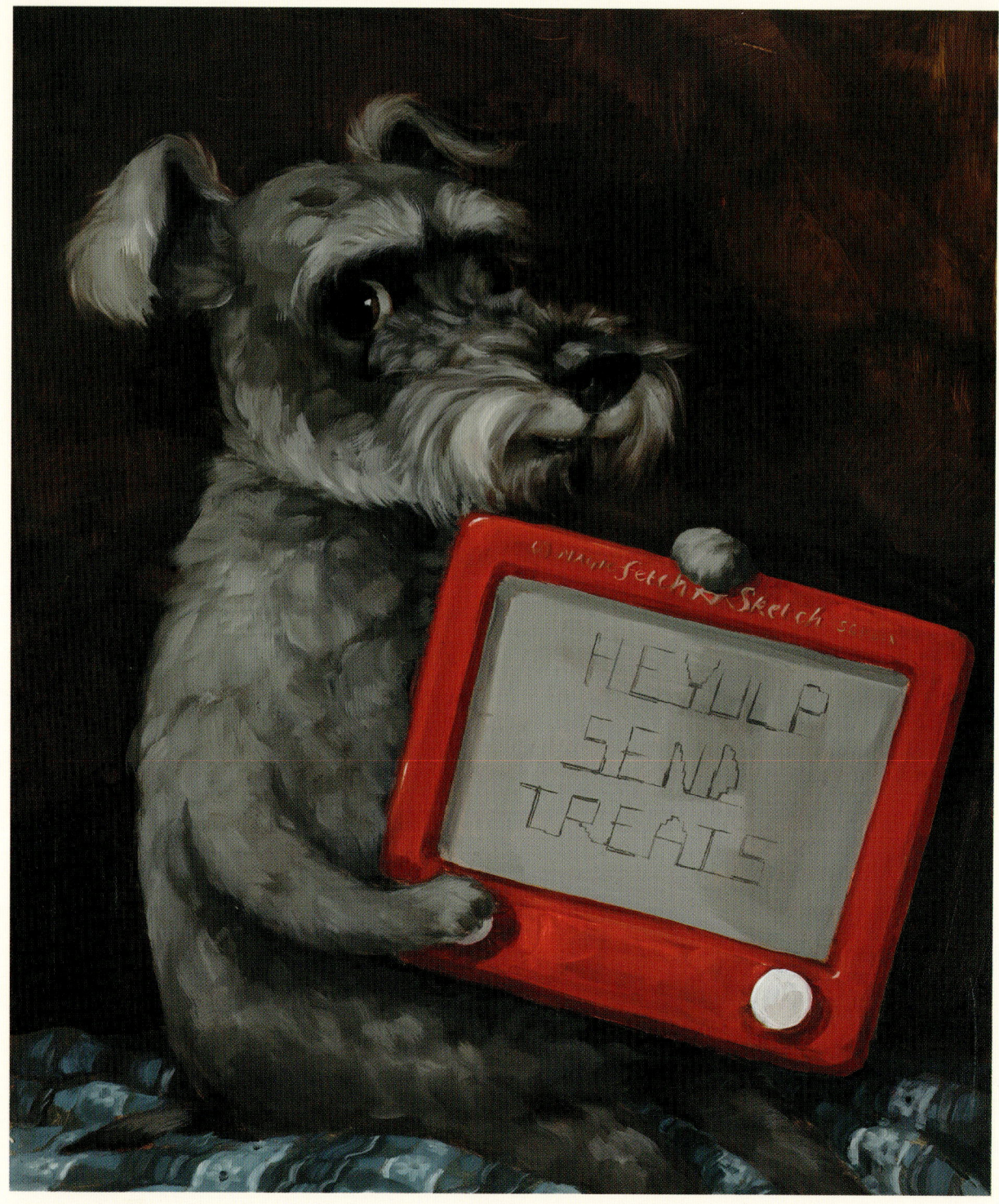

HEYULP SEND TREATS | Anything with peanut butter

MIDGE | She likes to keep her mind busy

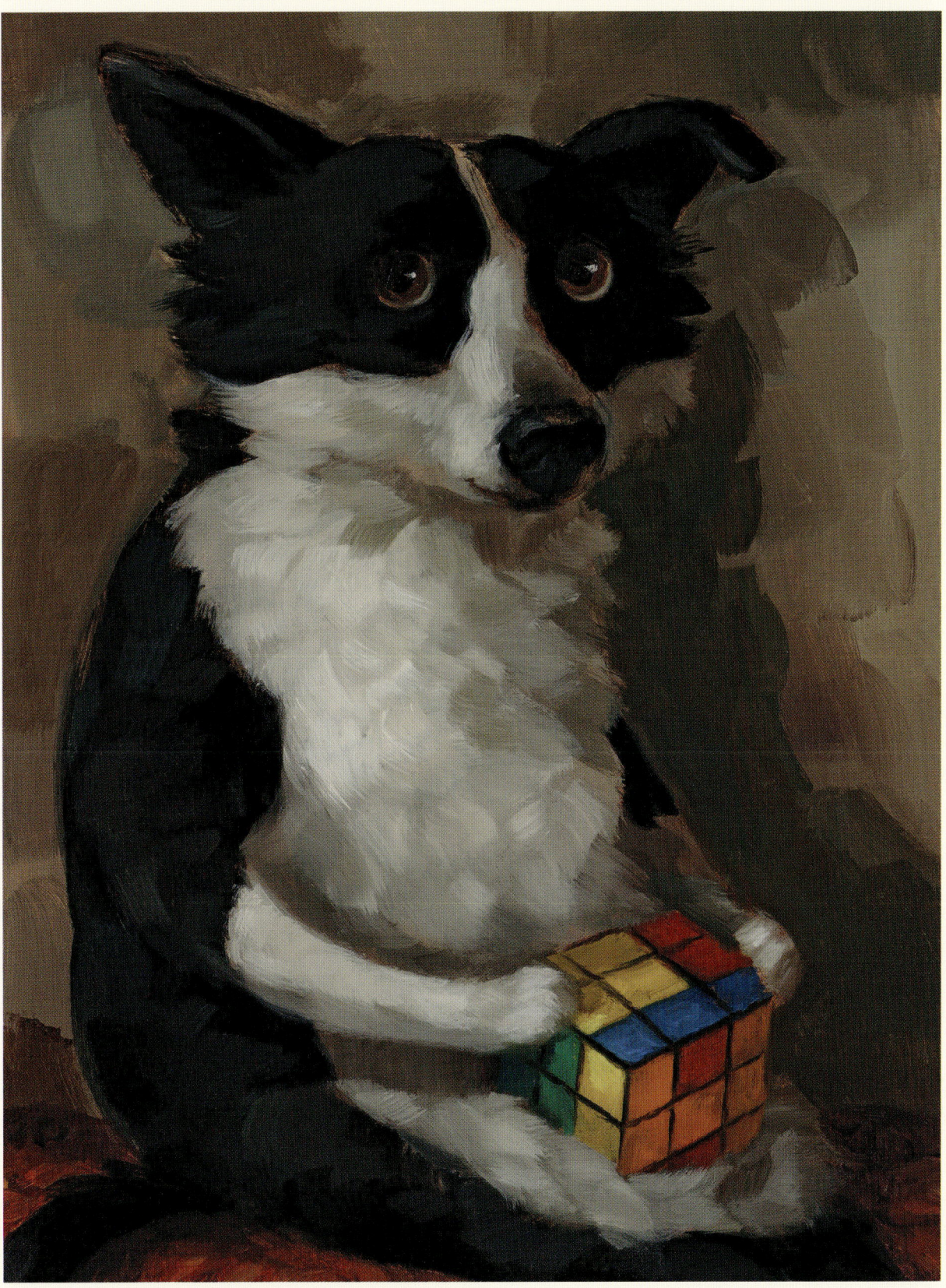

GOOD GIRL

Like a donut with sprinkles. Like cherry pie
and ice cream. Like a chocolate-covered profiterole.
She is sweet—the sweetest, in fact!

From the soft floof on the top of her head to the tips of
her four dainty paws to the very end of her pompom tail,
she is a good girl through and through.

Oh, until it's time to leave the park and she's a little sh*t!

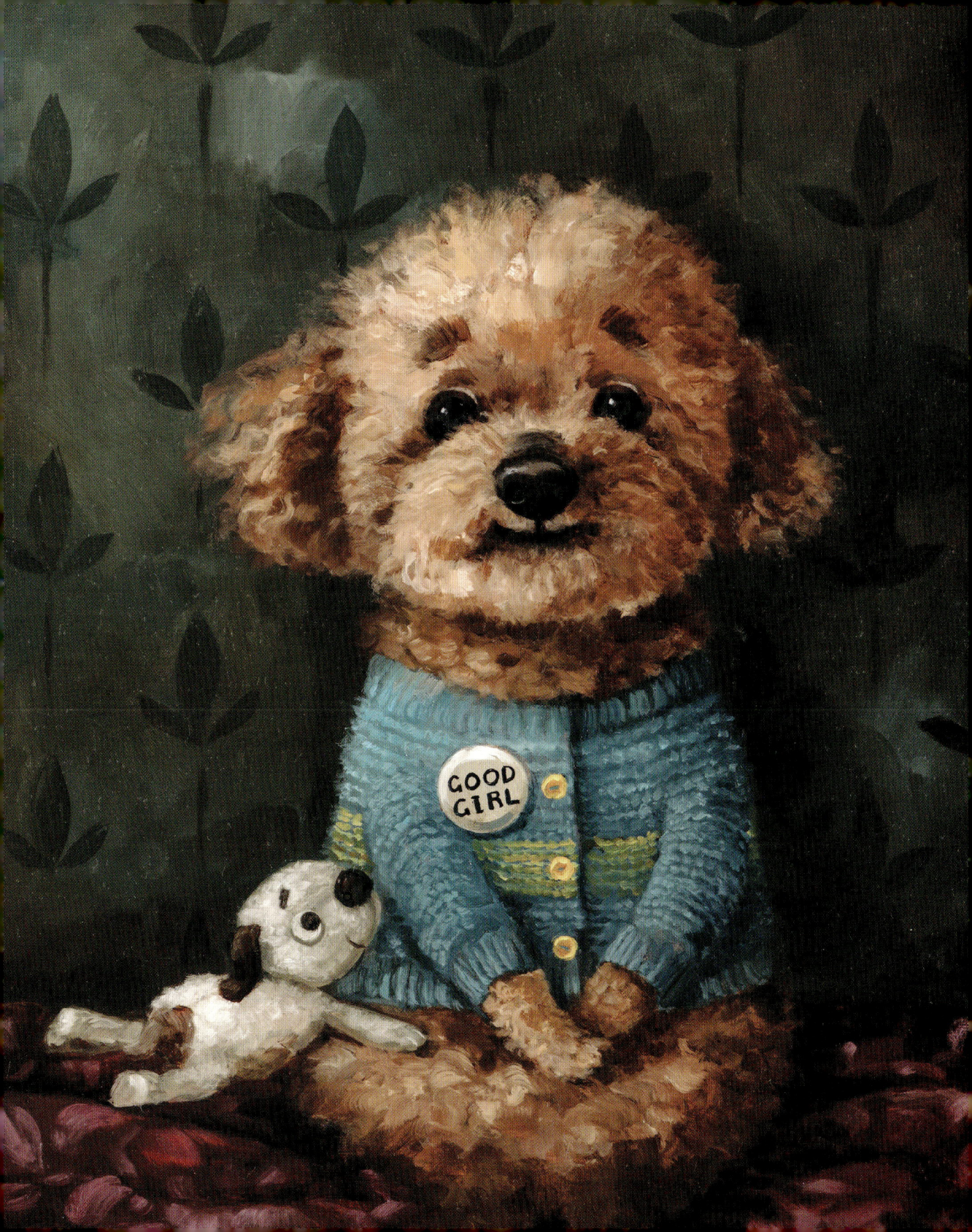

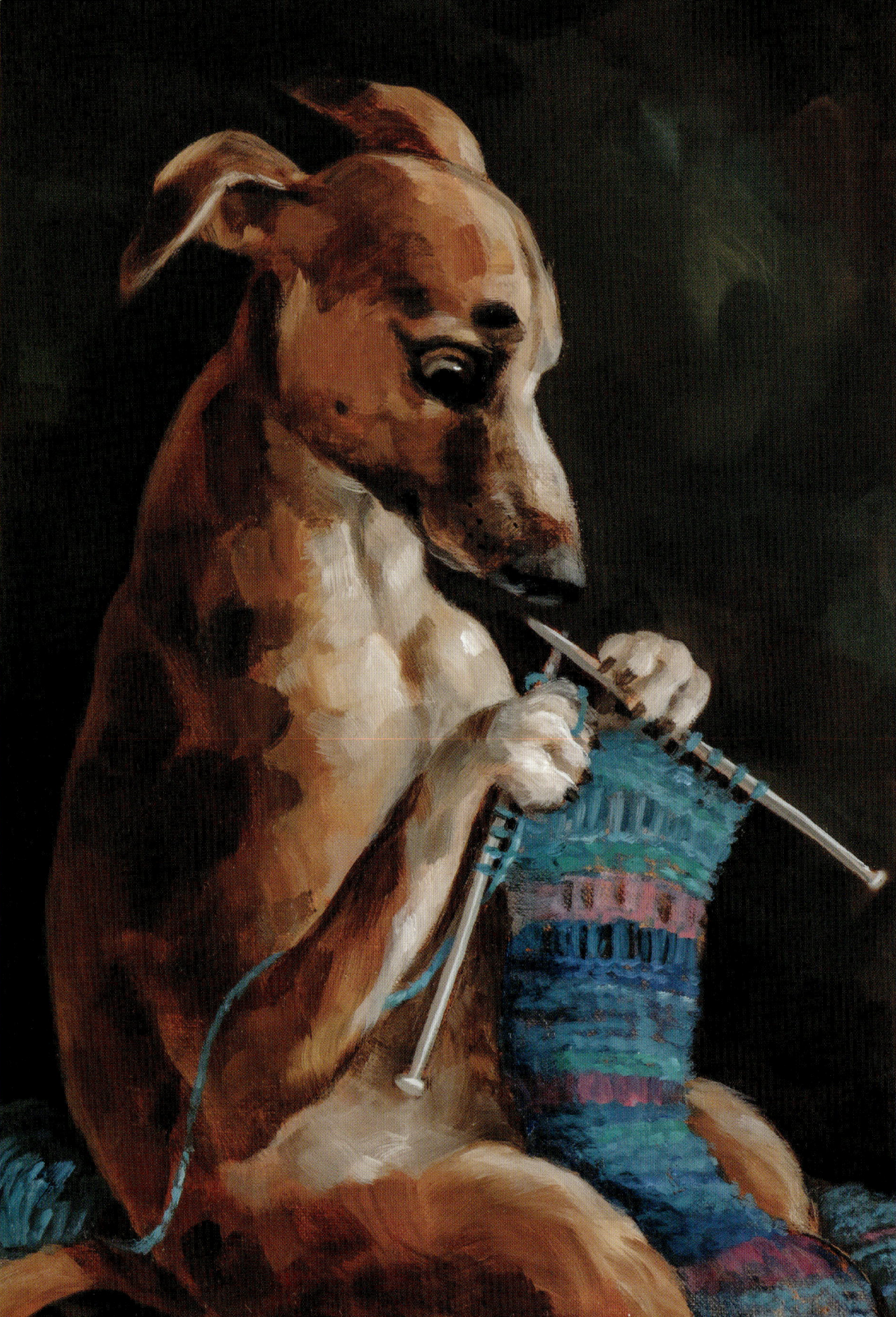

KNITTING WHIPPET

Friday night, Netflix and knitting

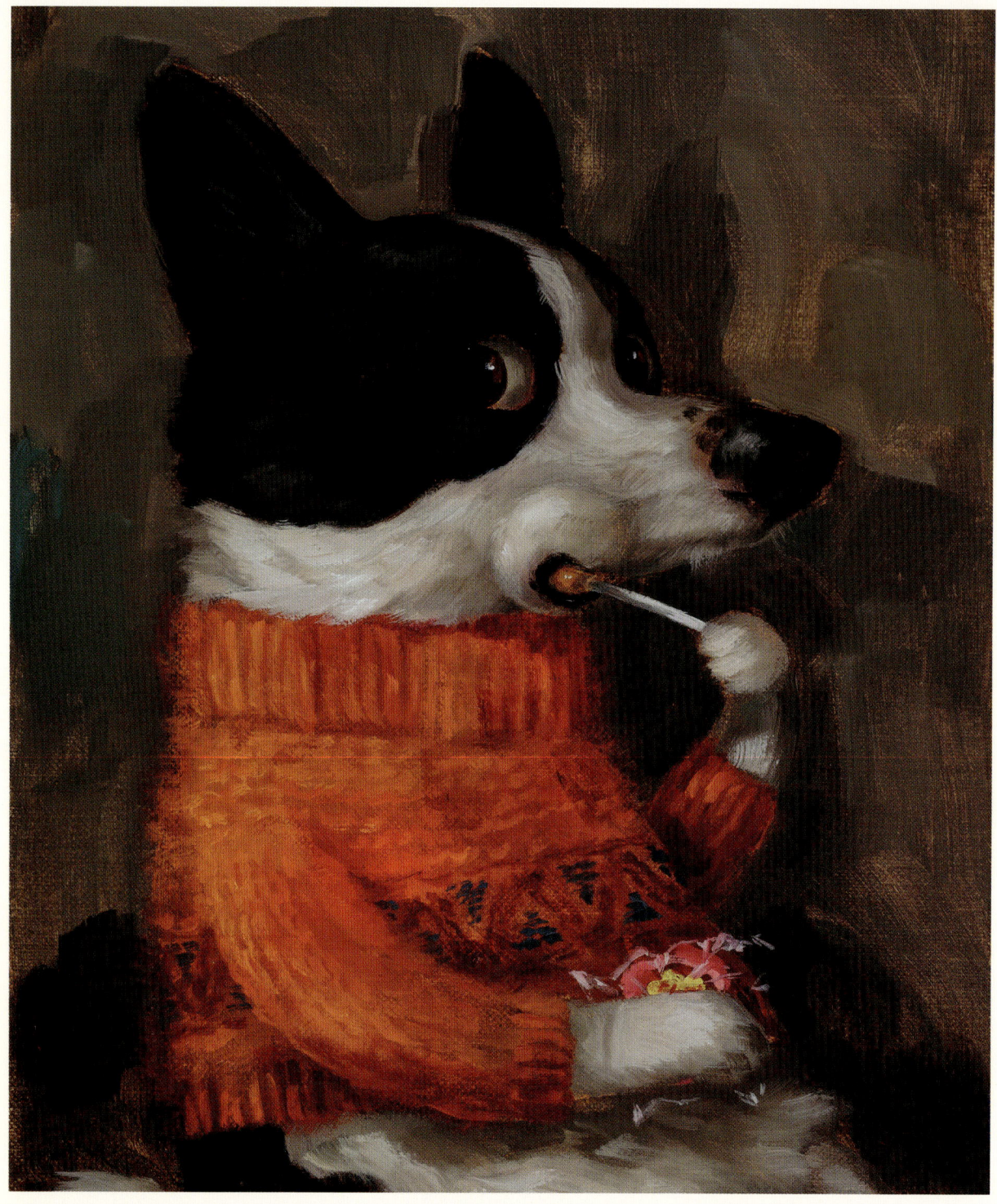

CHUPA CHOPS | No idea how he unwrapped it

LOLLY LOVER | She knows how to keep cool

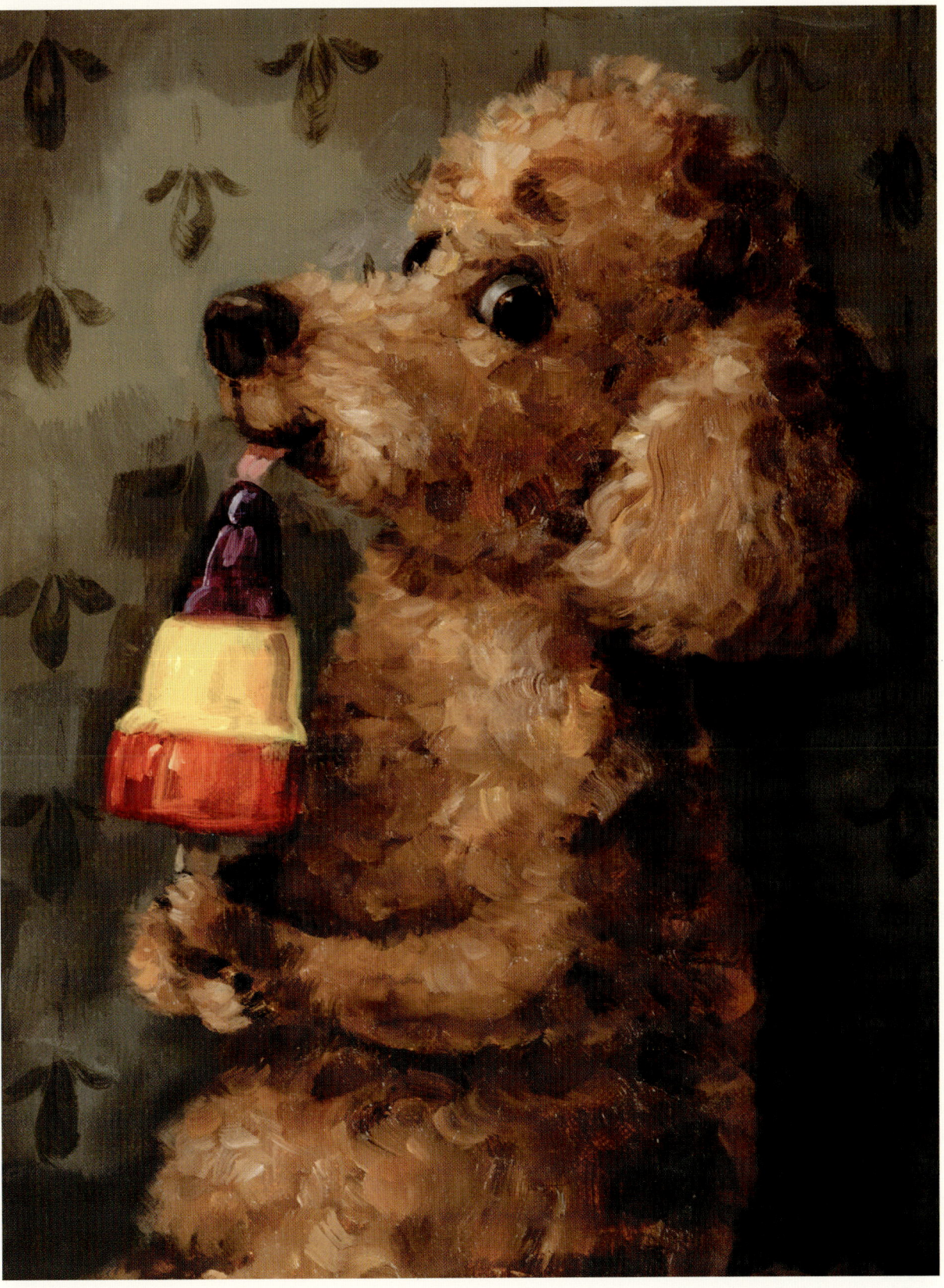

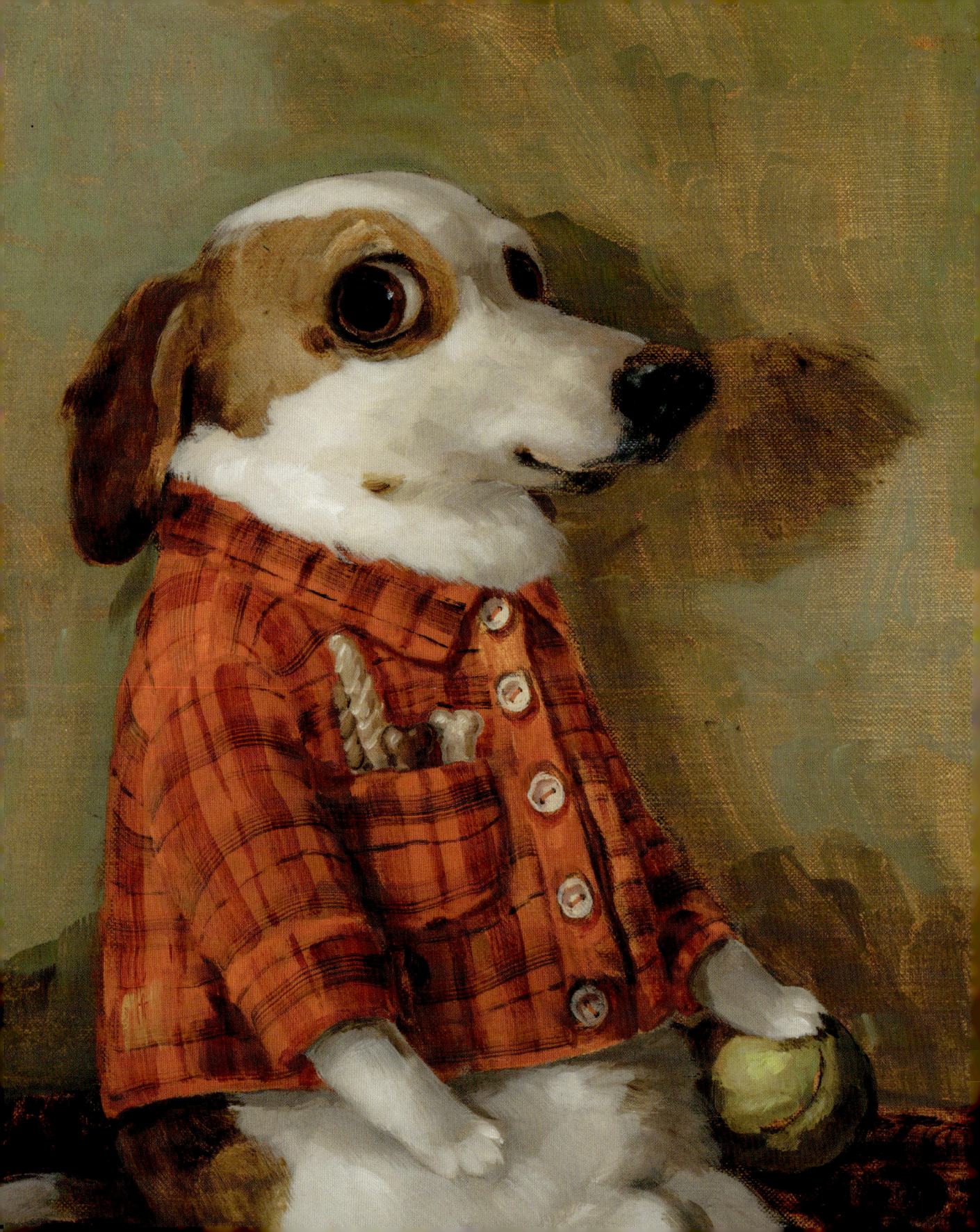

NORMA

She is always park ready

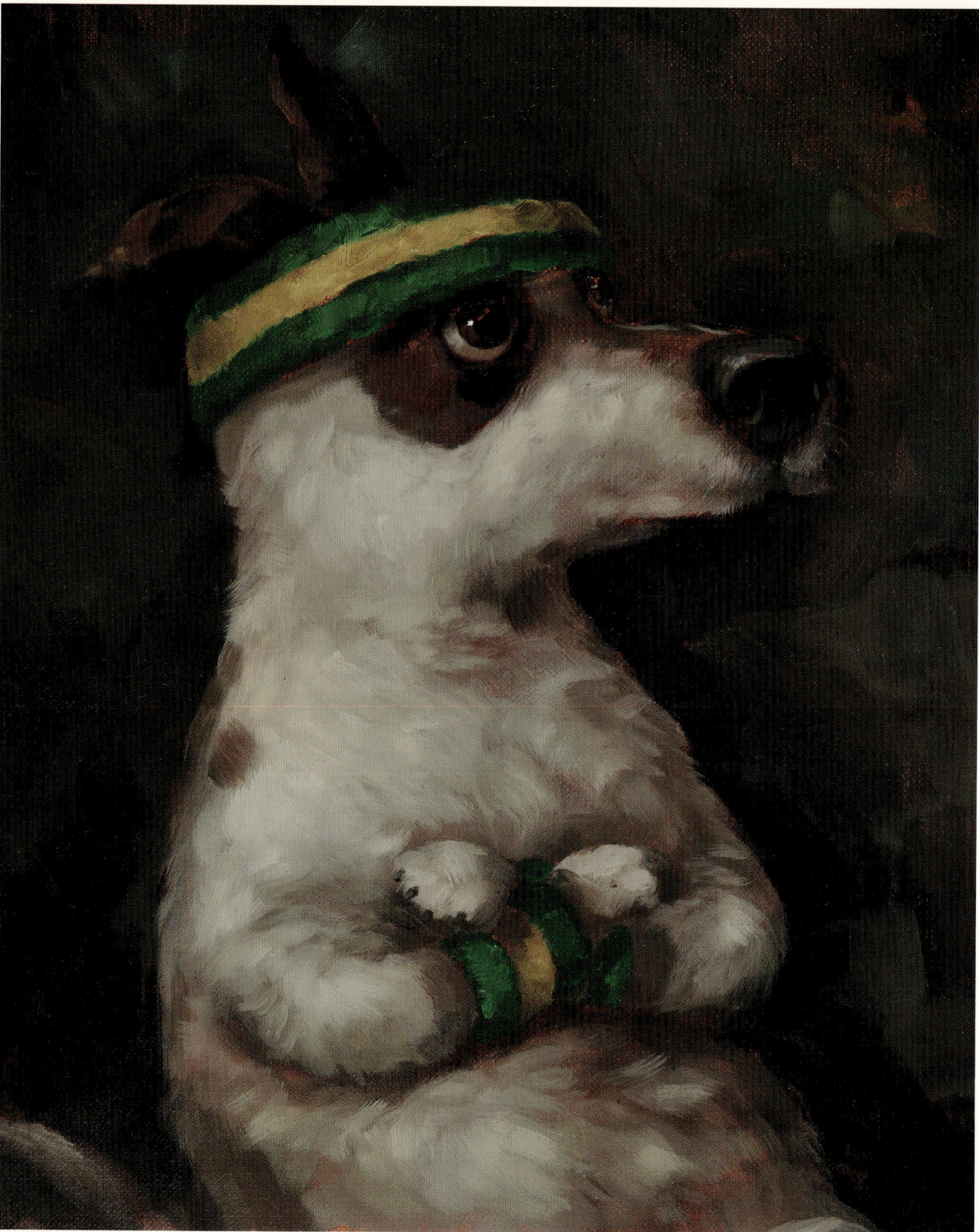

CLIVE

He is serious about everything—
biscuit eating, squirrel chasing,
and ball fetching

LOLA

People to see, bums to sniff

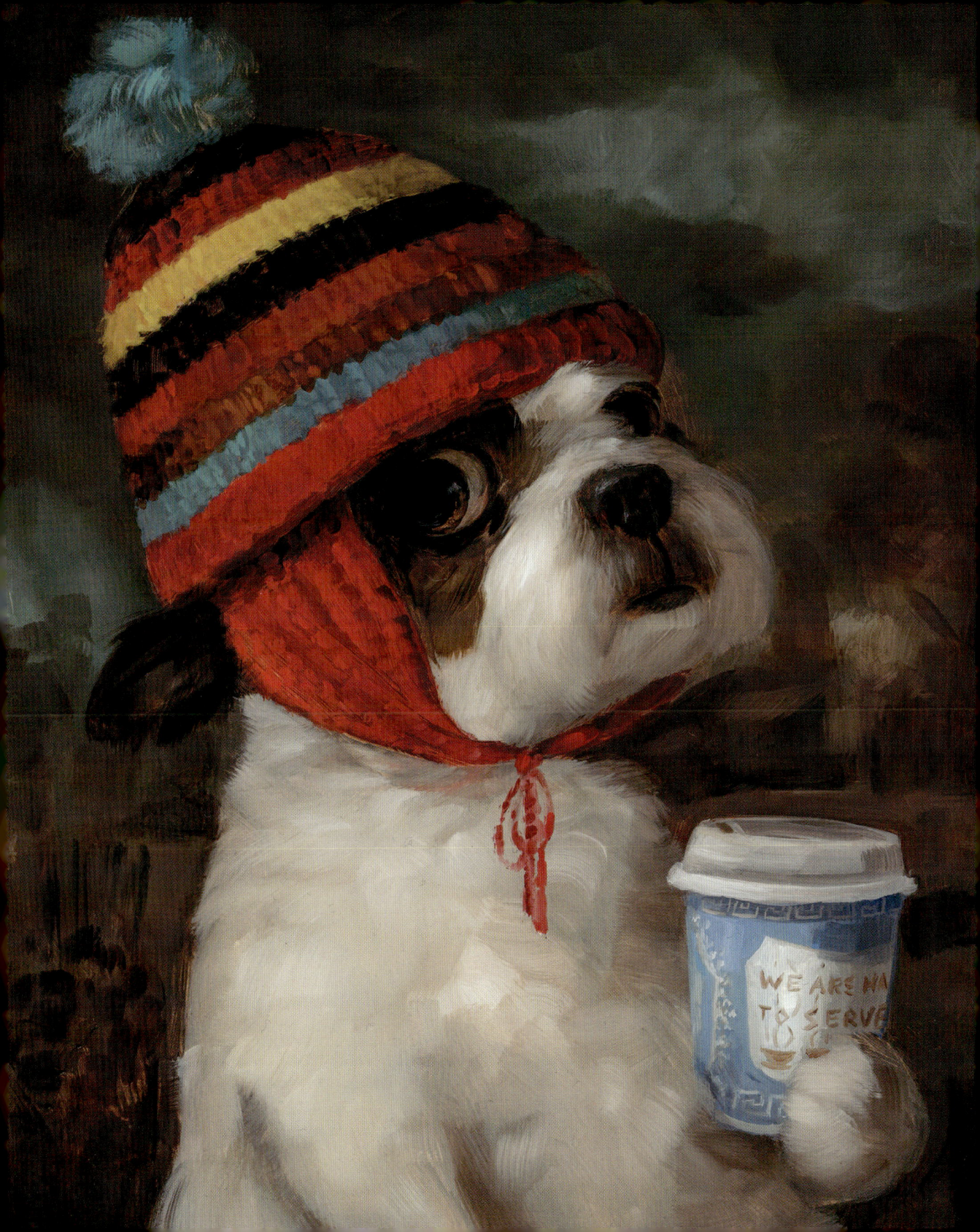

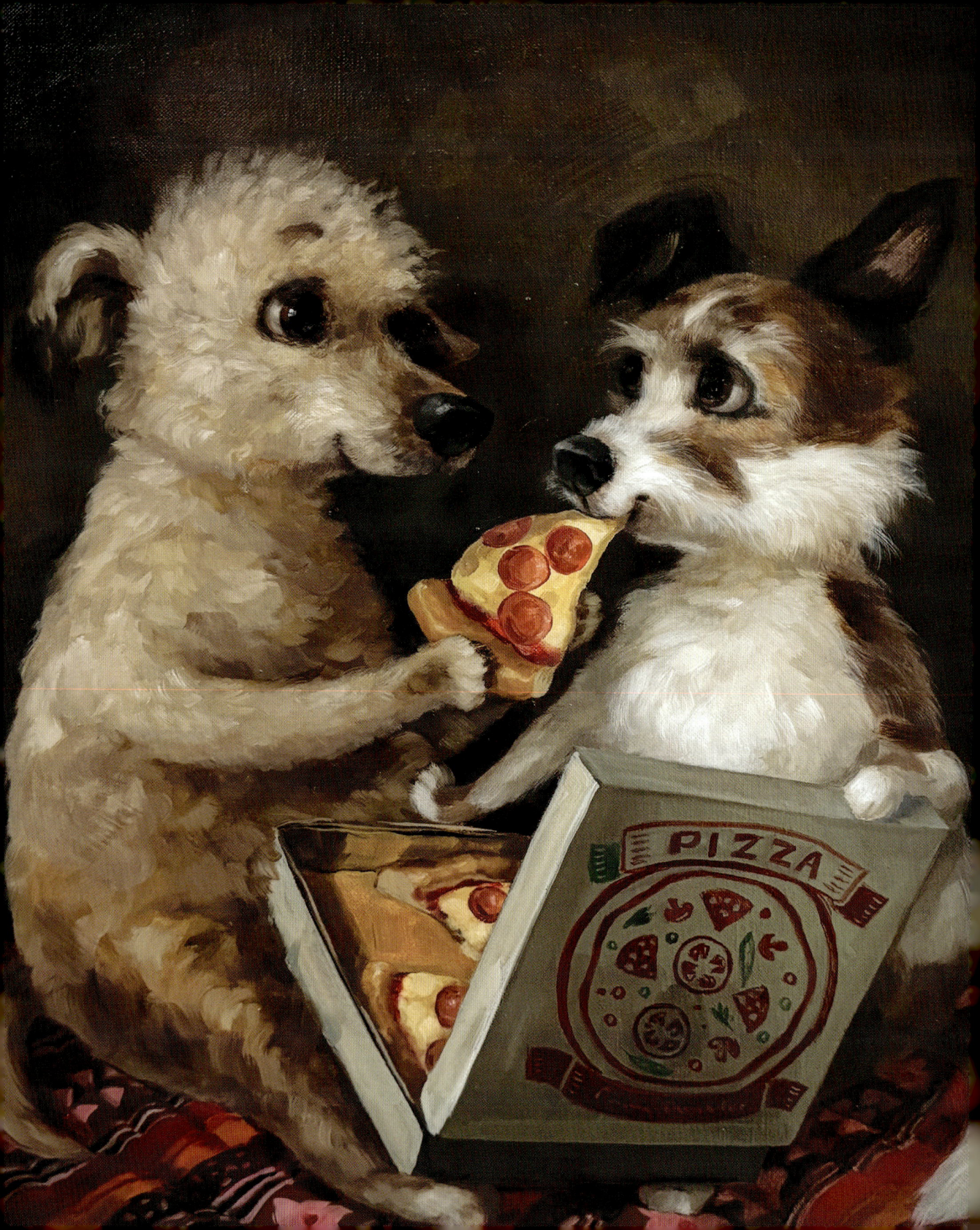

PIZZA LOVERS

Pupperoni for two

STEVIL KNIEVEL

The little-known canine counterpart of the famous Evel Knievel.

Some would say jumping rows of cats is not quite so daring as jumping rows of cars, but let me just ask: Can a car lash out and take a swipe at your undercarriage with razor-sharp claws? I don't think so!

This makes Stevil by far the braver of the two. Just a slurp of orange juice and he's ready! (At least, we think it's just orange juice.)

Go STEVIL!!!

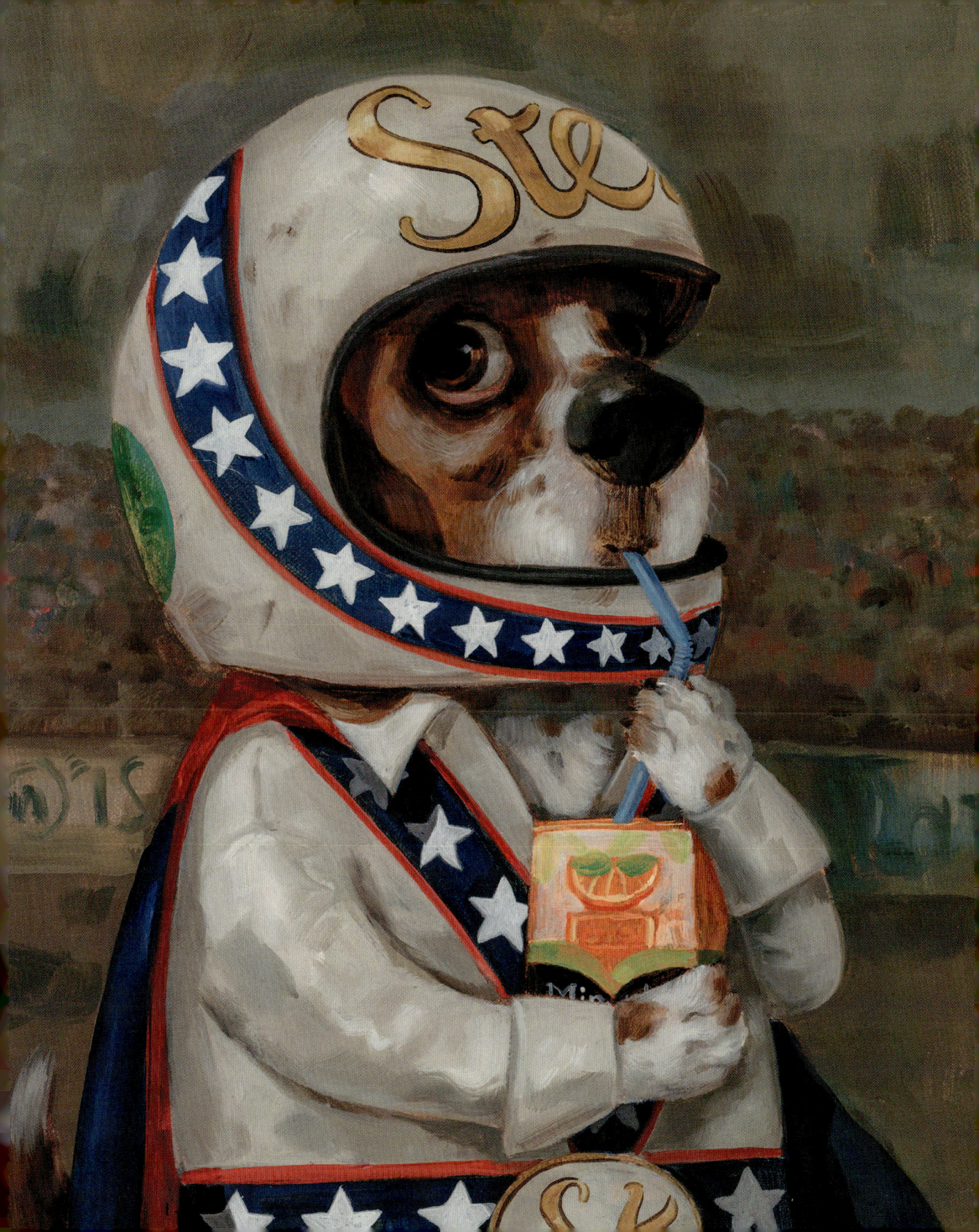

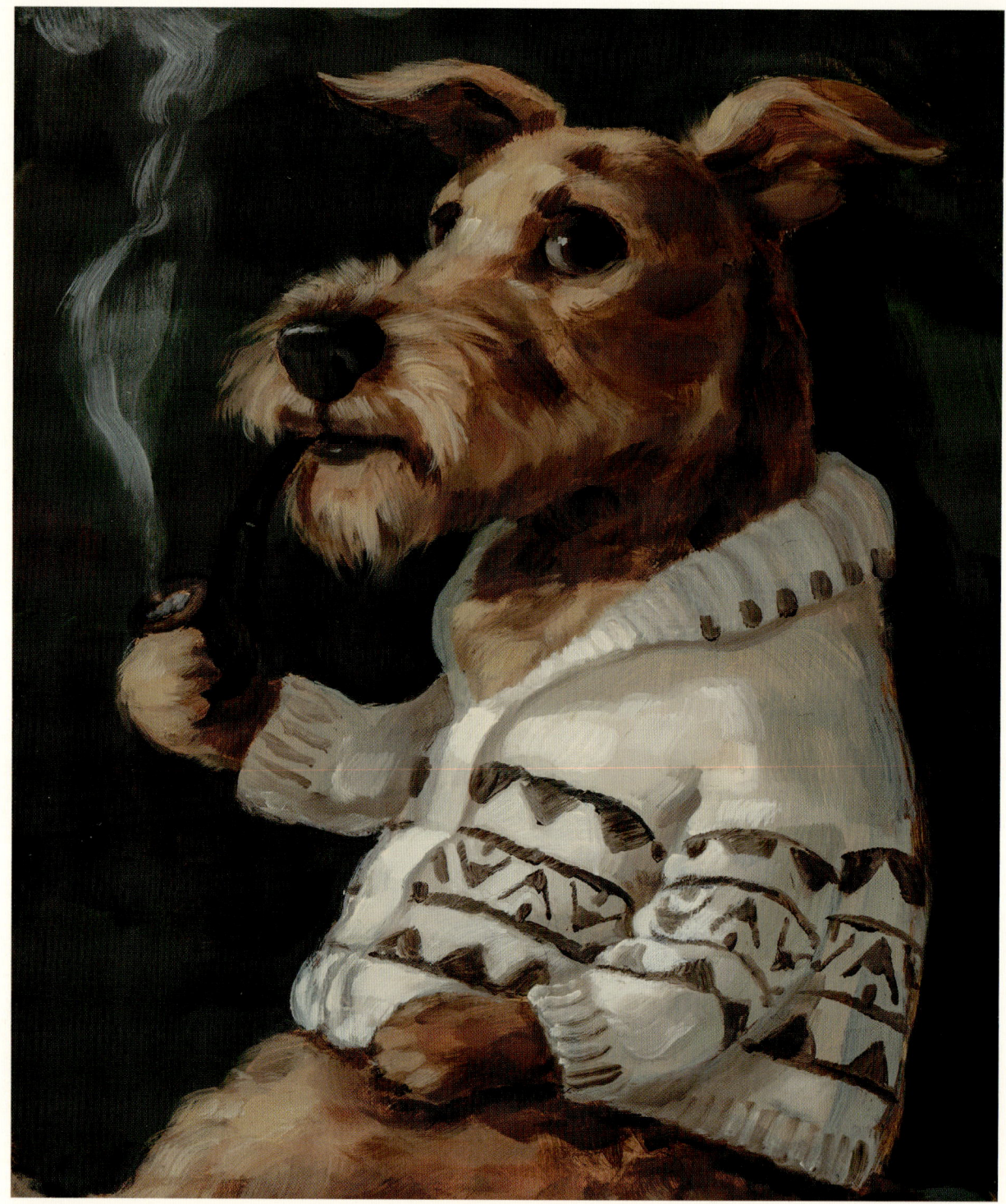

SEAMUS | With a taste for good sweaters and perhaps a dram of something strong

SAUSAGE LOVER | A sausage aficionado

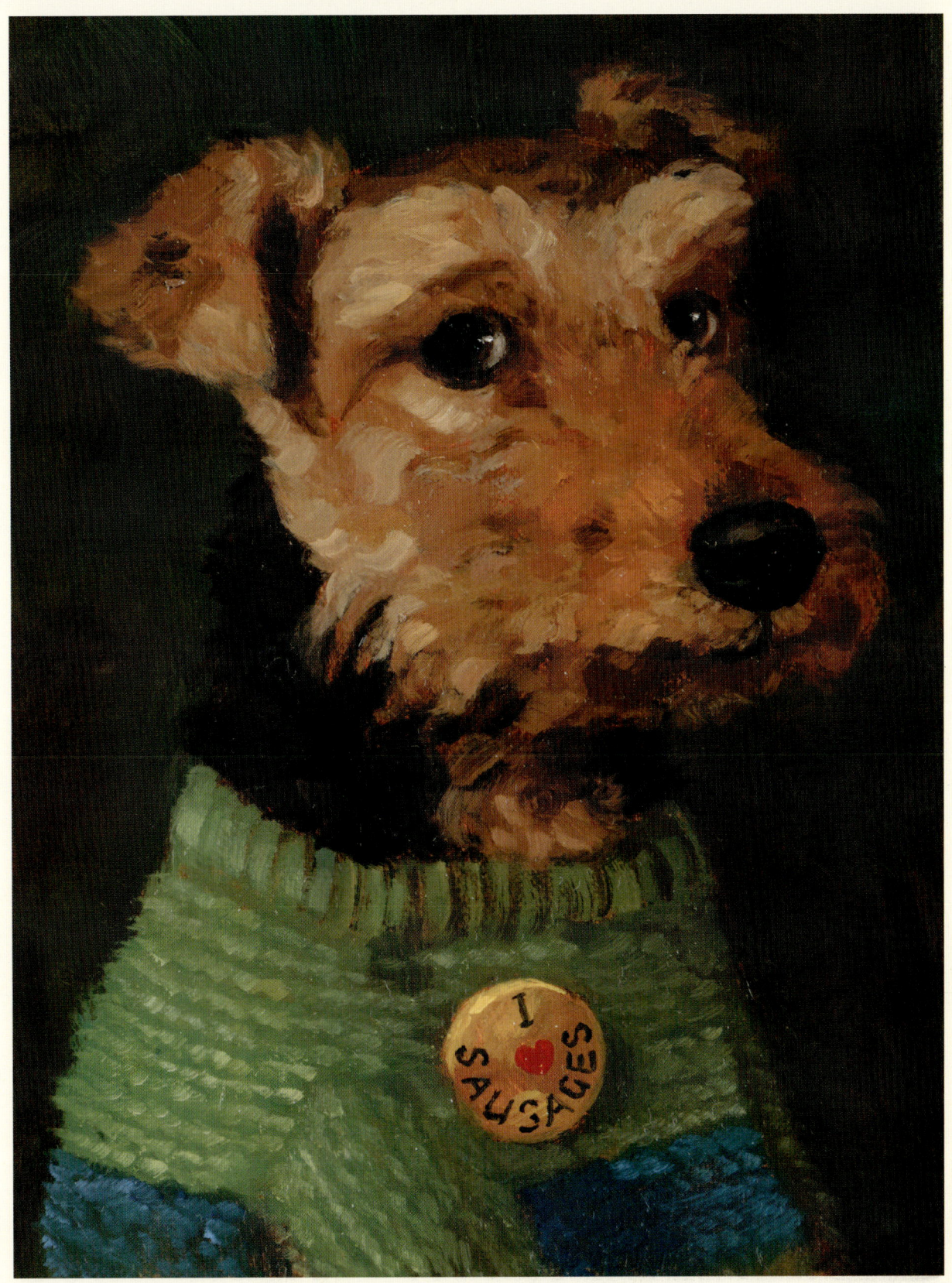

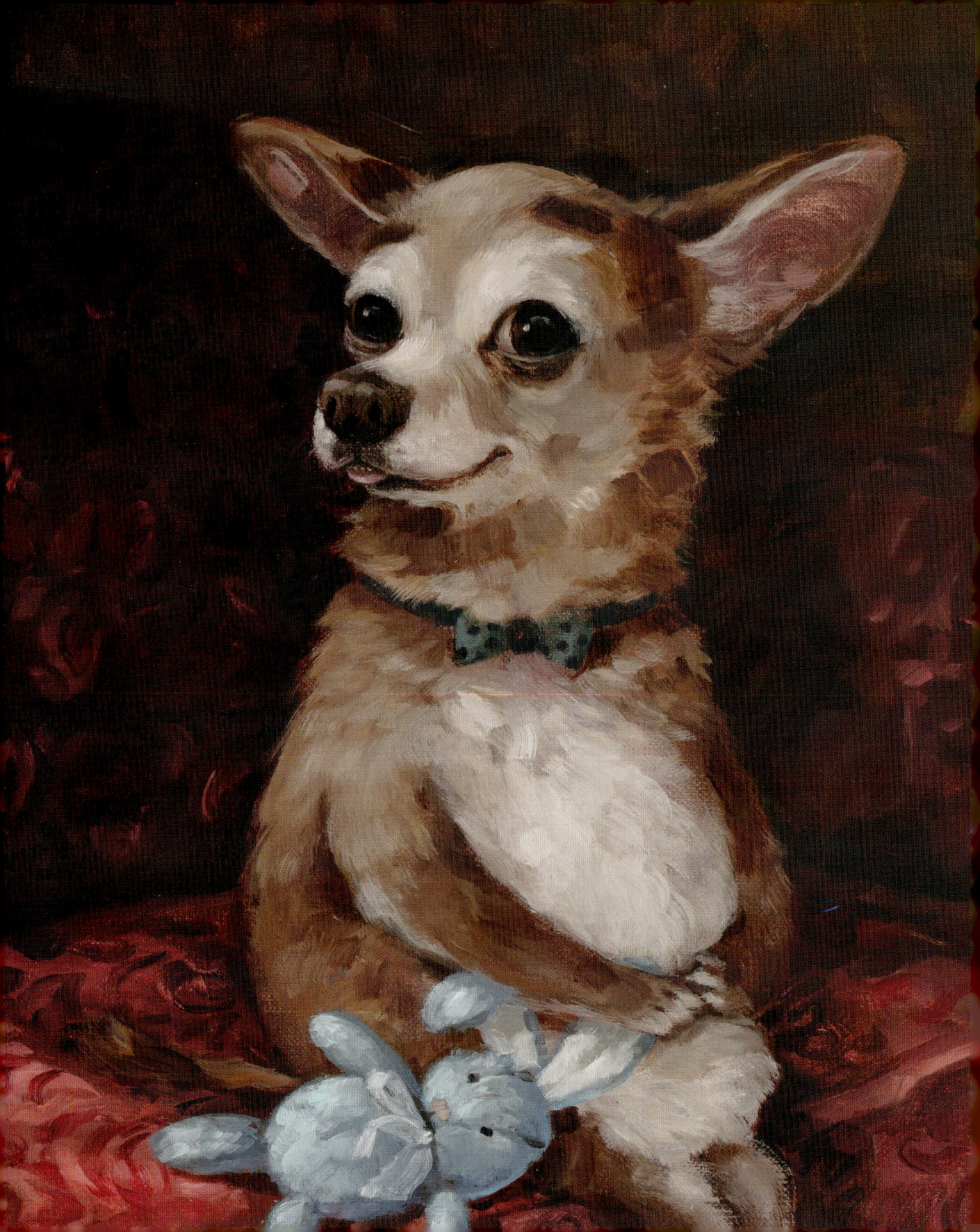

OTTO

He loves romance novels

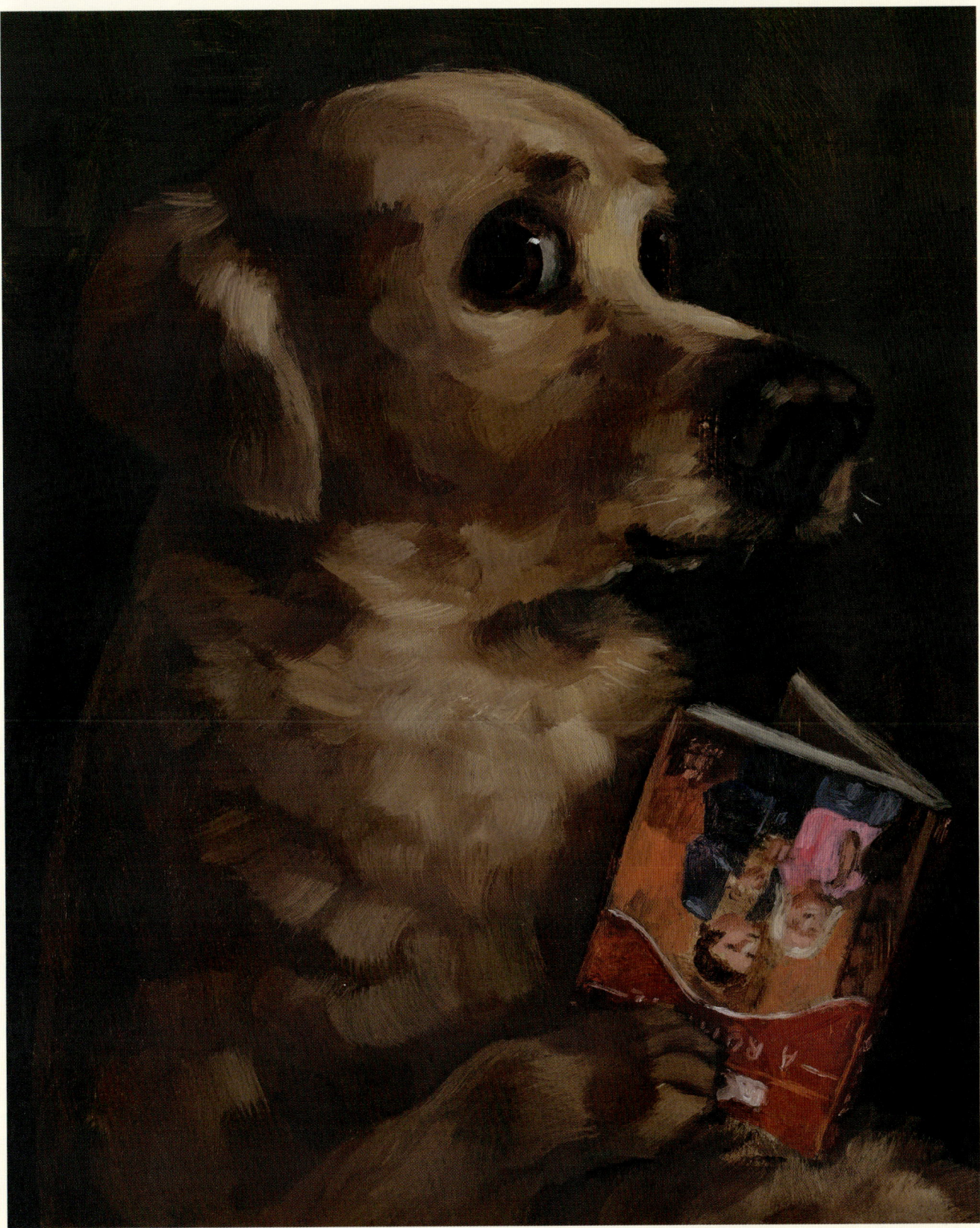

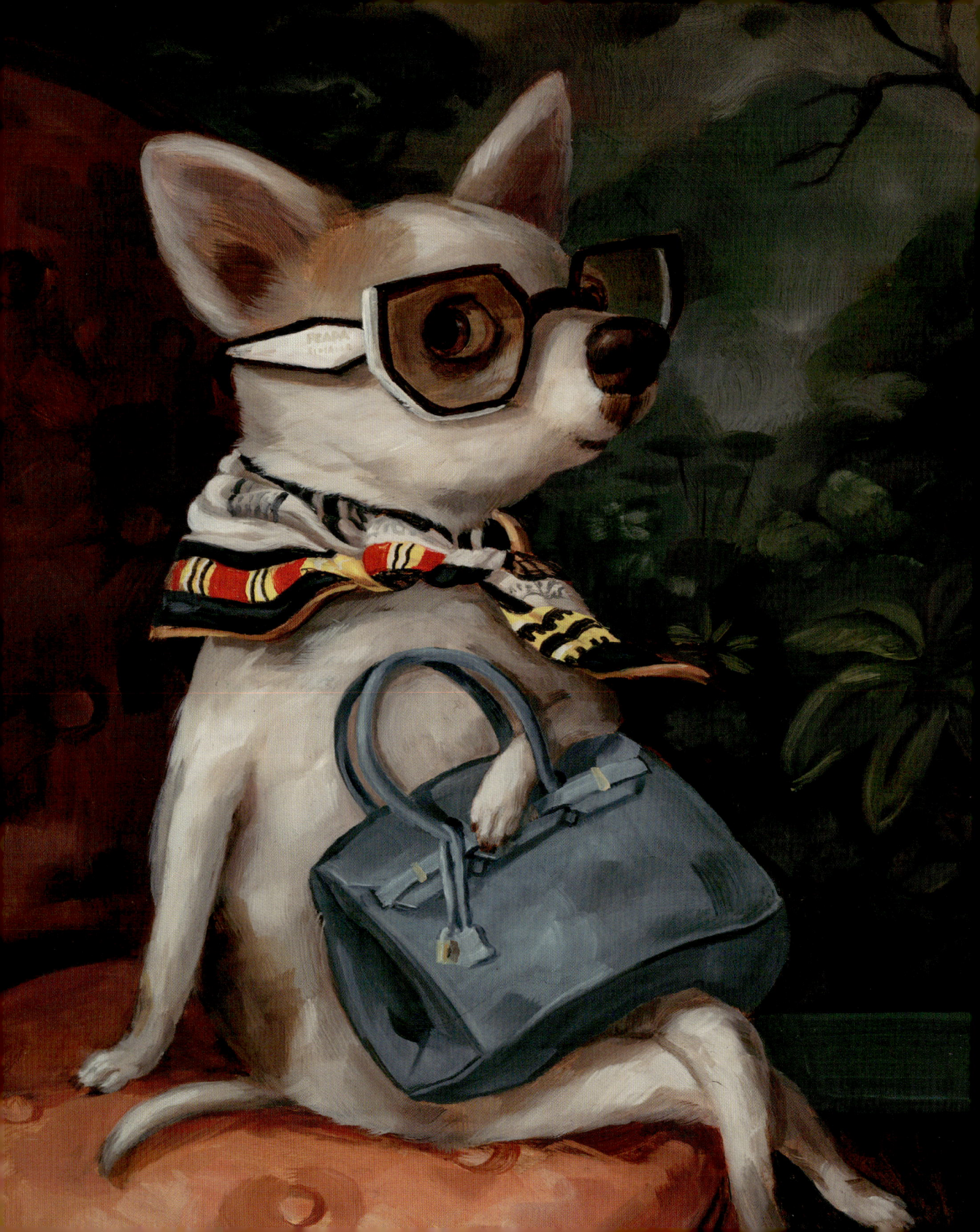

LITTLE JANE

This iconic pup knows that the bag everyone wants was named after her. The scarf? A gift . . . and the glasses too!

She's an influencer, you know, so she gets it all for free.

She drinks only mineral water from Alpine springs. She eats duck liver macarons for dinner (she skips breakfast) and takes a private jet to Paris Fashion Week. But under all of this, she is just a normal dog.

She loves a good sniff of a lamppost!

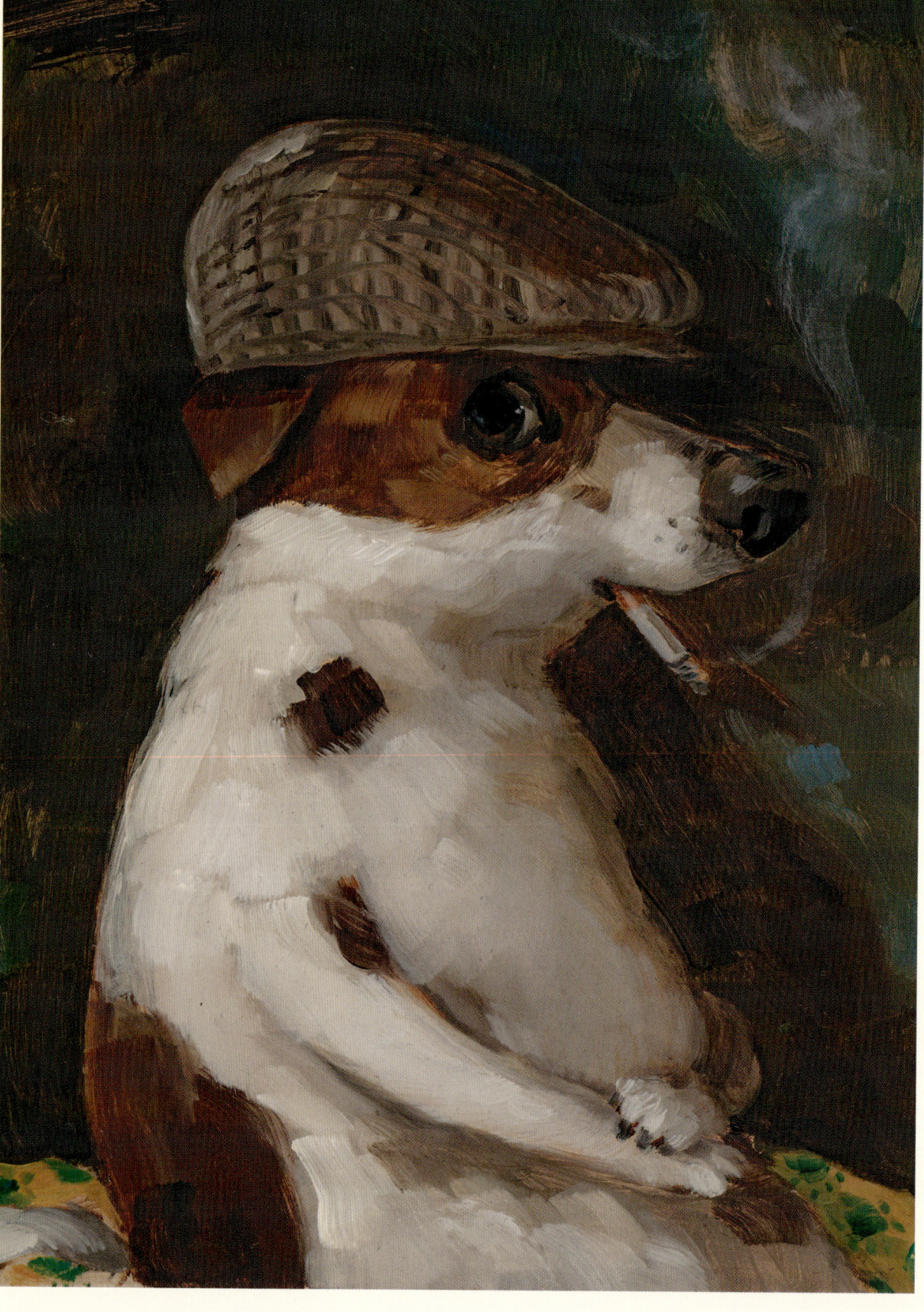

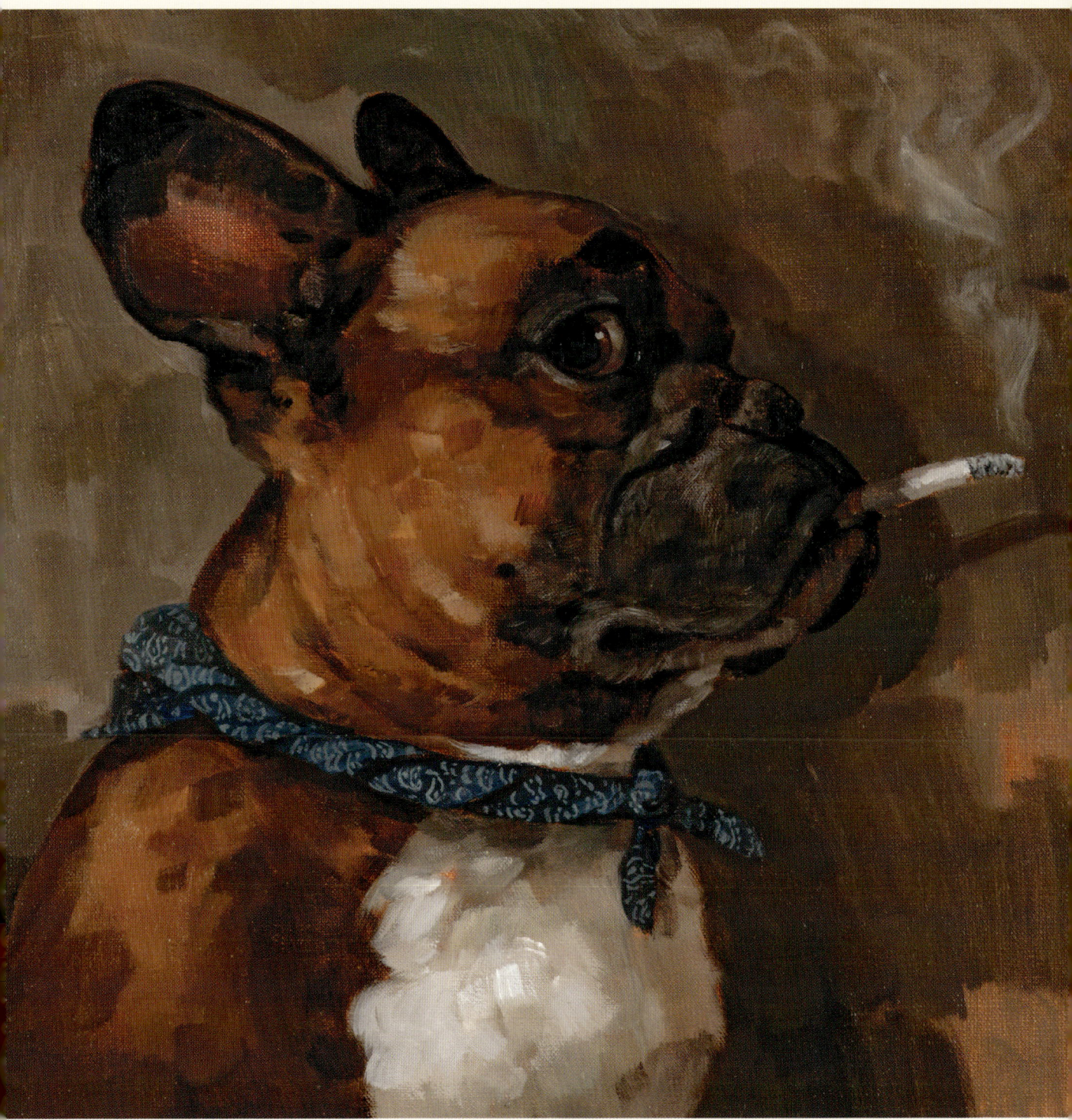

MARCEL | No plans to quit!

SMOKING JACK | Intends to quit!

TILLY

She comes from a long line
of lolly lovers

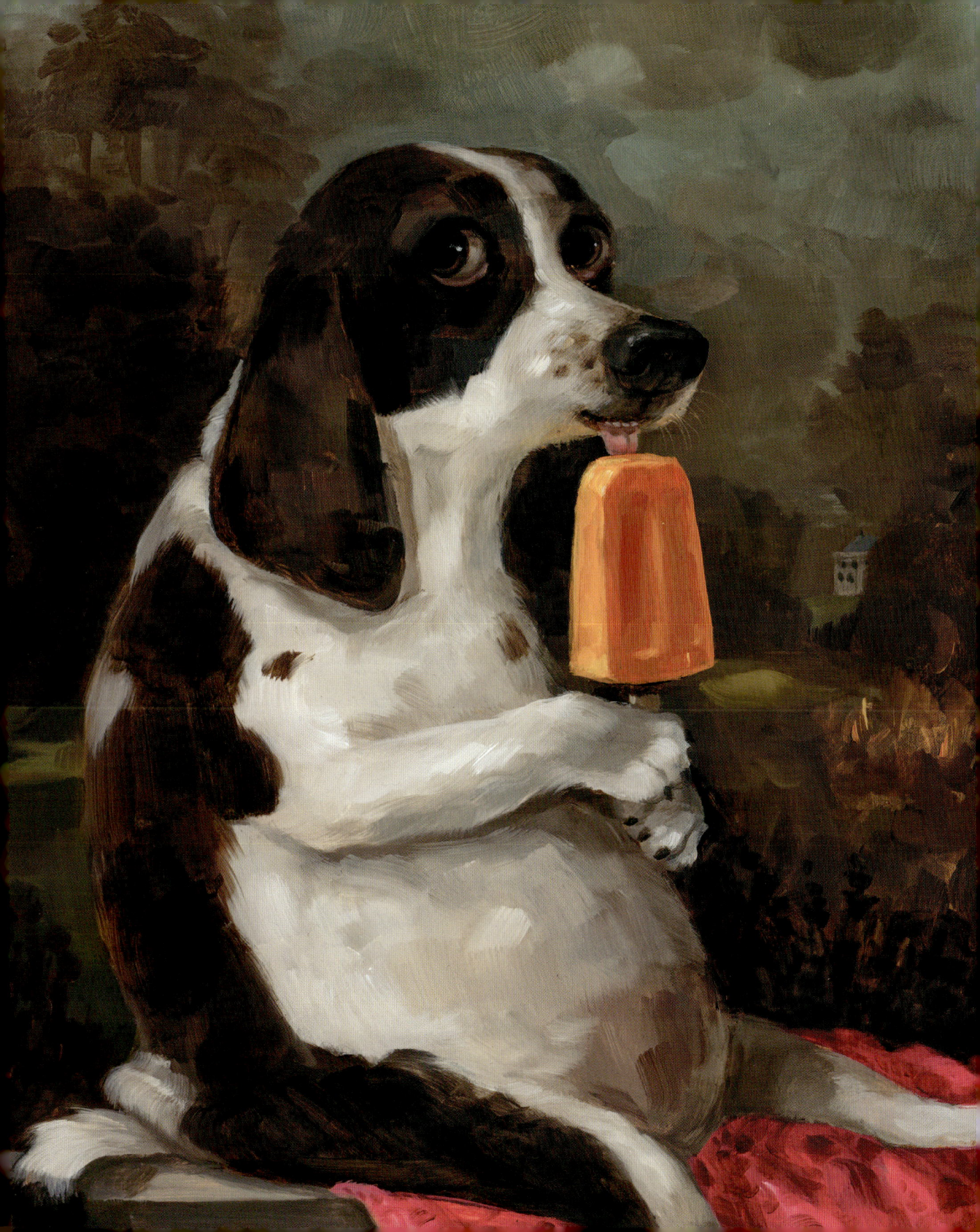

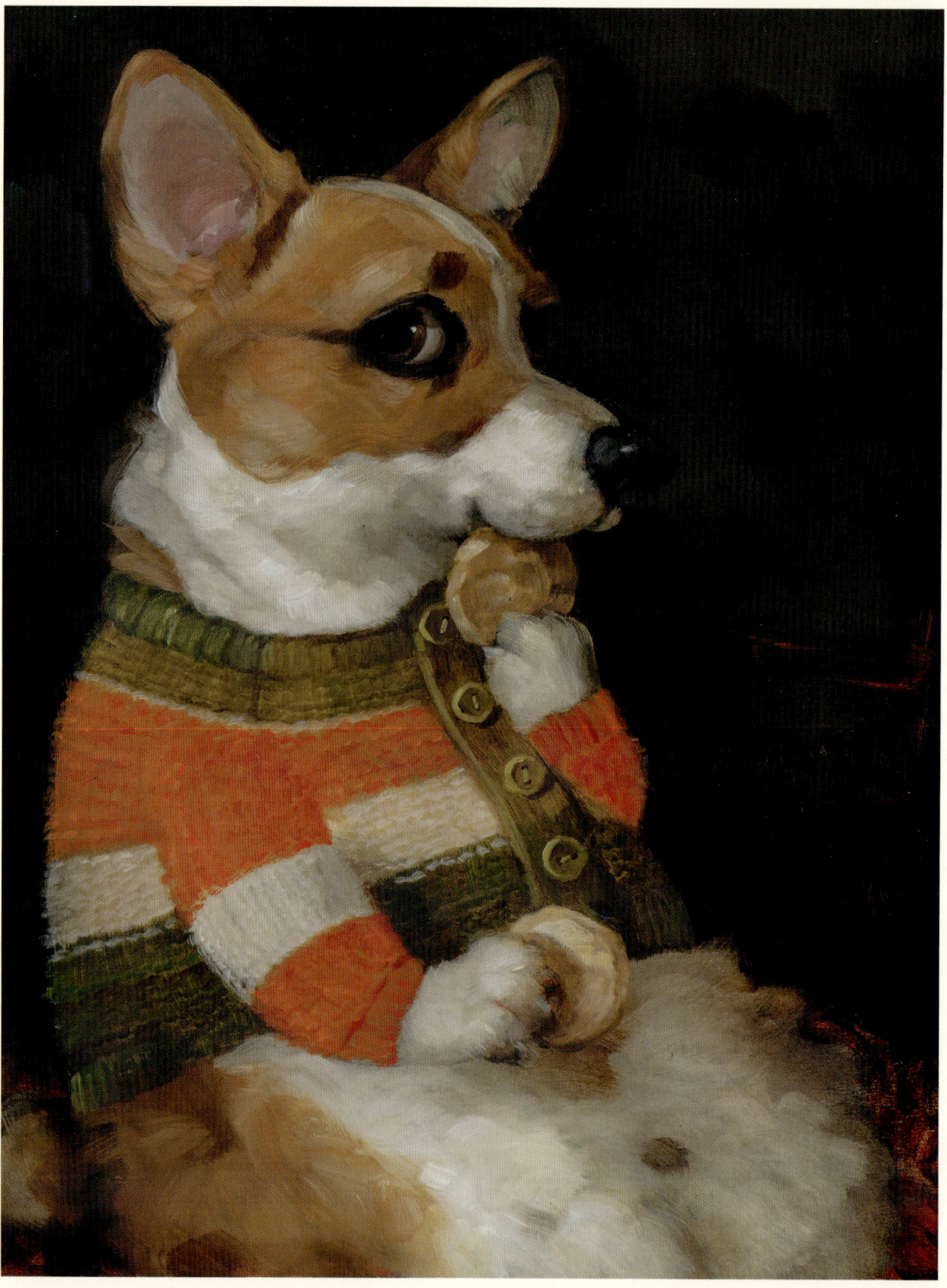

CARDIGAN CORGI

Cashmere only and
all-butter shortbread

COULD YOU REPEAT
THE QUESTION, PLEASE?

"I didn't quite catch you
the first time"

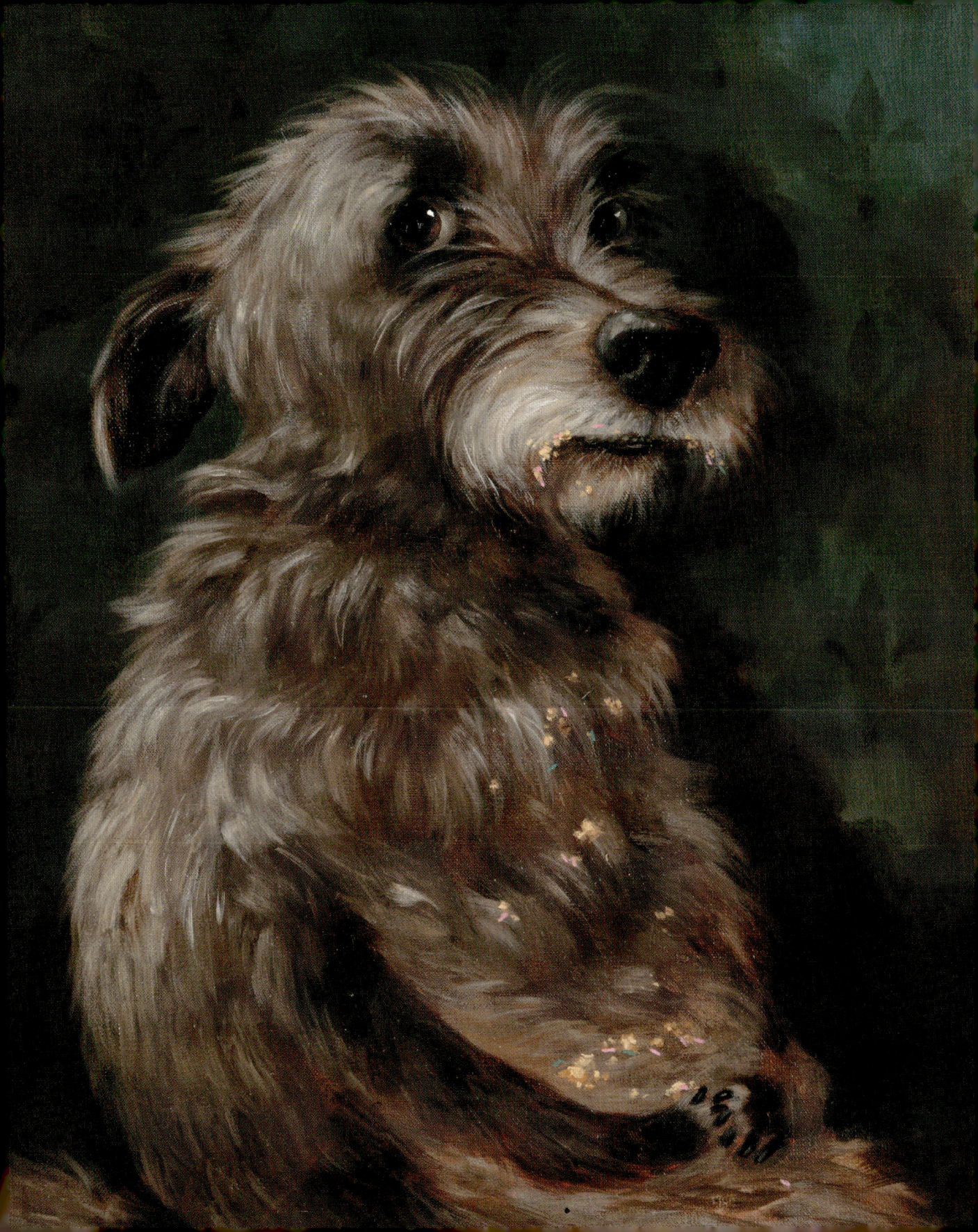

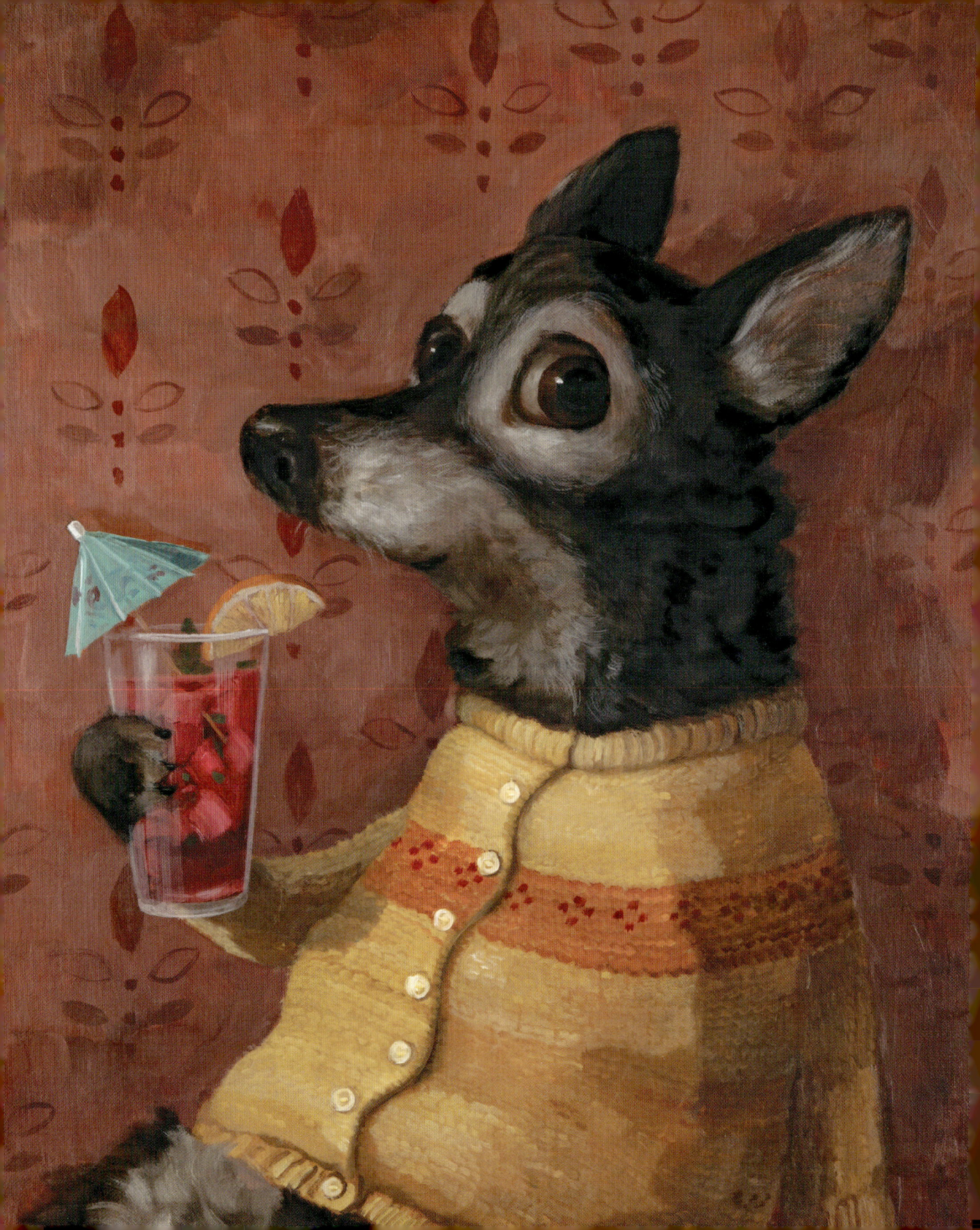

DEBBIE

She loves cocktail night

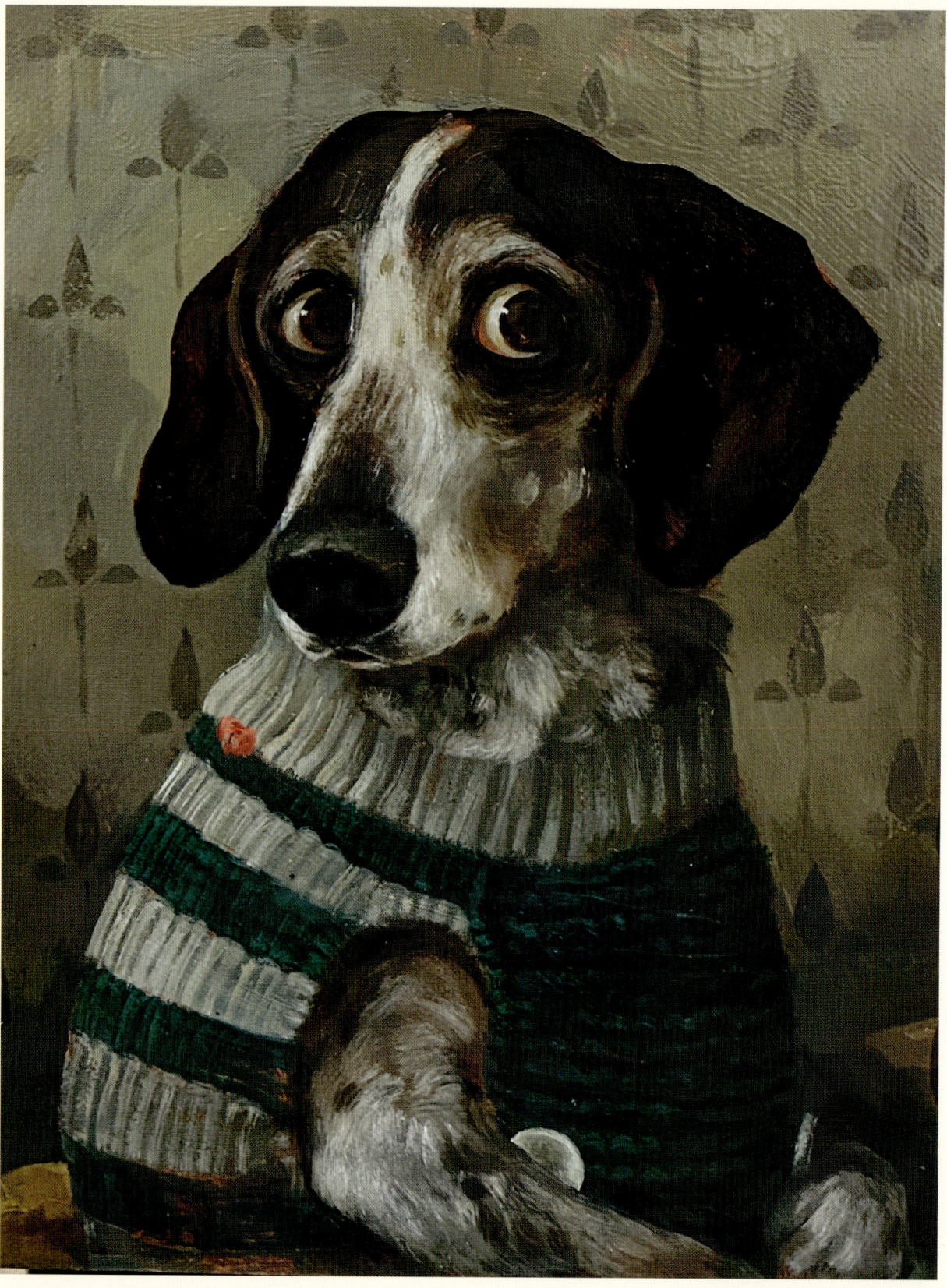

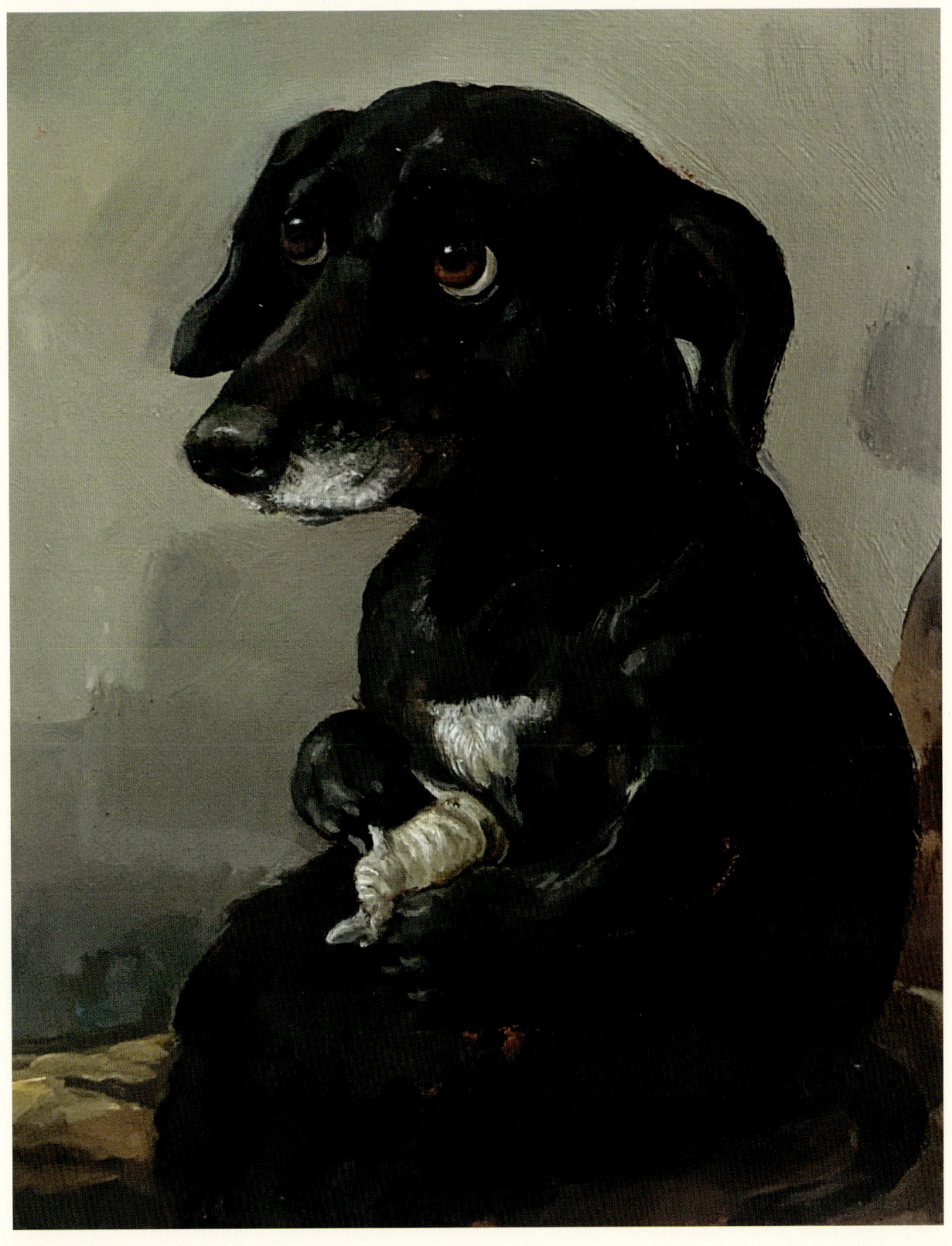

HATTIE AND CHIVA | Sisters from different misters

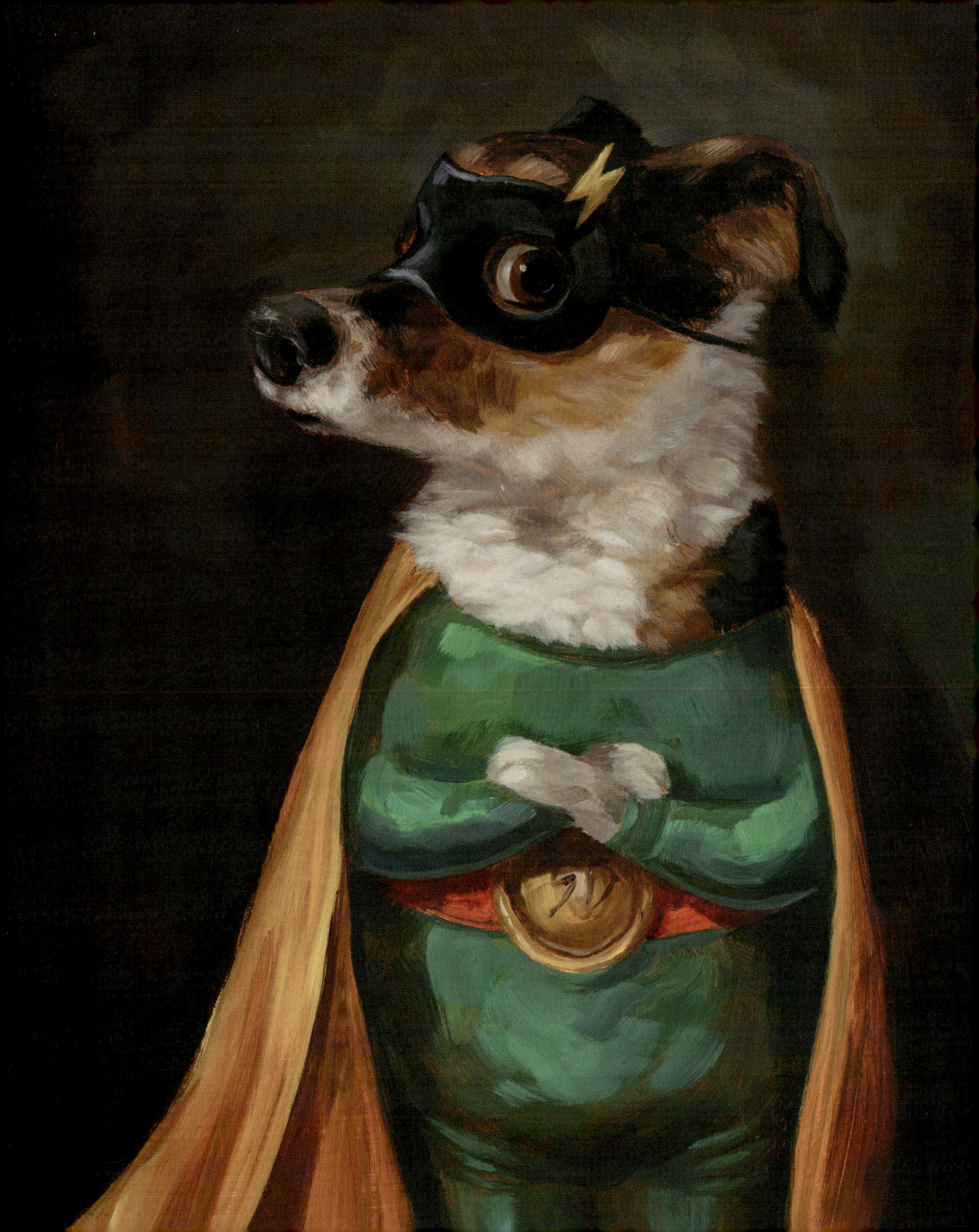

SUPER DOG

VISION: 98/100
Can see a snack packet being opened from a mile away.

SMELL: 99/100
Can smell a snack packet being opened from a mile away.

HEARING: 50/100
Can hear a snack packet being opened from a mile away
but struggles to hear when asked to sit, stay, or fetch.

SPEED: 95/100
As a Jack Russell cross, he can run up to 32 miles per
hour (true JRT fact). Even faster when there's a tennis
ball to chase!

SPECIAL SUPERPOWER: 100/100
This boy can do toots that will clear a room in seconds.

PATRICK

He loves his hat—"It's nobody's
business but mine"

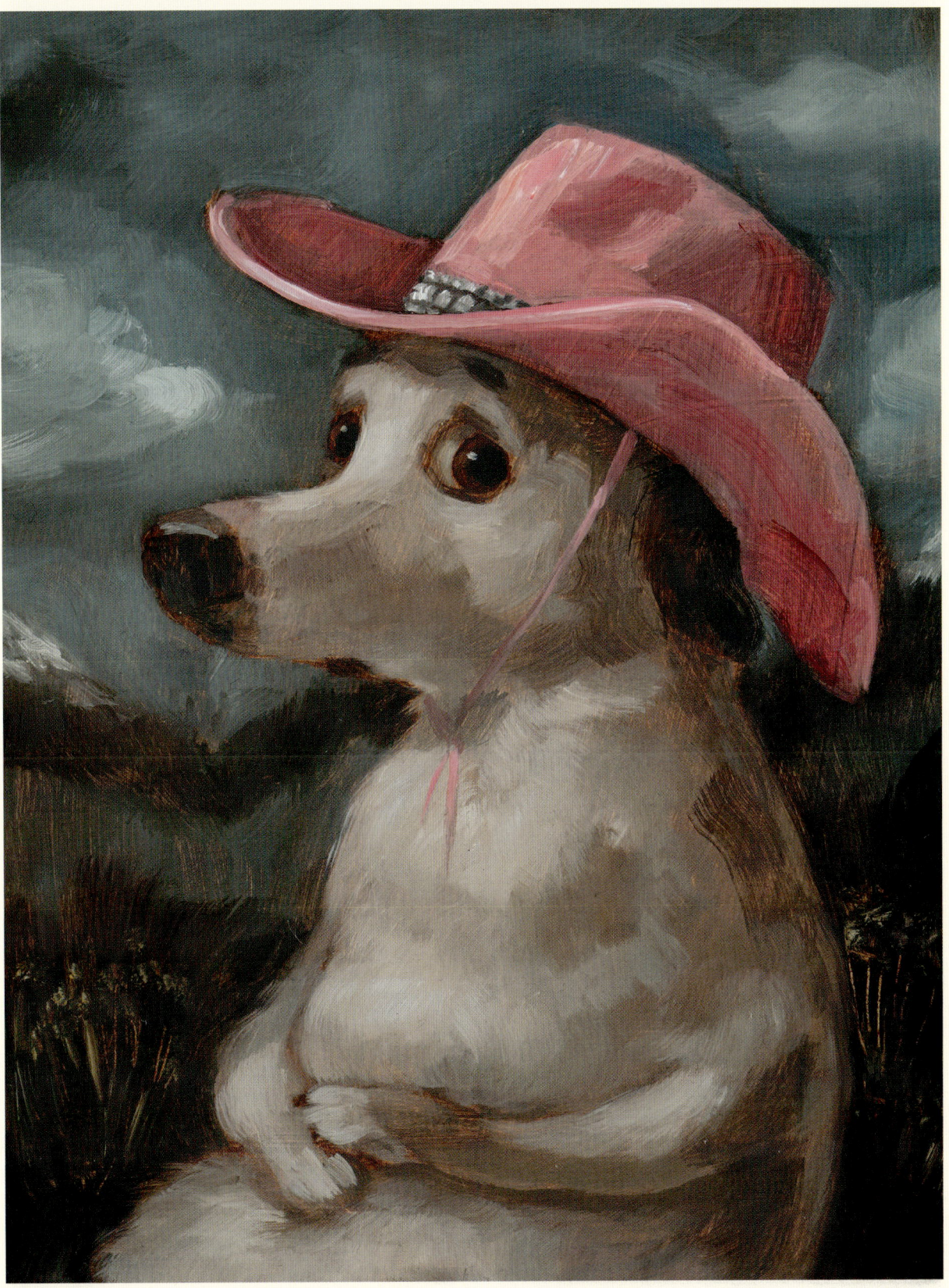

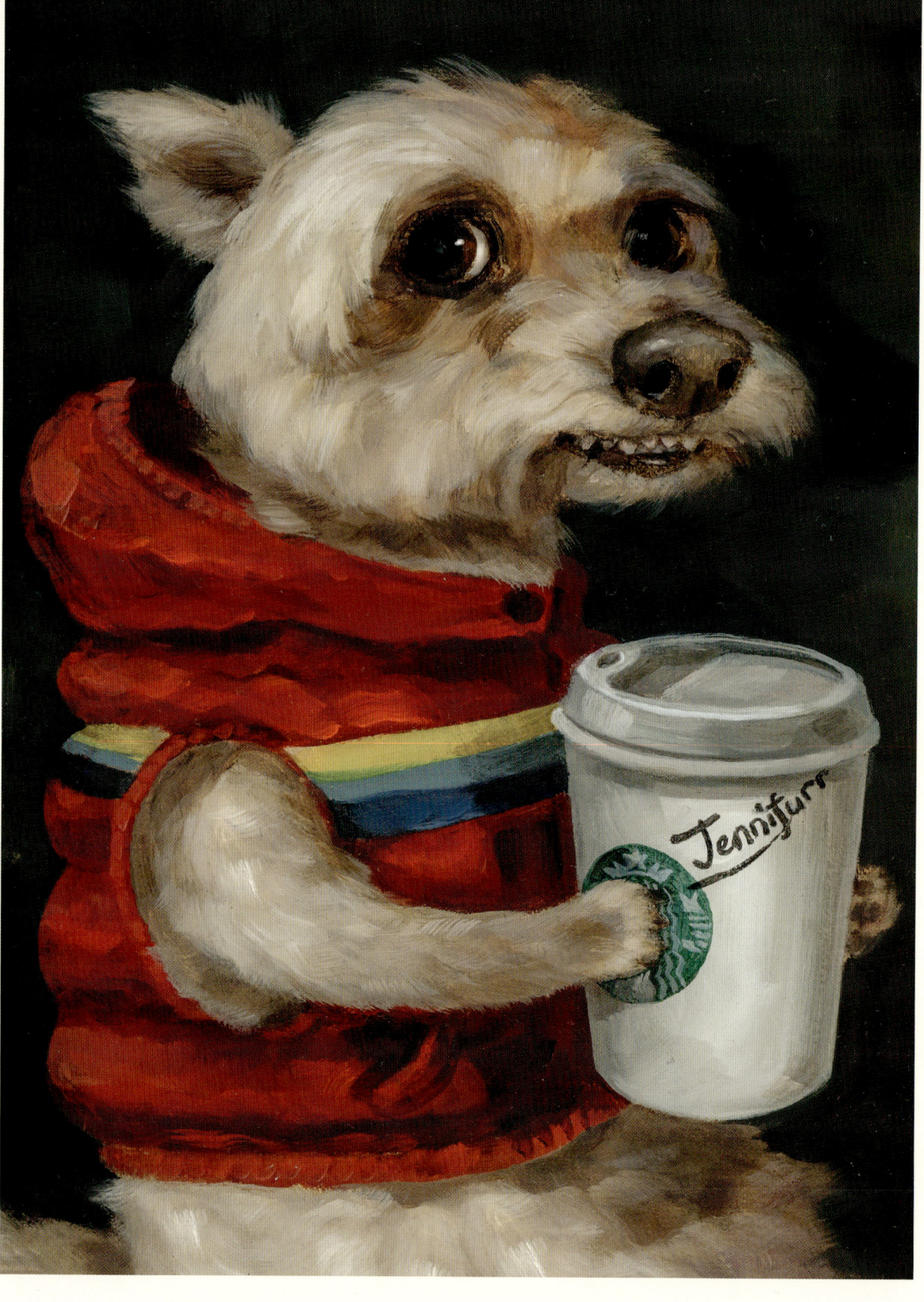

JENNIFURR

She loves her crisp morning walks
in the park with a stop-off for a
tasty puppuccino

ALAN LOVES HIS NEW JUMPER

. . . but not as much as biscuits

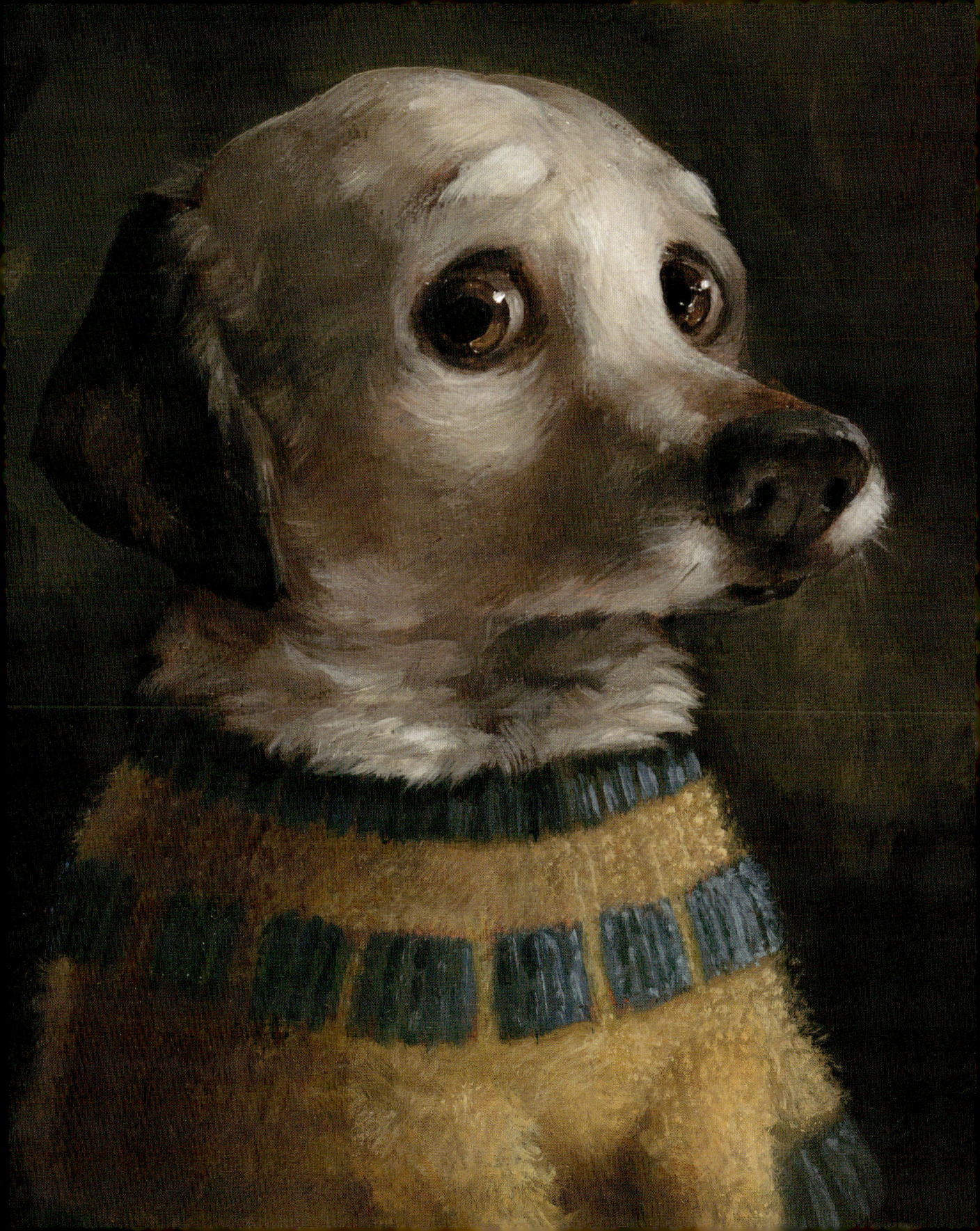

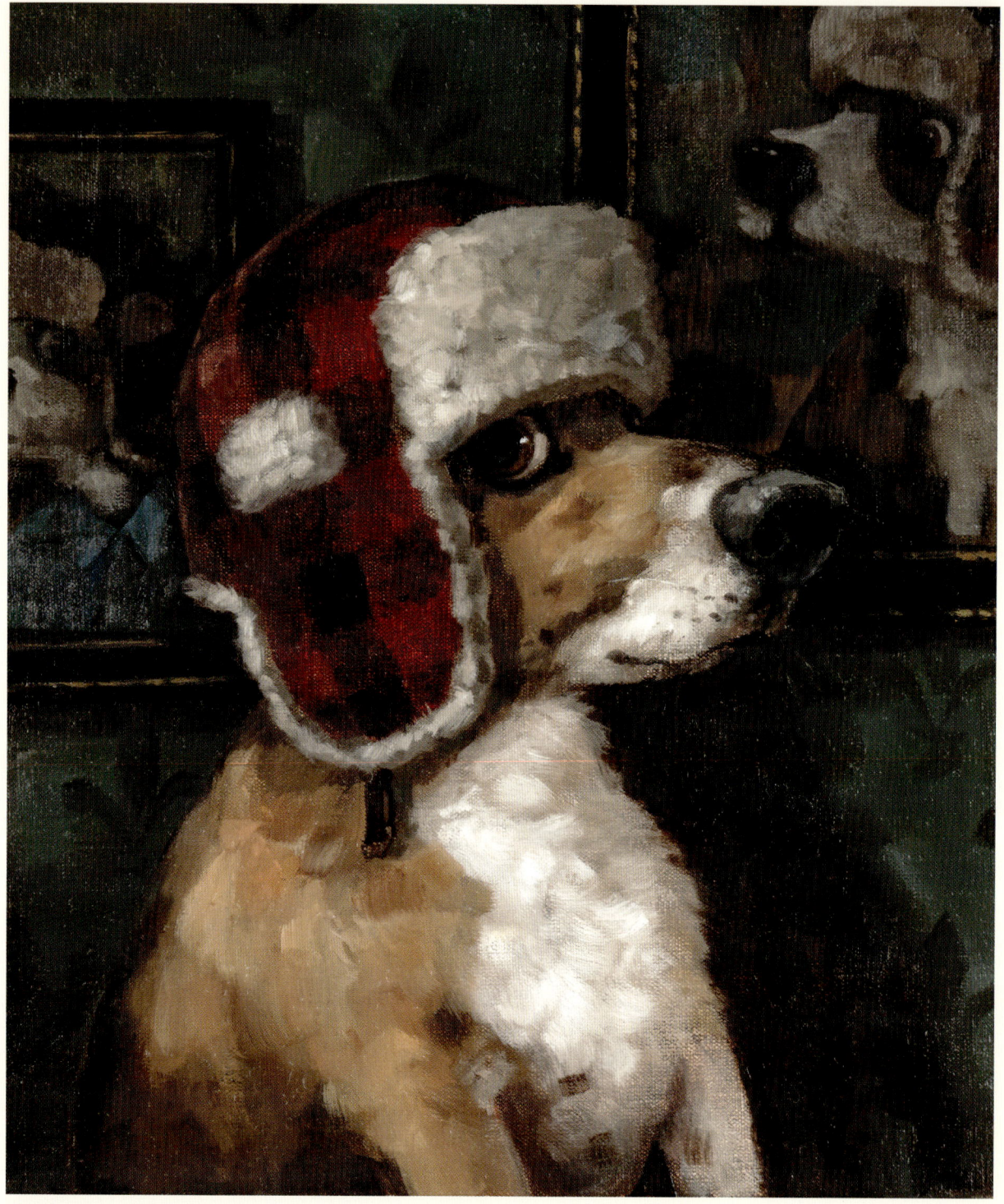

HAT GENERATIONS | It was the only inheritance

I LOVE MY DUCKIE TOO | "Paws off!"

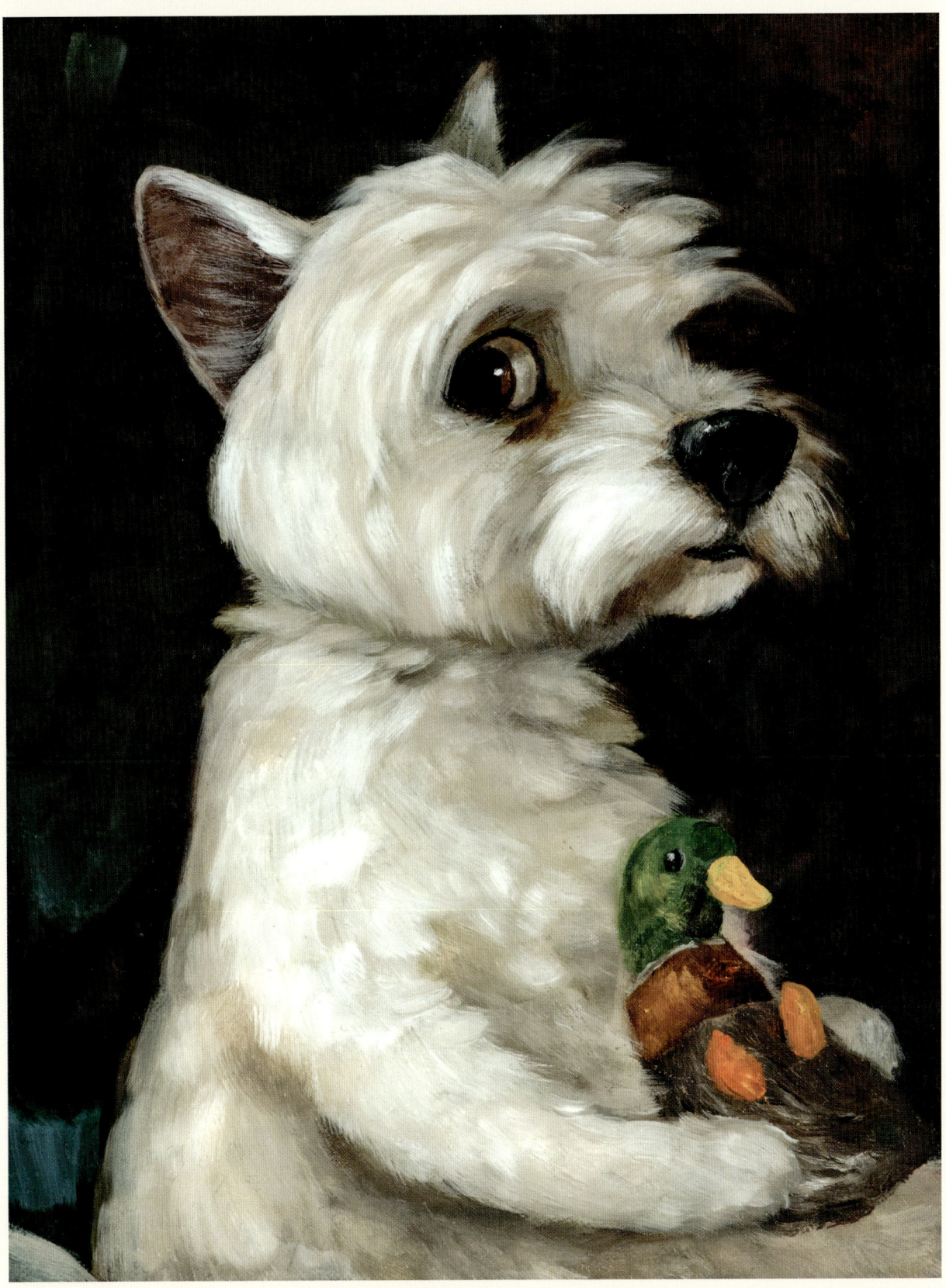

PAWTAGONIA

This little pup is ready for all the outdoor action, as long as Duck can come too!

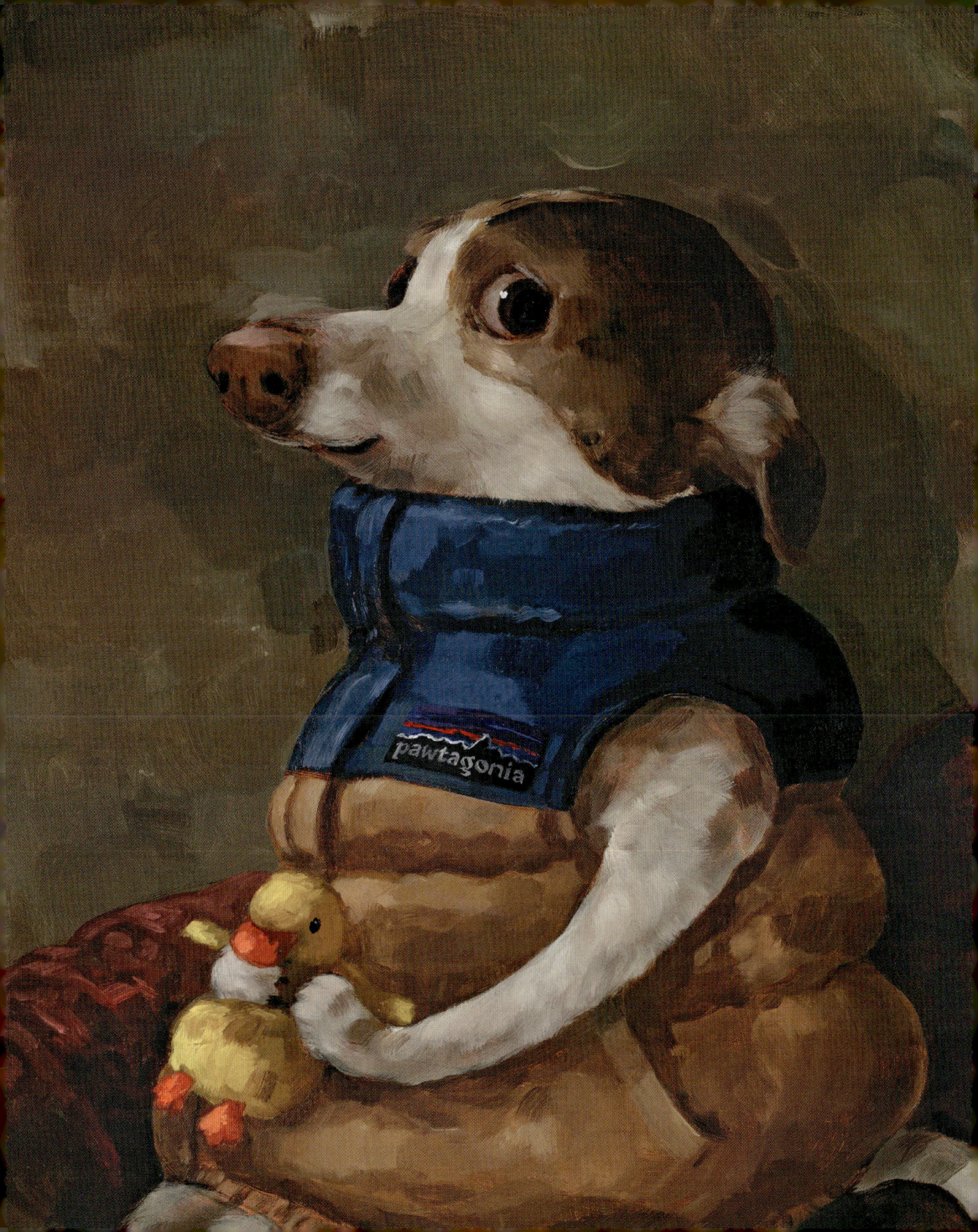

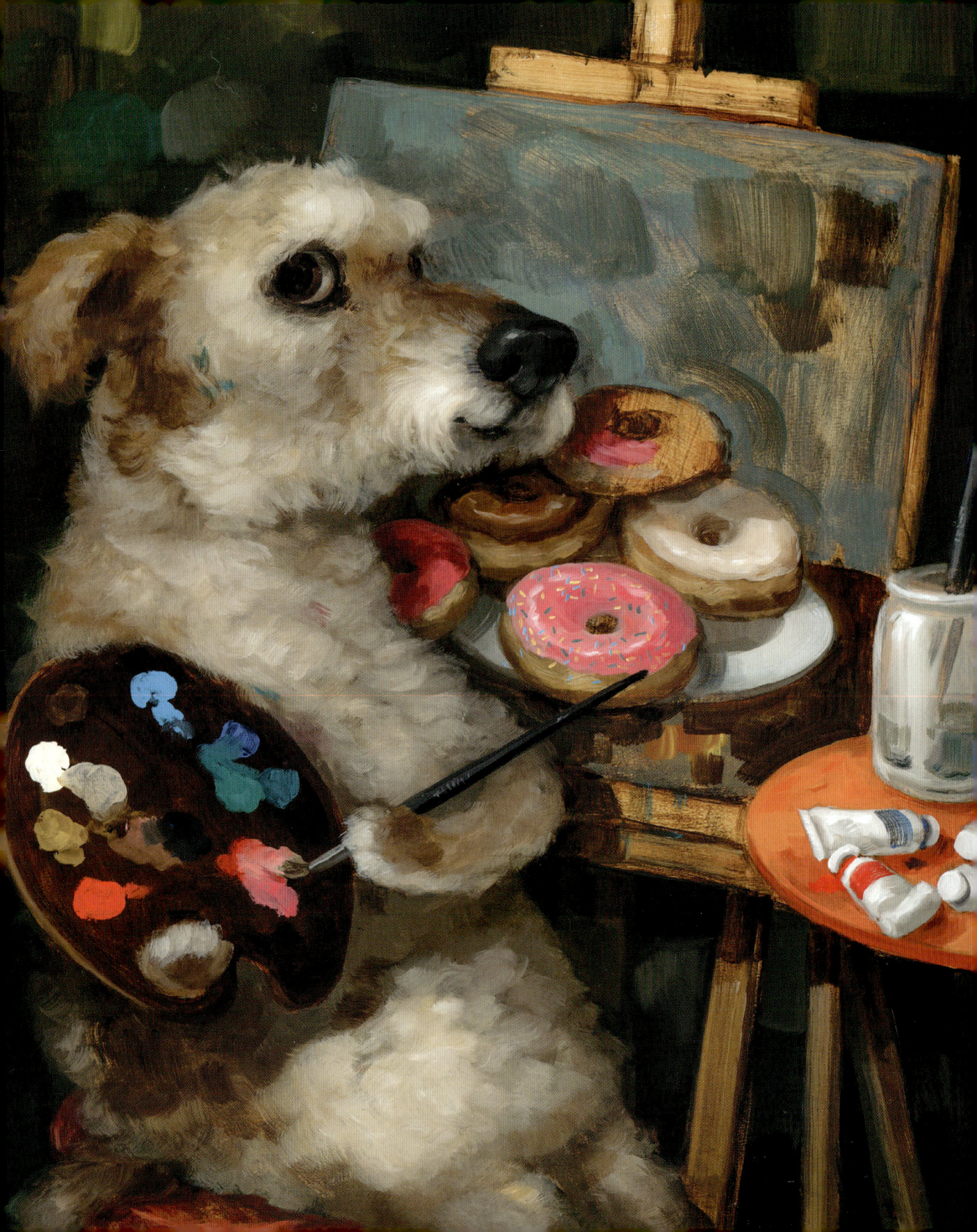

THE ARTIST AS A DOG

A self-portrait with donuts

I LOVE THIS STICK

". . . and my ball, and my bunny"

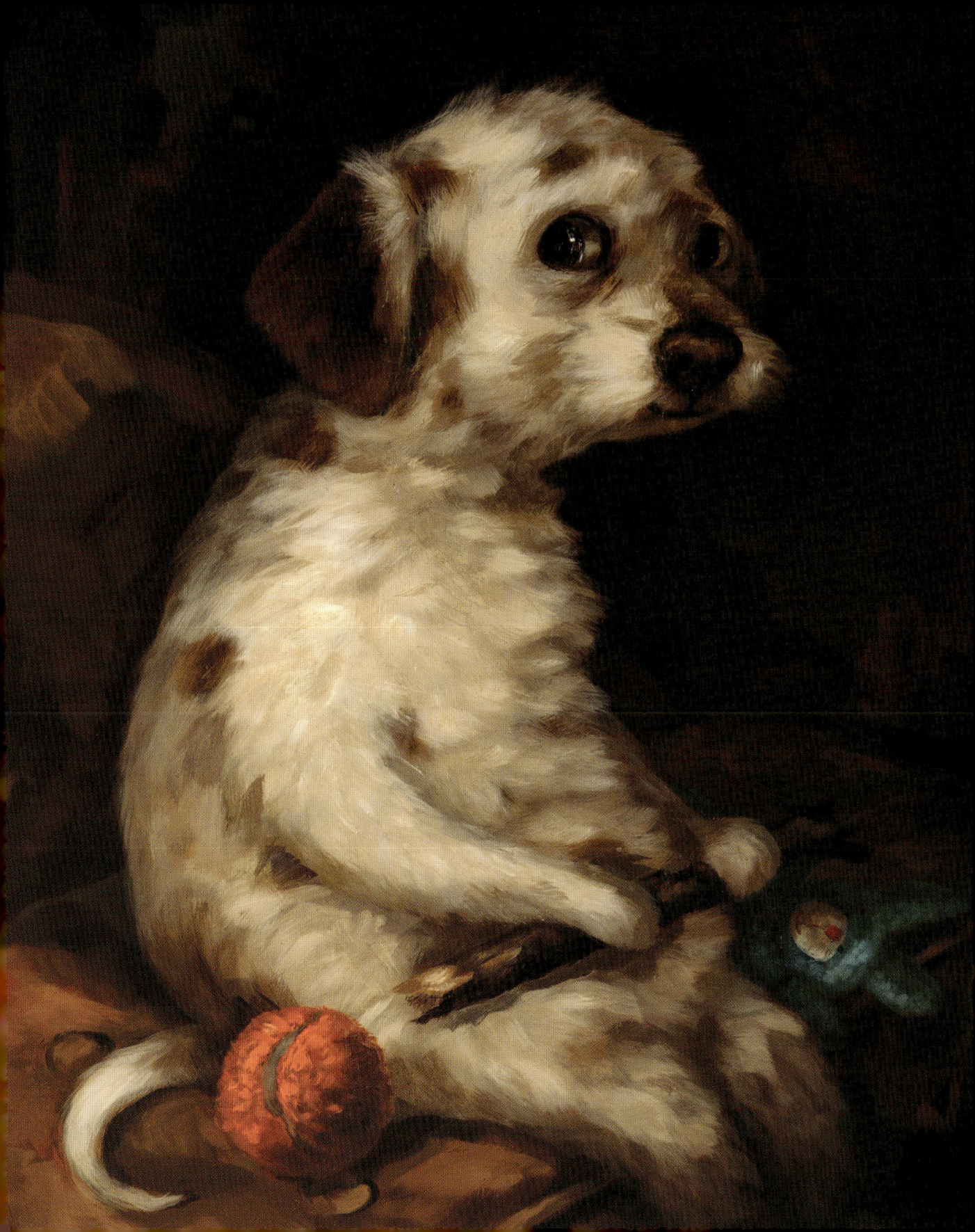

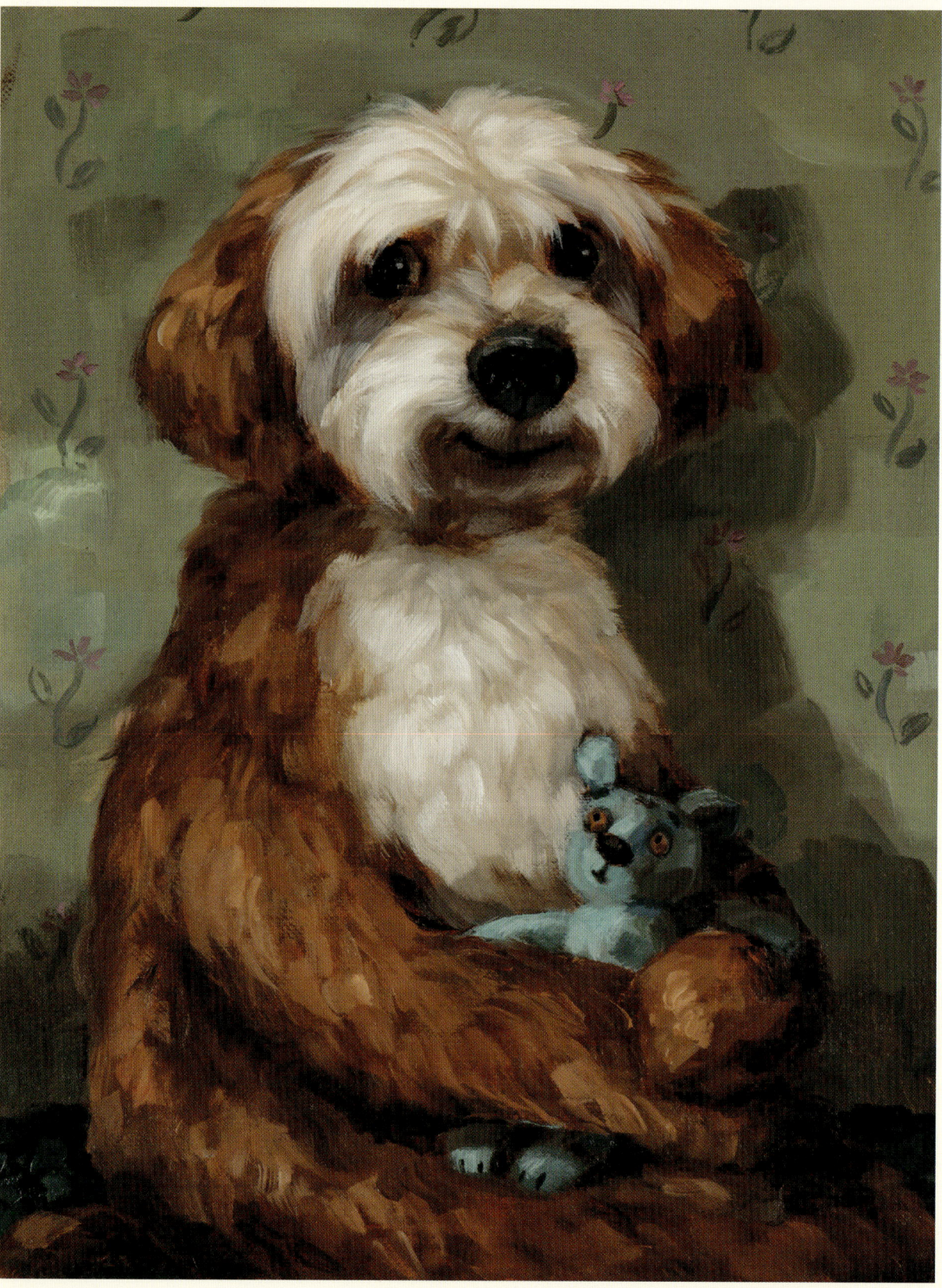

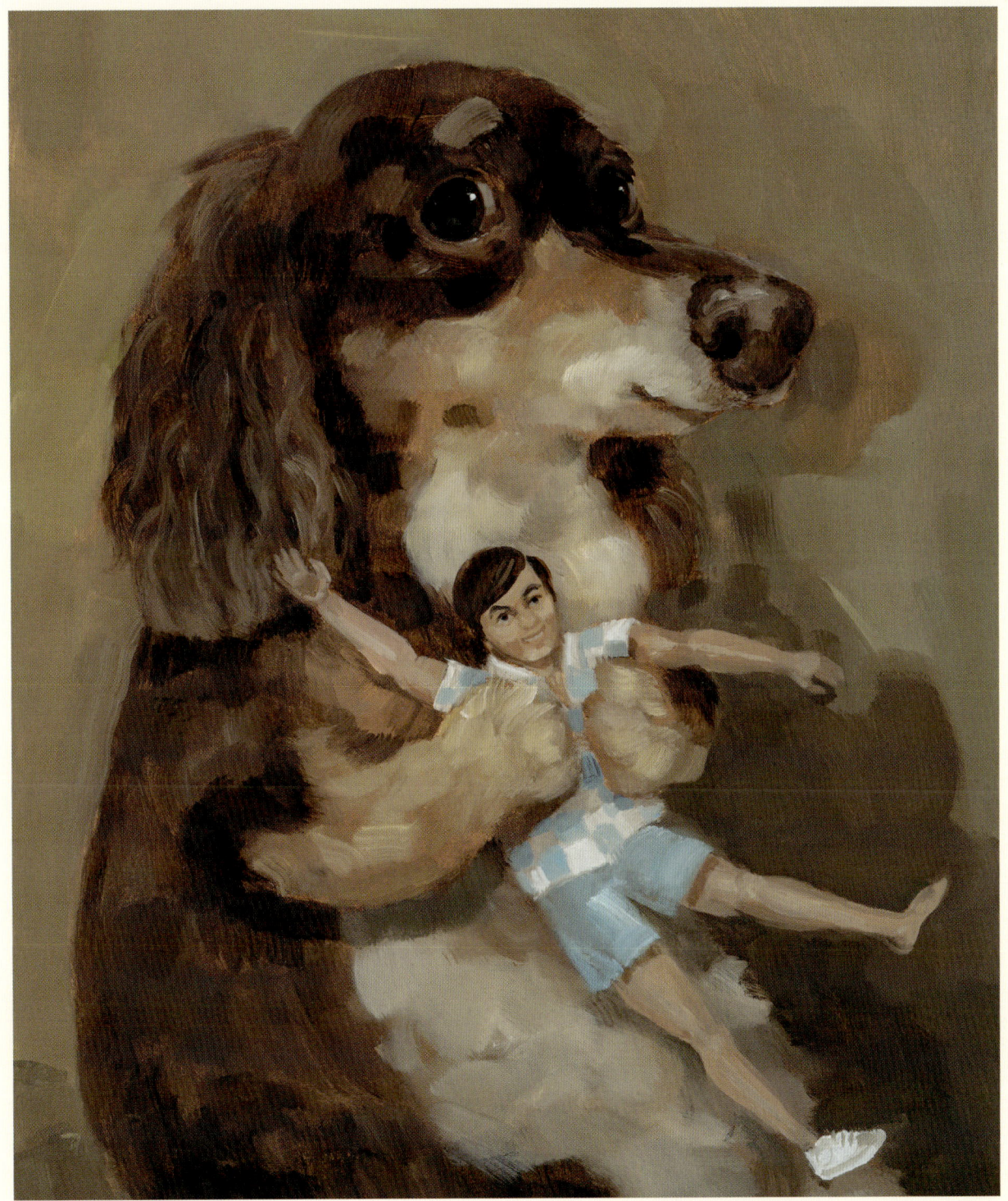

TUBEY LOVES KEN | And Jenn too

DOODLE LOVES BLUE TED | And Blue Ted loves Doodle

PIZZA LOVER

Pizza Lover is taking his role as the new People's International Pizza Aficionado (PIPA, for short) very seriously. He's now the go-to for the one-bite review.

All this fame, however, has definitely gone to Pizza Lover's head. This morning he listed his rider requirements for his dressing room:

Extra pizza—extra pupperoni

Sausages

Peanut butter biscuits

A case of beer—Corona

Extra limes

Sparkling water with ice

Six tennis balls

A pig's ear

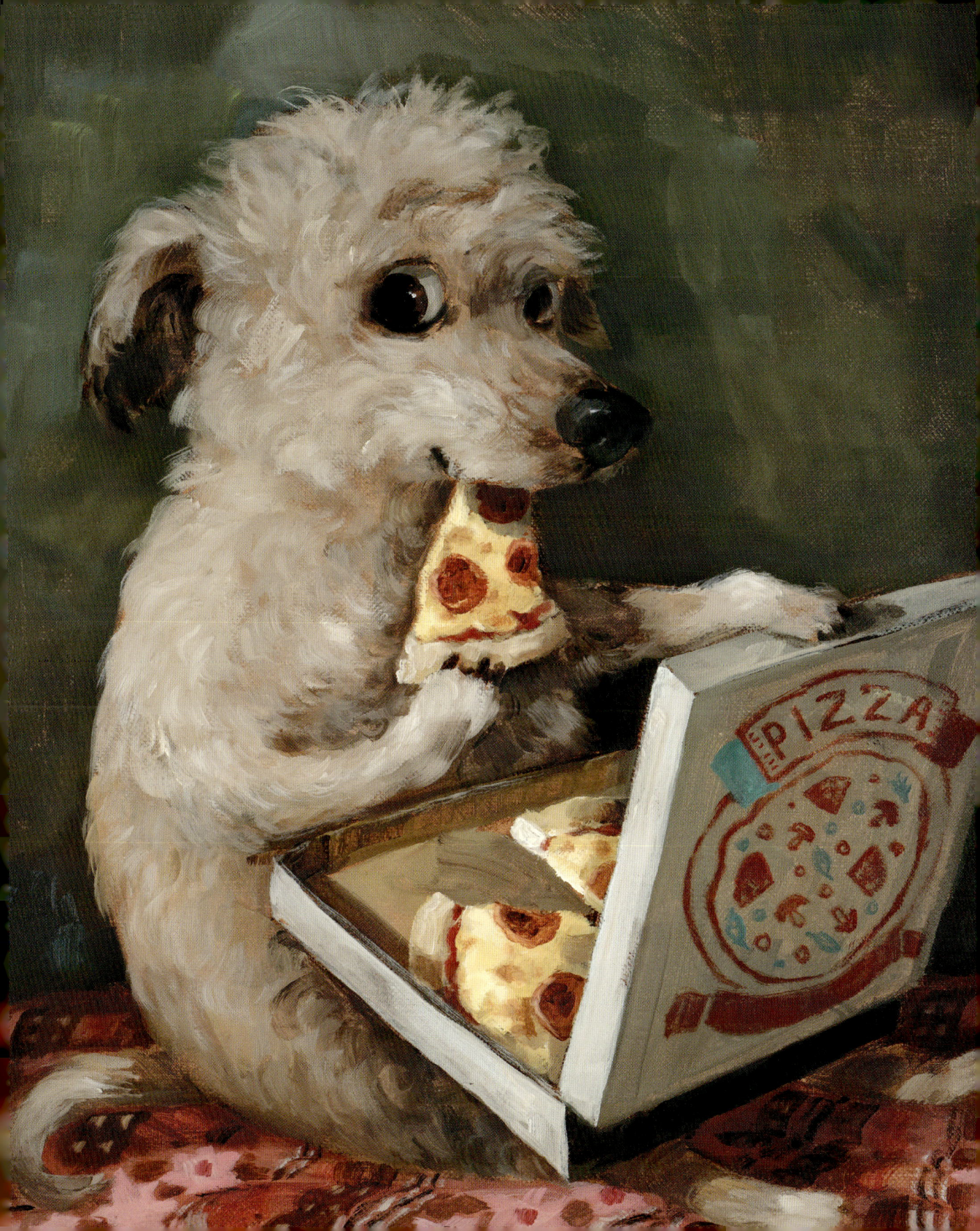

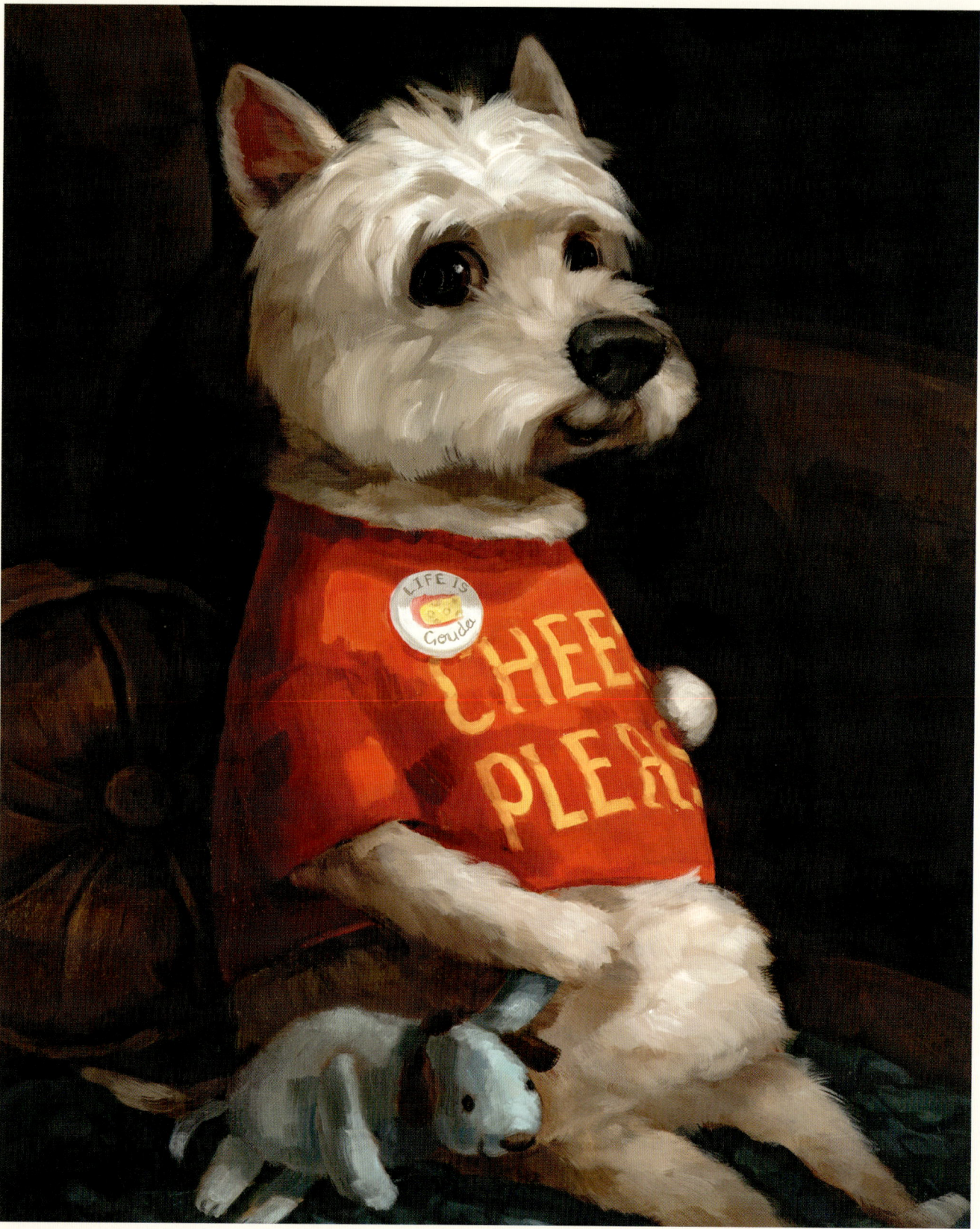

LIFE IS GOUDA

. . . while he's getting cheese
treats, at least!

FABIO

Oh, so fabulous

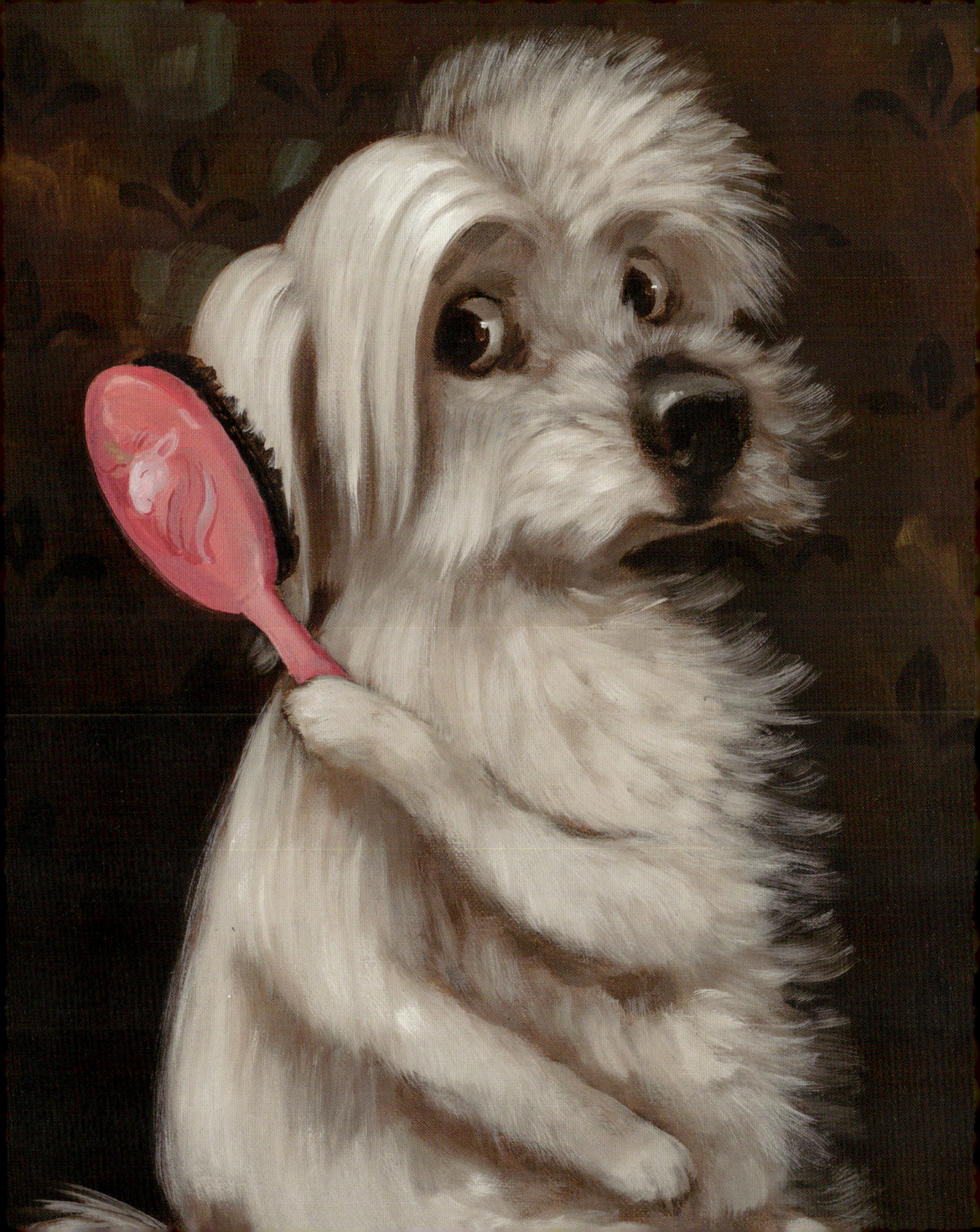

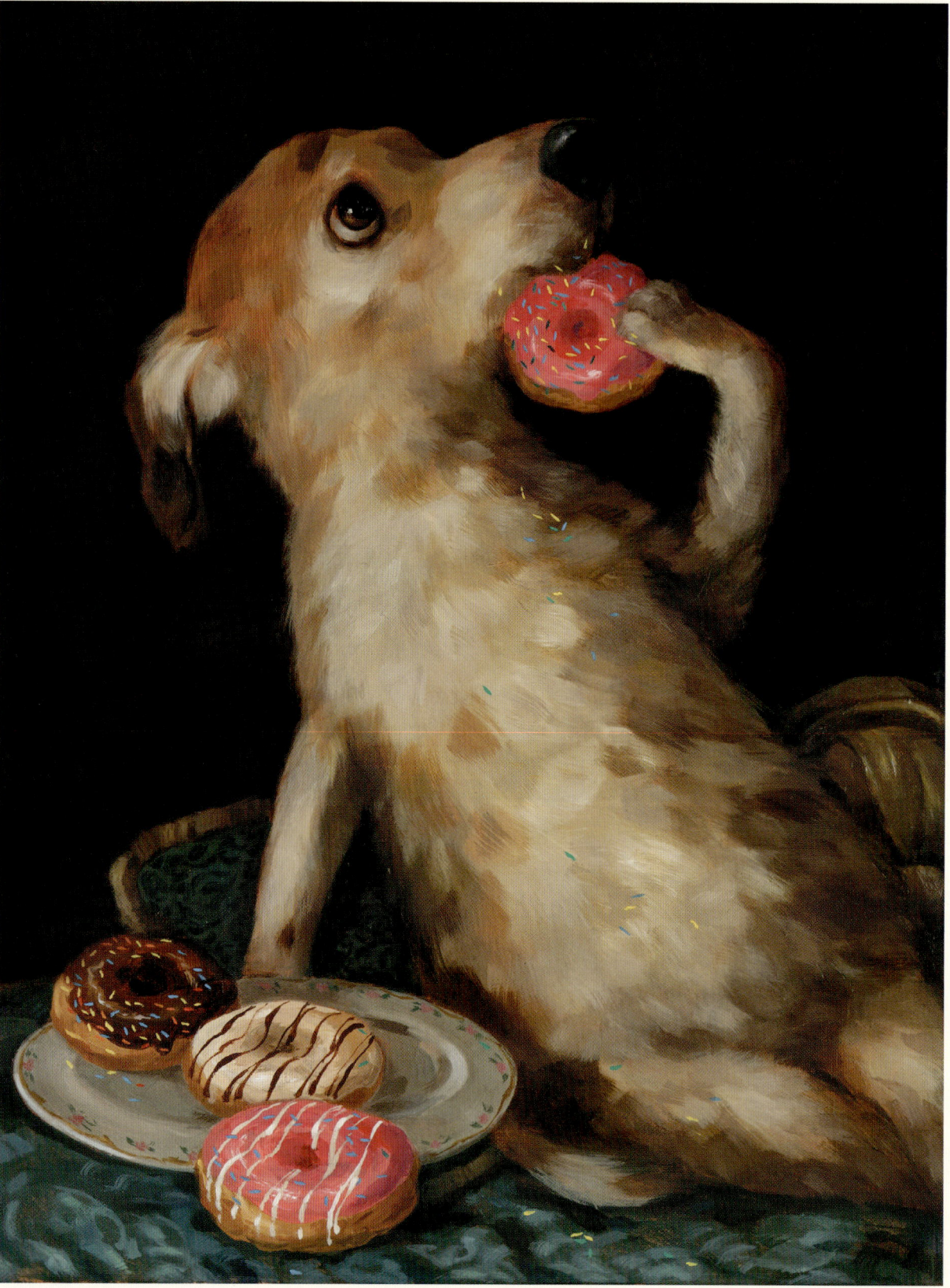

THE FIRST BITE IS THE SWEETEST

And so is the second, third, and fourth

LITTLE LOUIS

"Who are you looking at? . . . Me? Yes, I'm smoking a cigarette. What of it?"

Little Louis—Chihuahua, thirty-five years old (in dog years).

Single.

Lover of espresso, cigarettes, and art house cinema, particularly existential dramas.

Constantly pondering the absurdity of the canine condition.

"Non, je ne regrette rien" is the soundtrack to his life.

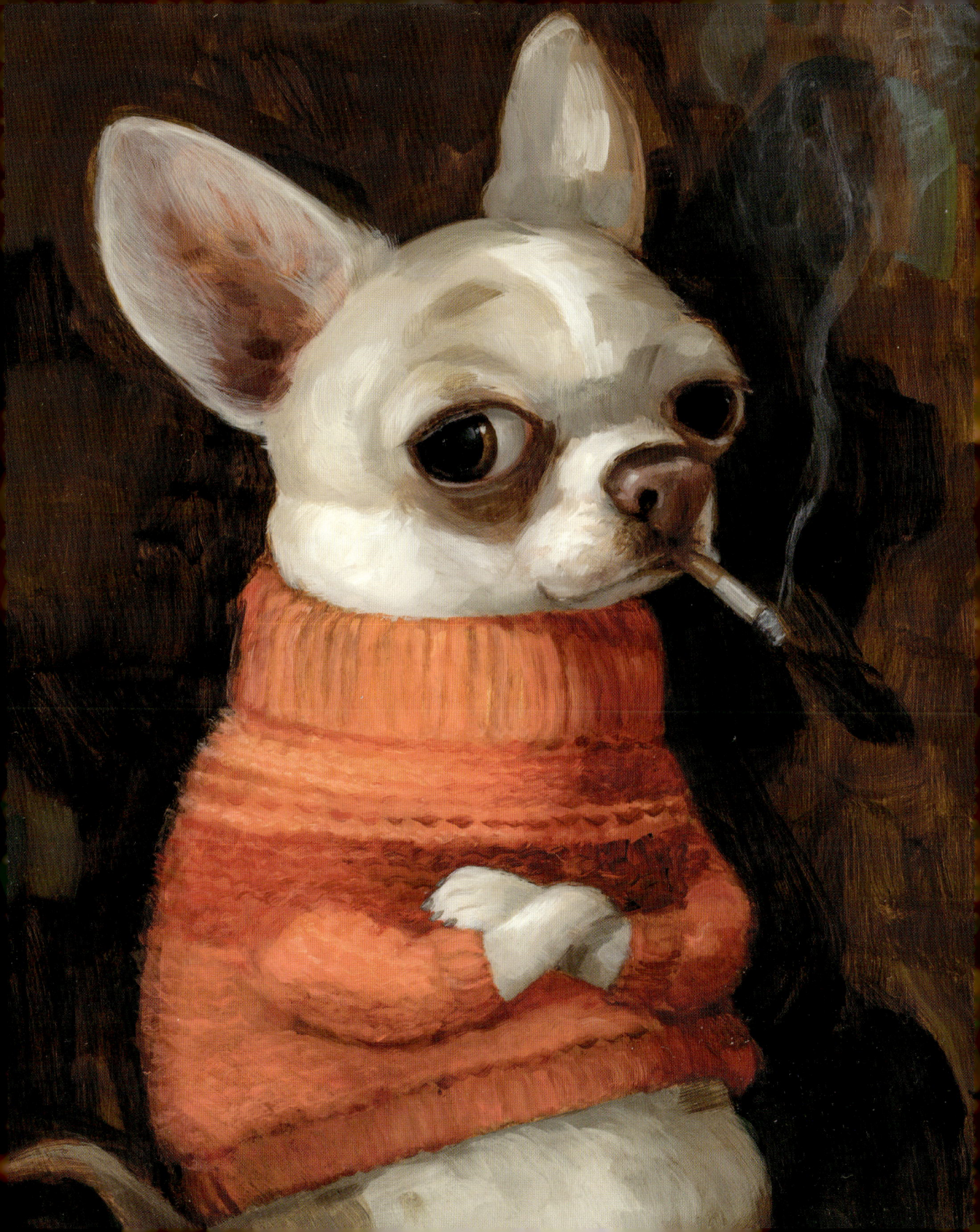

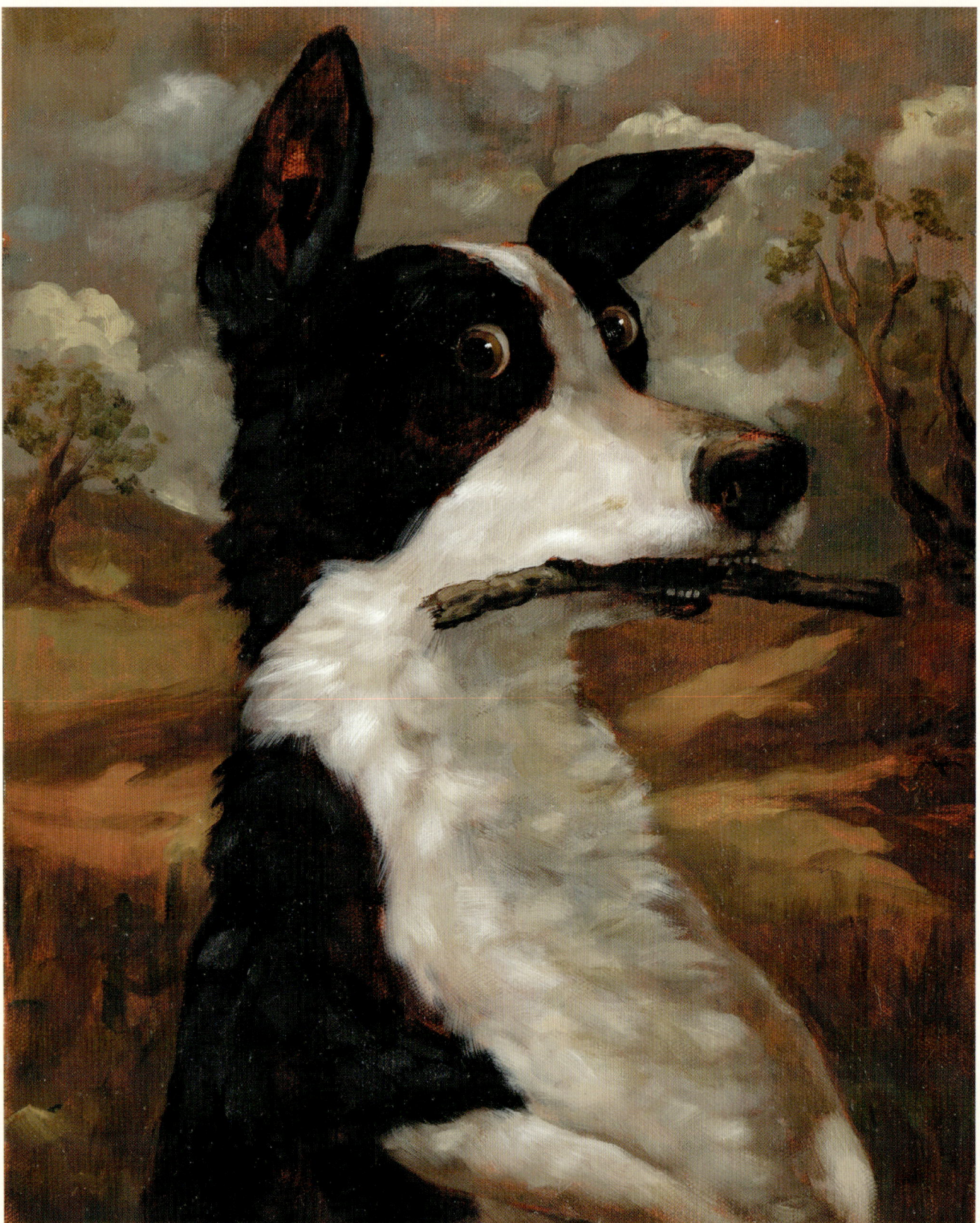

STICK IS LIFE

It's why he wakes up in
the morning

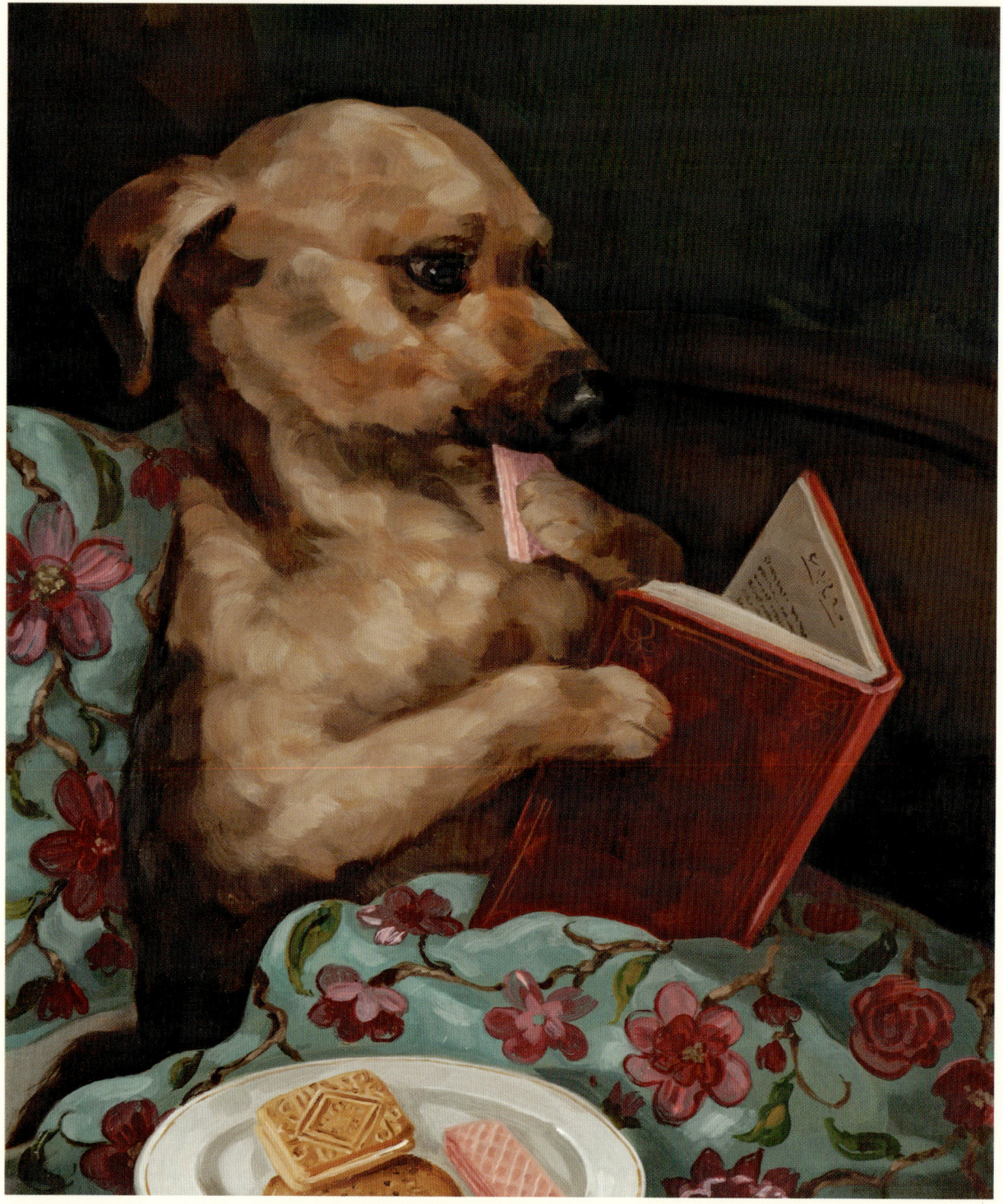

DUVET DAY | Always includes biscuits and a book

RON IN YELLOW JUMPER | It's one of Alan's hand-me-downs

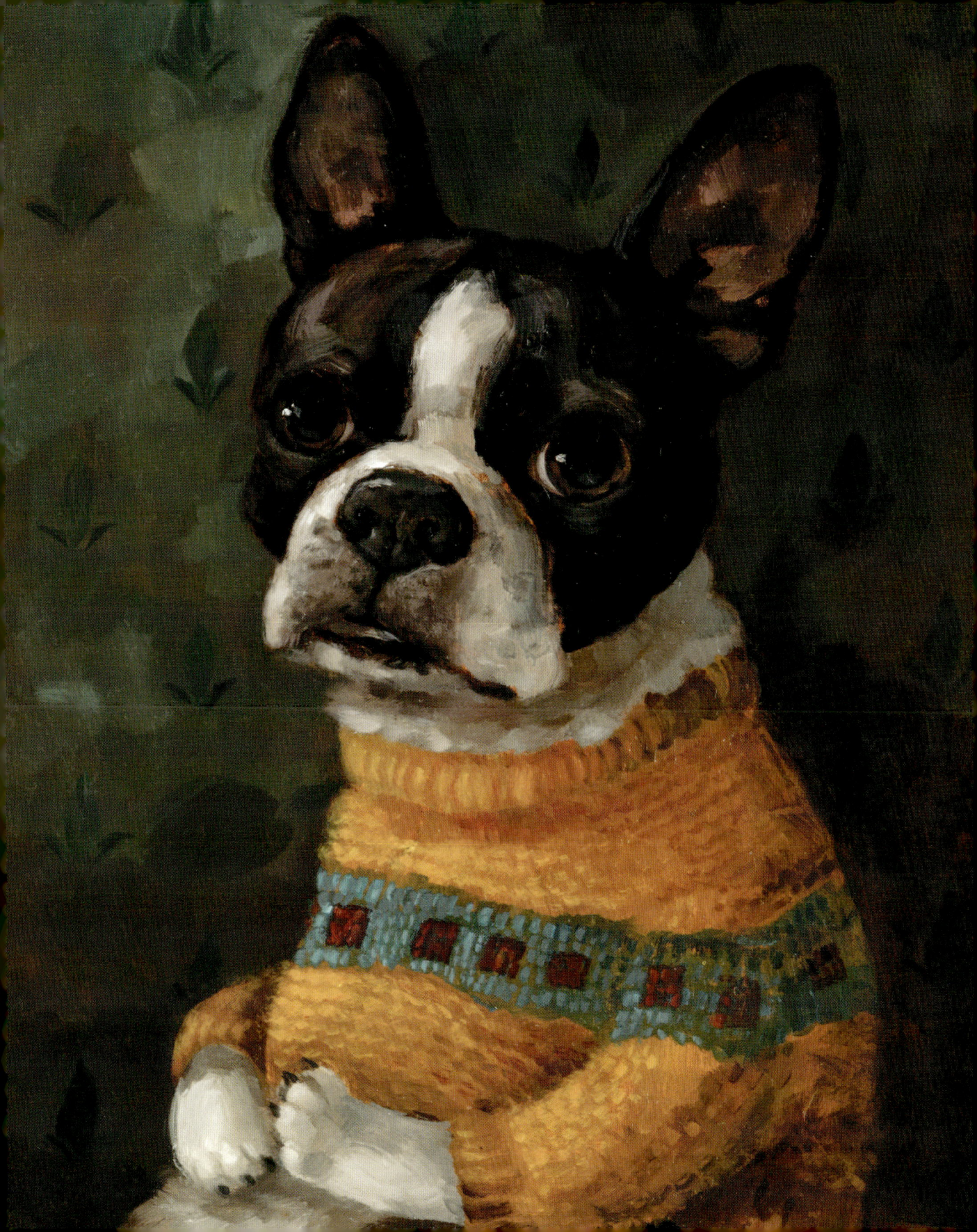

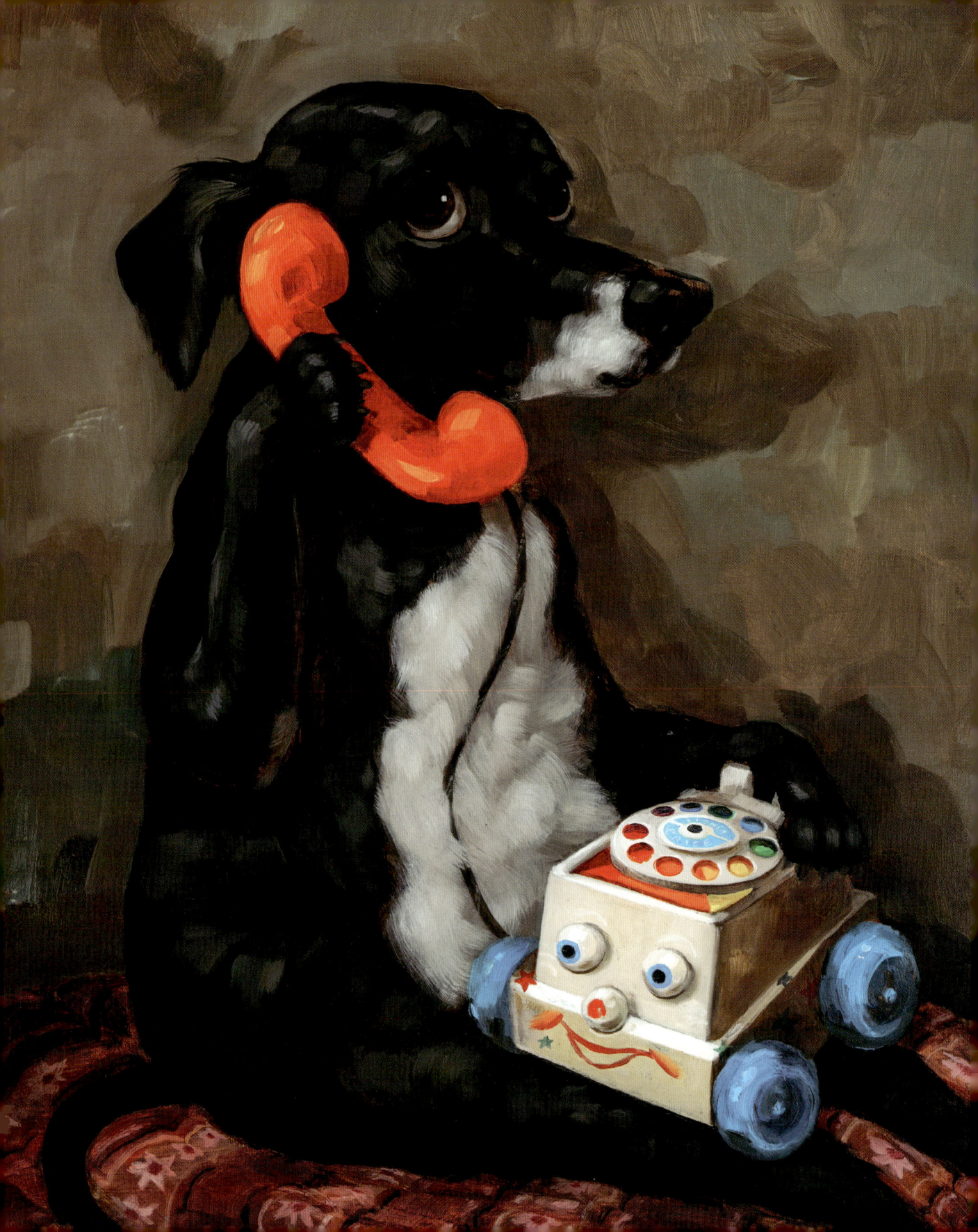

BETSY

She's been on hold for over an hour

MARLDON

Shining shoes is his passion

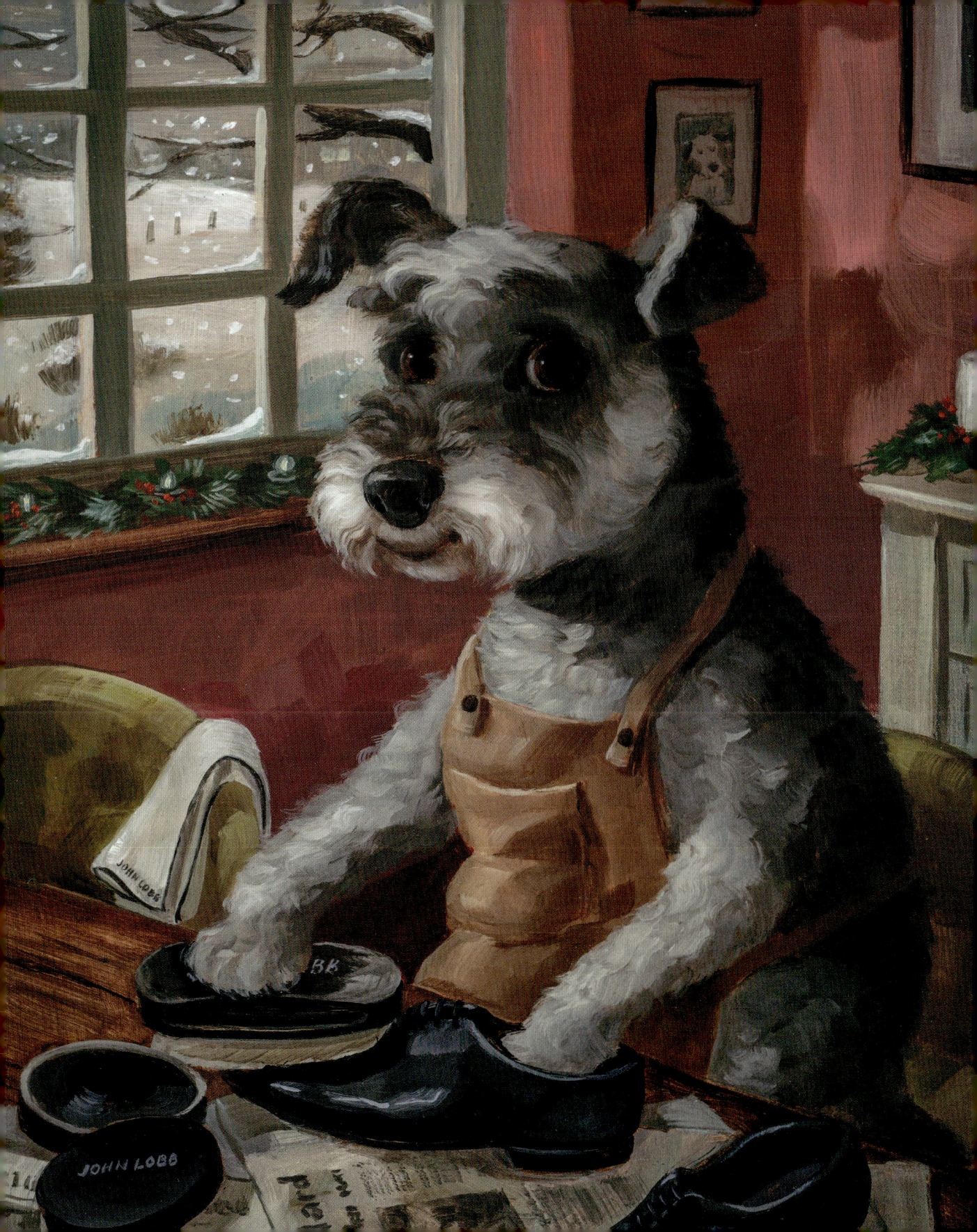

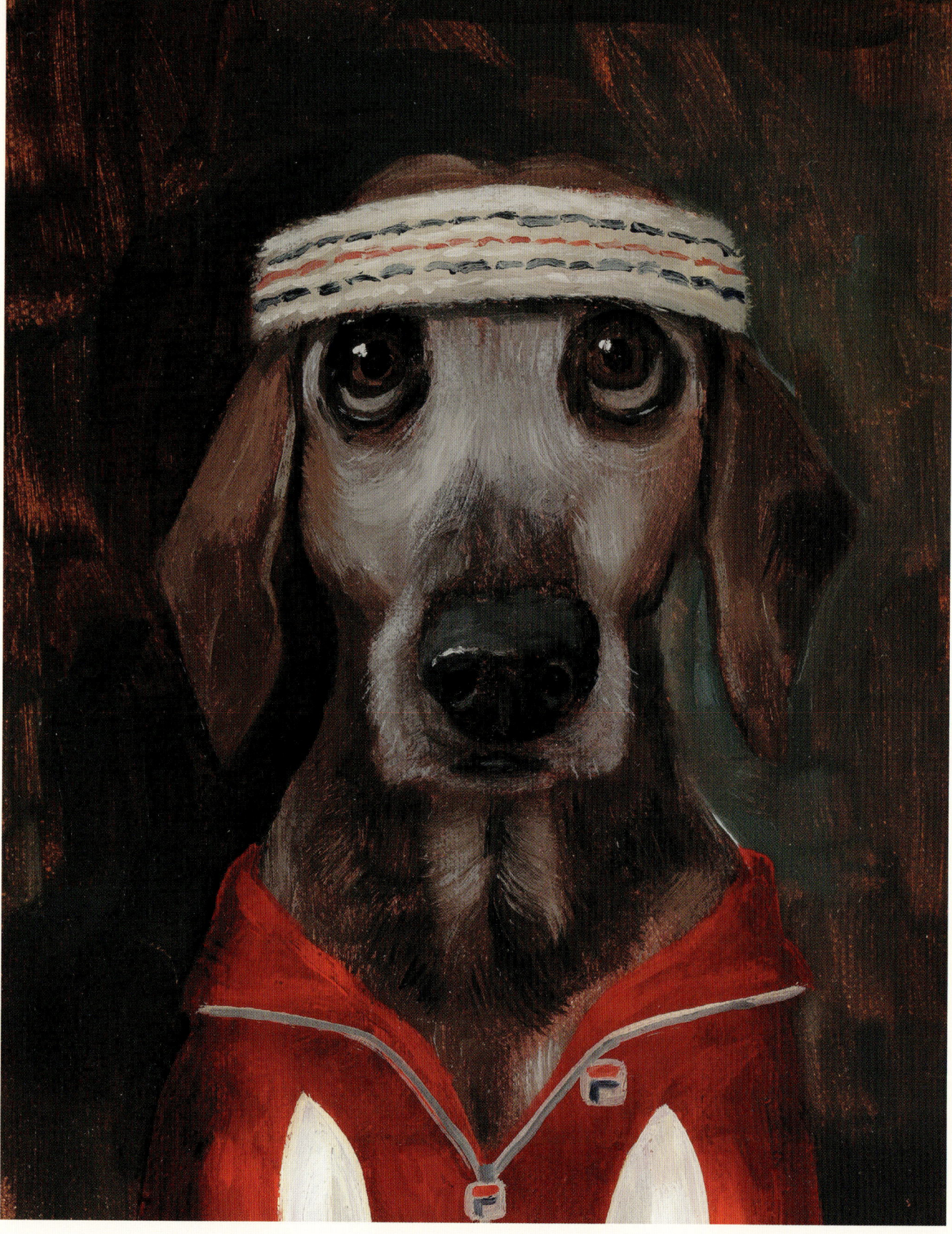

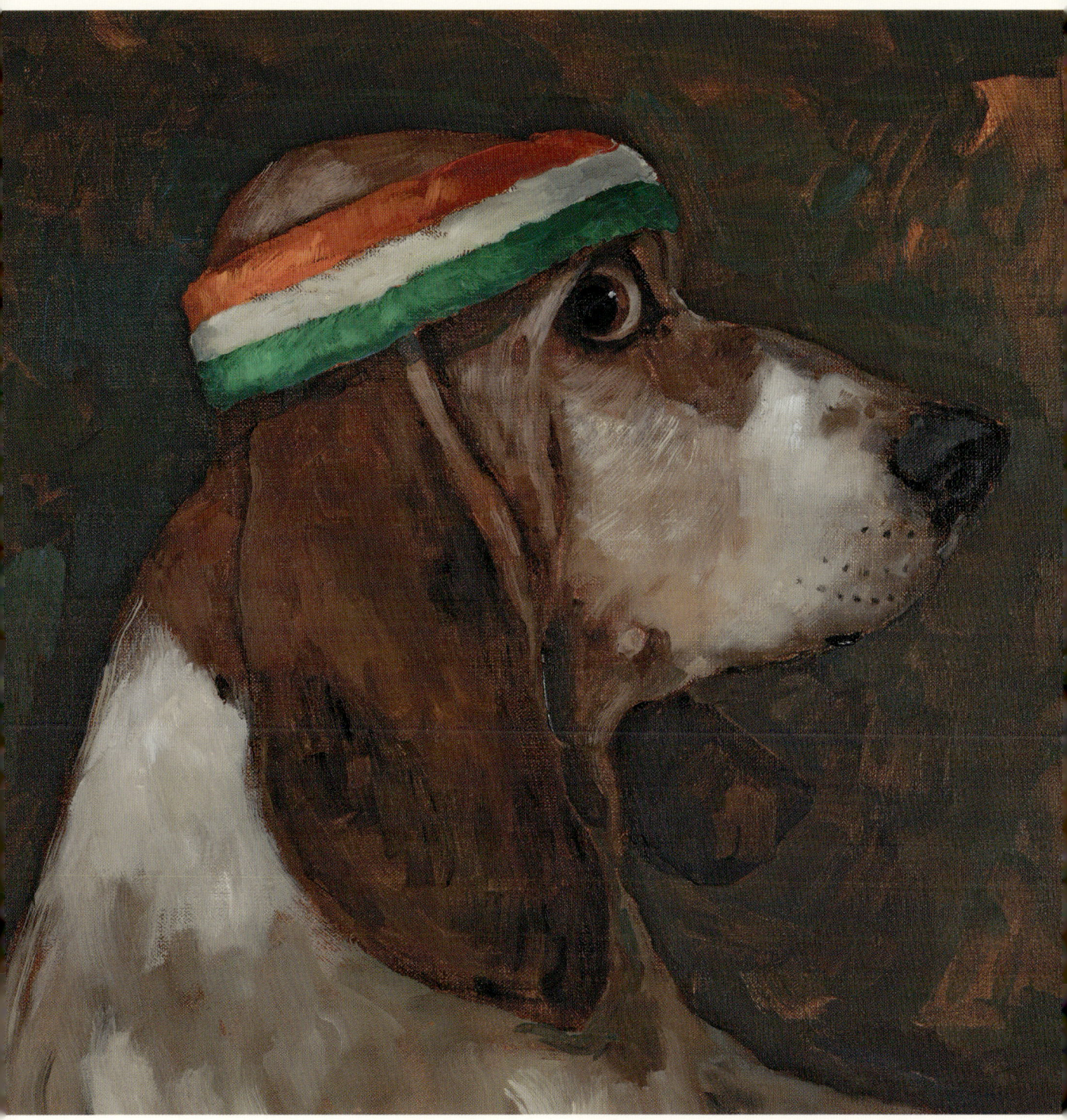

BASSET IN SWEATS | All the kit and no fit

LIFE IN THE OLD DOG | In vintage Fila

ARCHIE

He lost a ball and found six

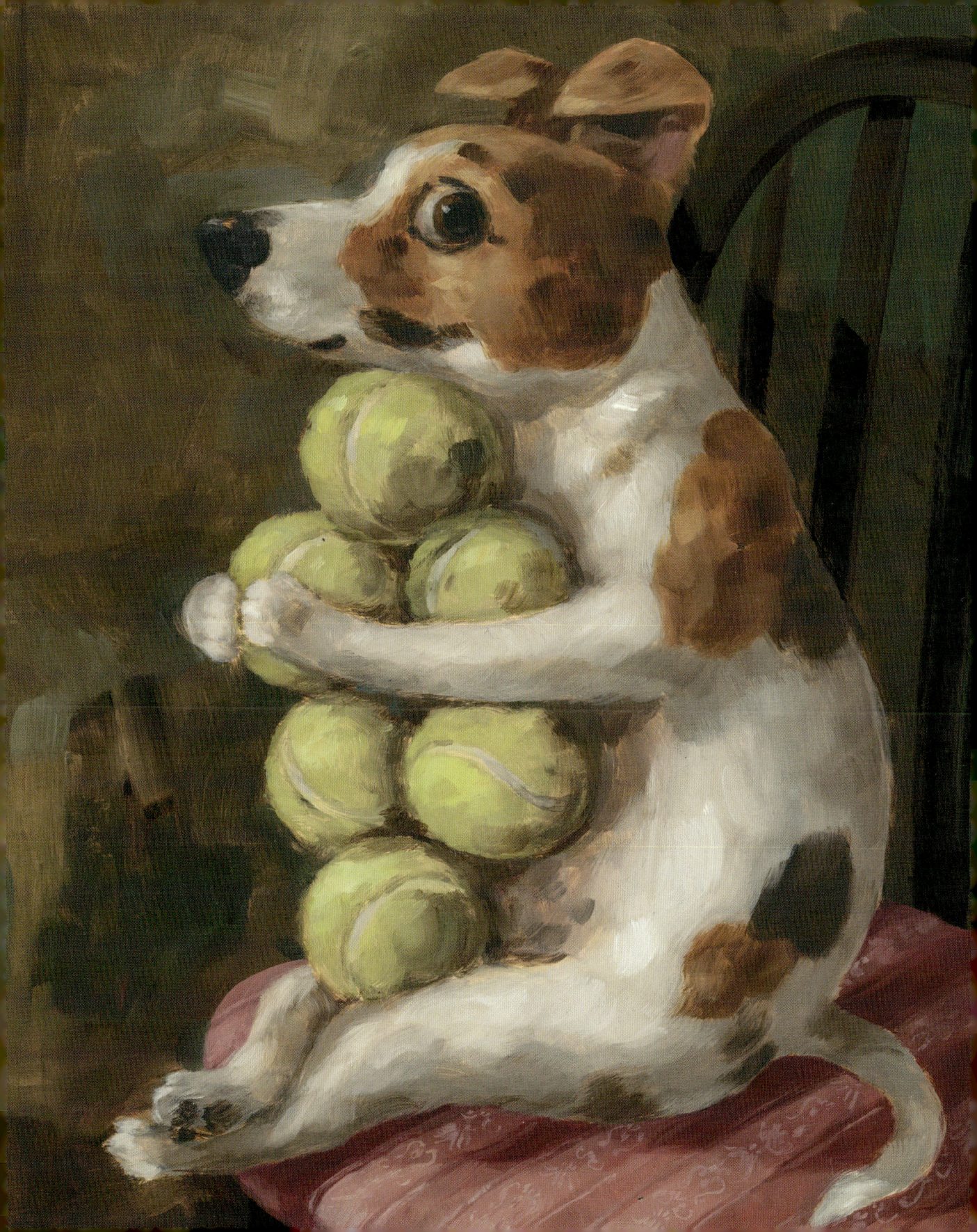

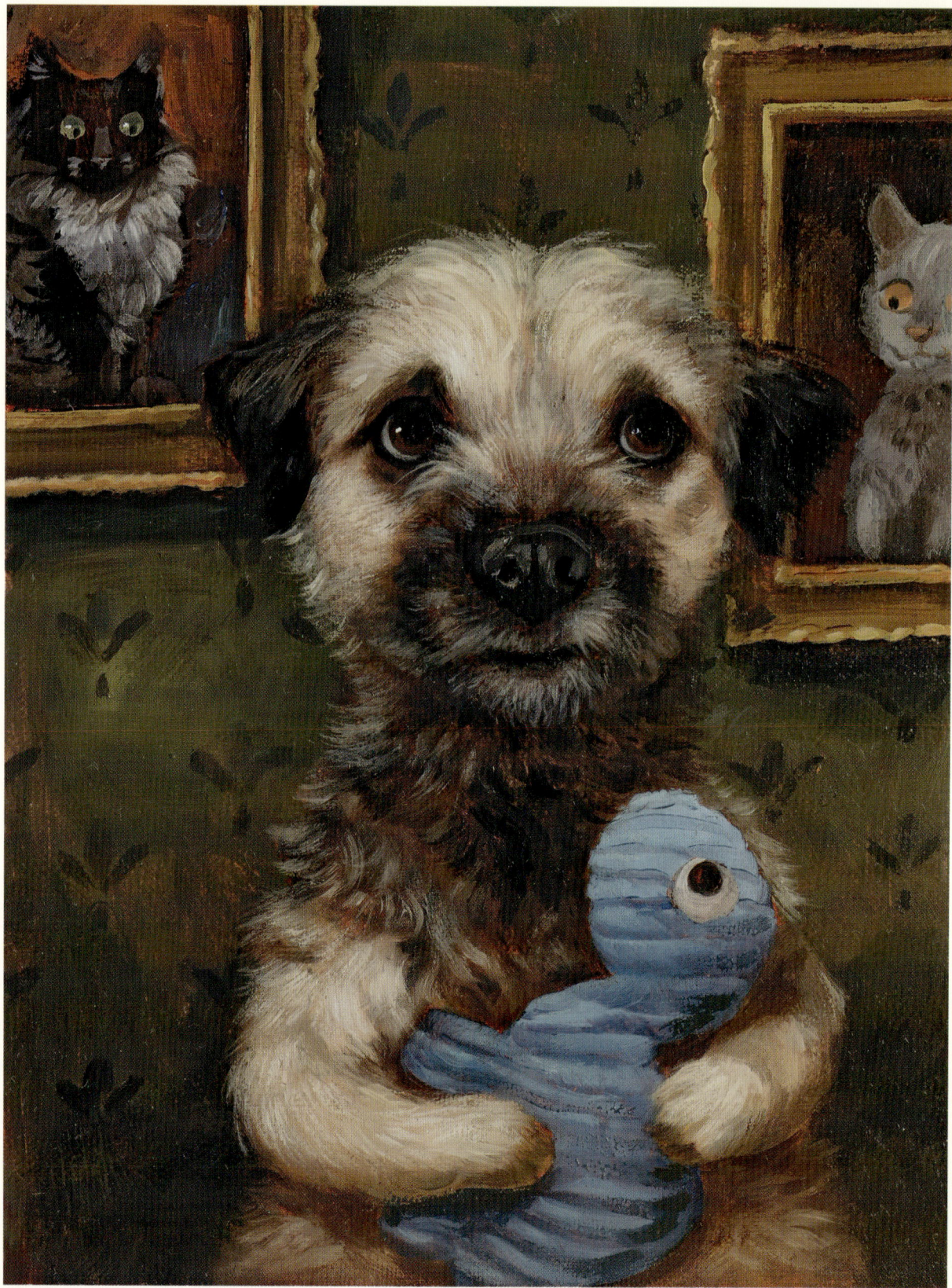

BISCUIT

And little blue dino

DAVE TINKLE

Tinkle by name, tinkle by nature

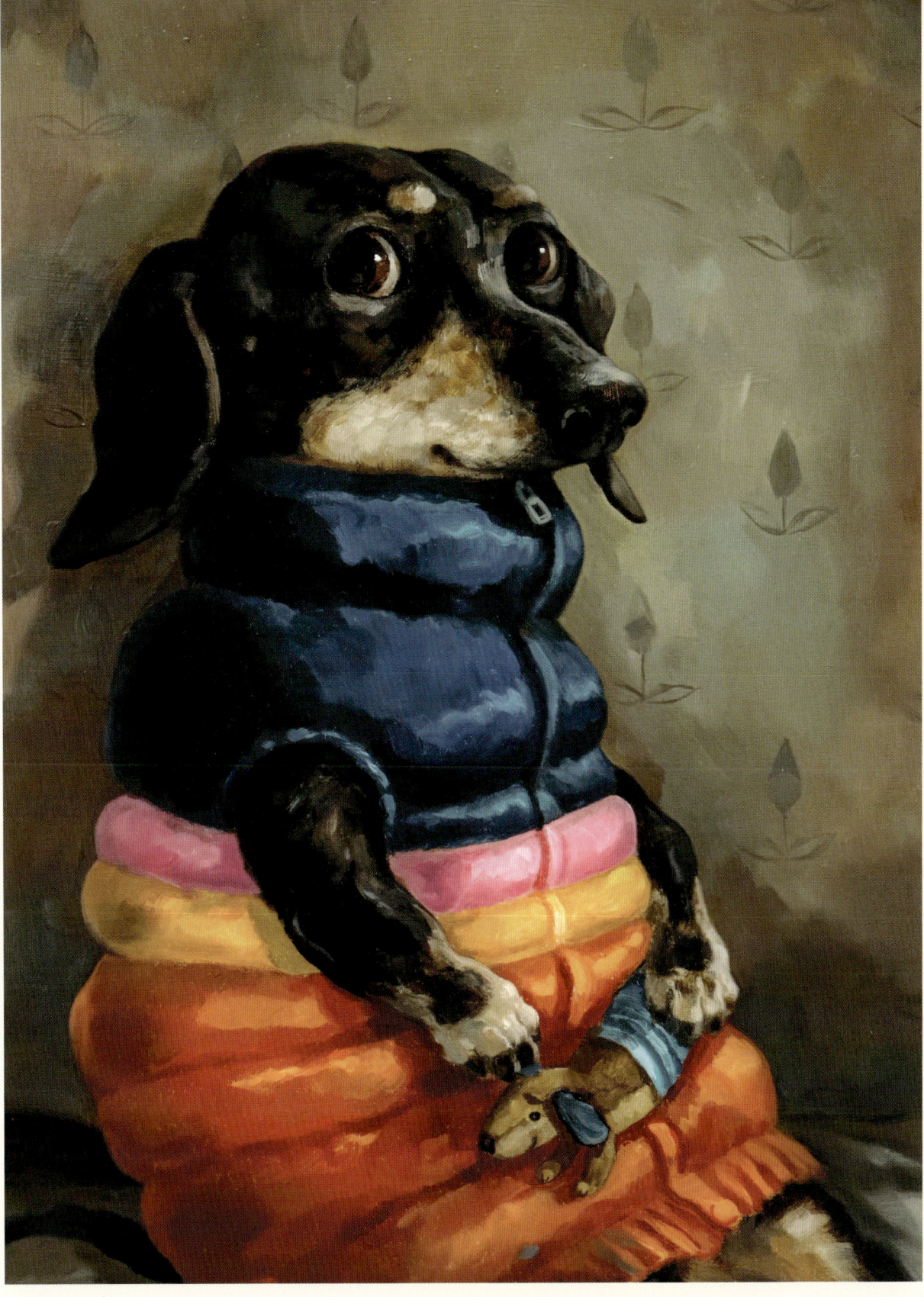

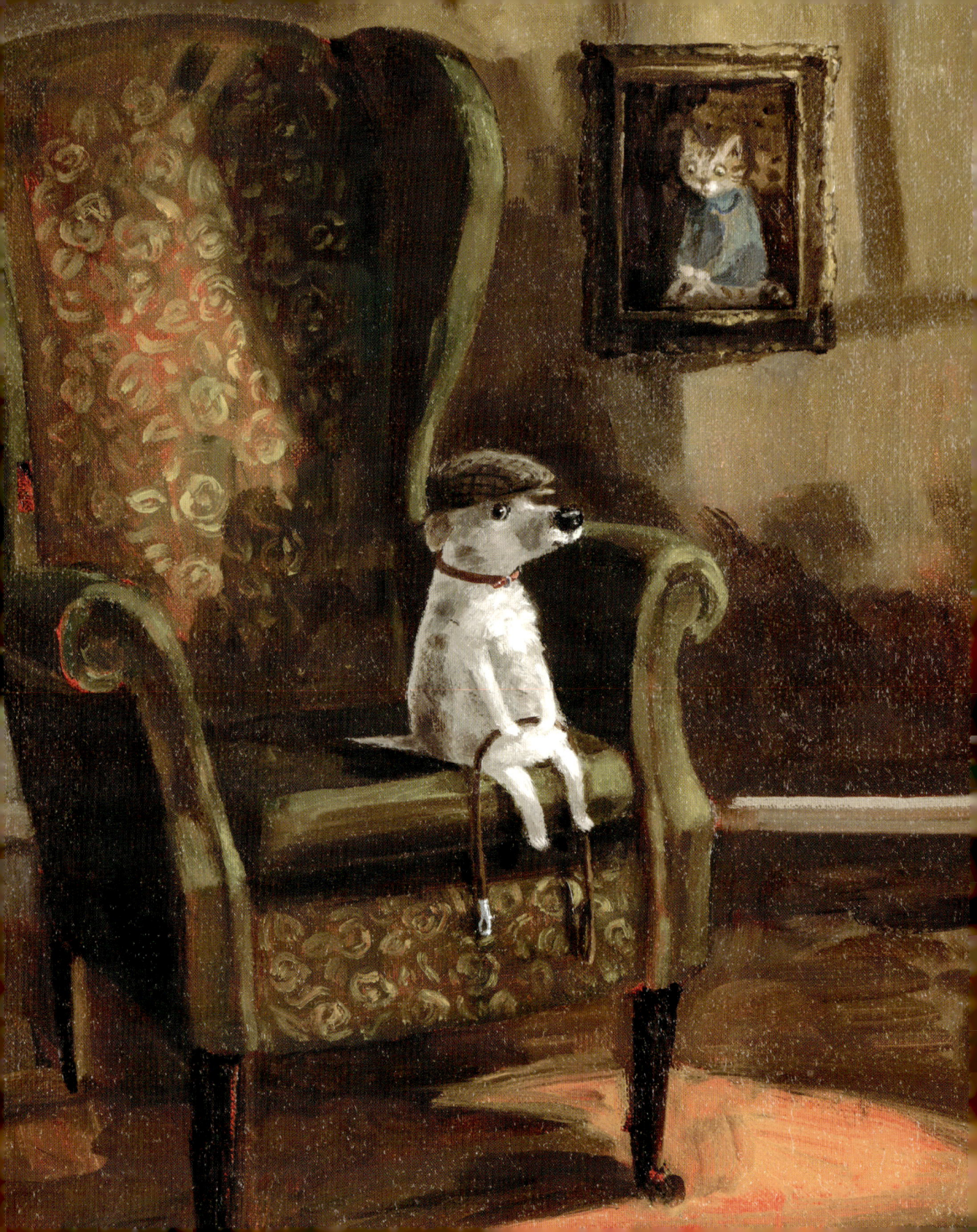

ERNEST

This is Ernest. He is, by anyone's standards, a very good boy. At 3:00 p.m. sharp he goes for a long walk with his human companion.

At 2:30 p.m. he finds his tweed cap and his leash, and he sits on the chair. His chair. Ready. The walk is the best part of his day, and he doesn't want to be late or scrambling at the last minute to find his things before they leave.

His human has a tweed cap too. They are quite the pair . . . inseparable . . . the best of friends. Their afternoon routine has been like this for the last ten years (that's seventy in dog years). Rain or shine. All that fresh air. All those hellos to people they know . . . and those they don't. All those smells.

When they get back home, Ernest is ready for his dinner.

YOGHURT CHOPS

Need a yoghurt pot cleaning? This little lady
has fourteen years' experience

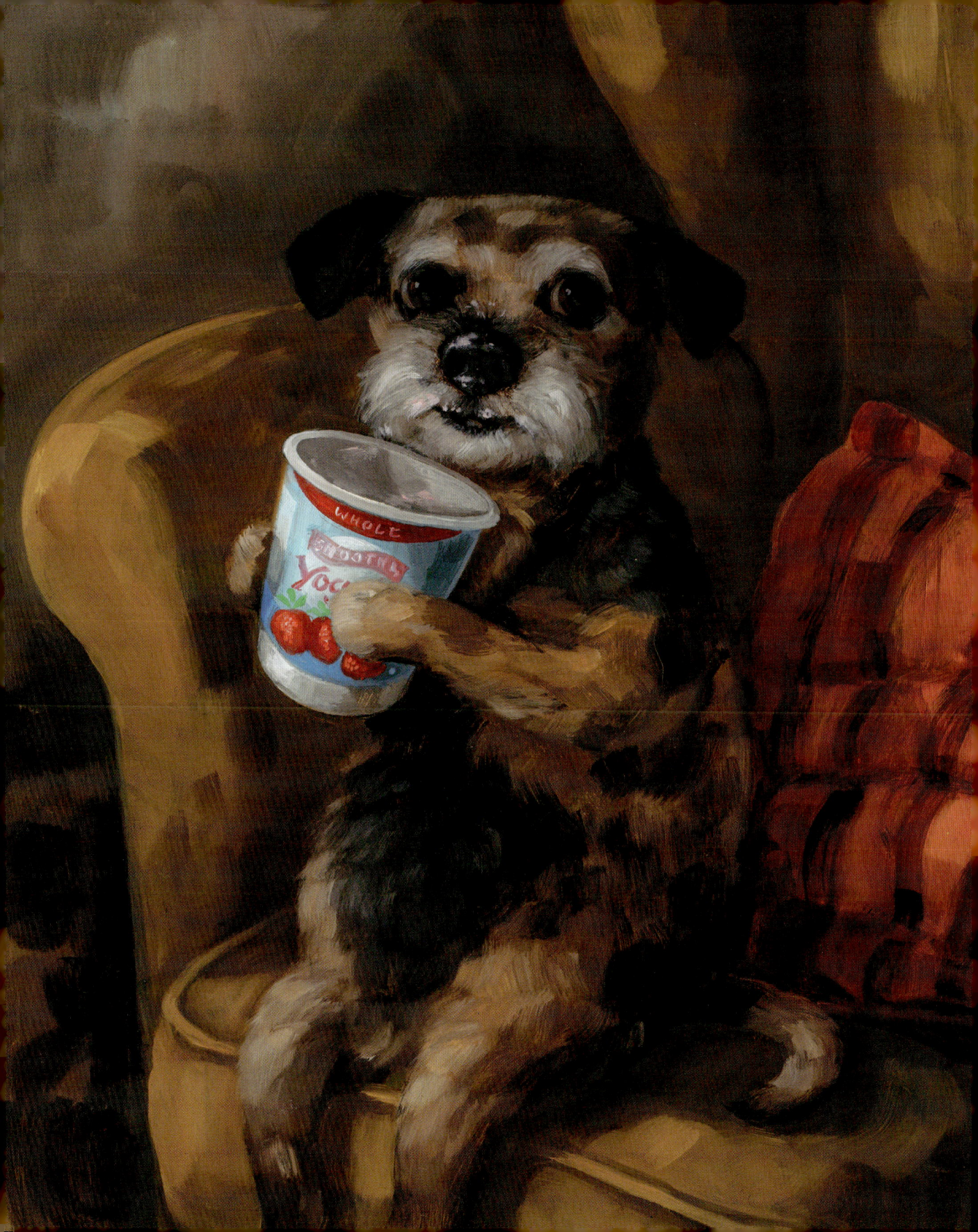

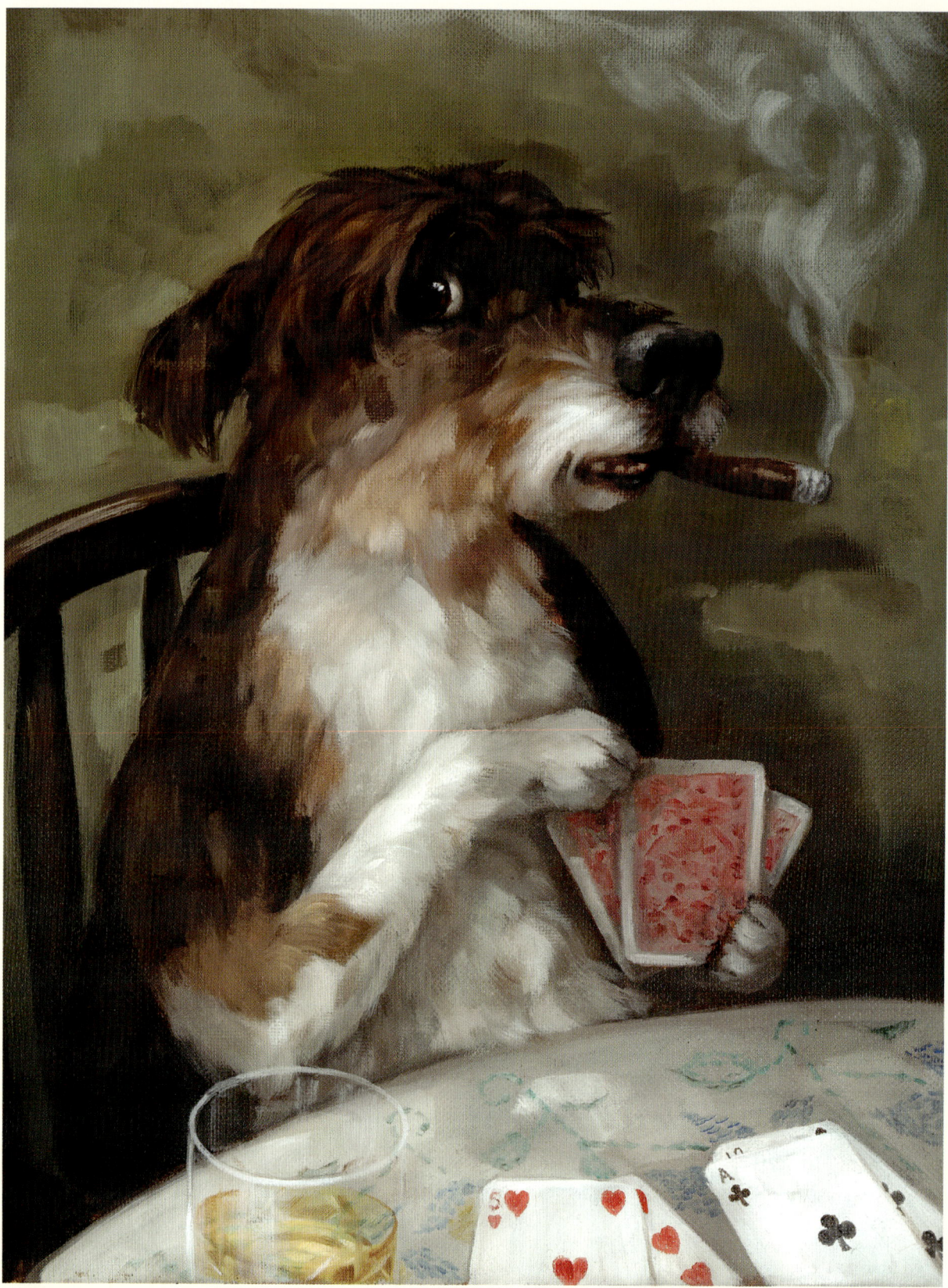

POKER NIGHT

He always plays his cards
close to his chest

HIS GRANNY KNITTED IT

And he loves it!

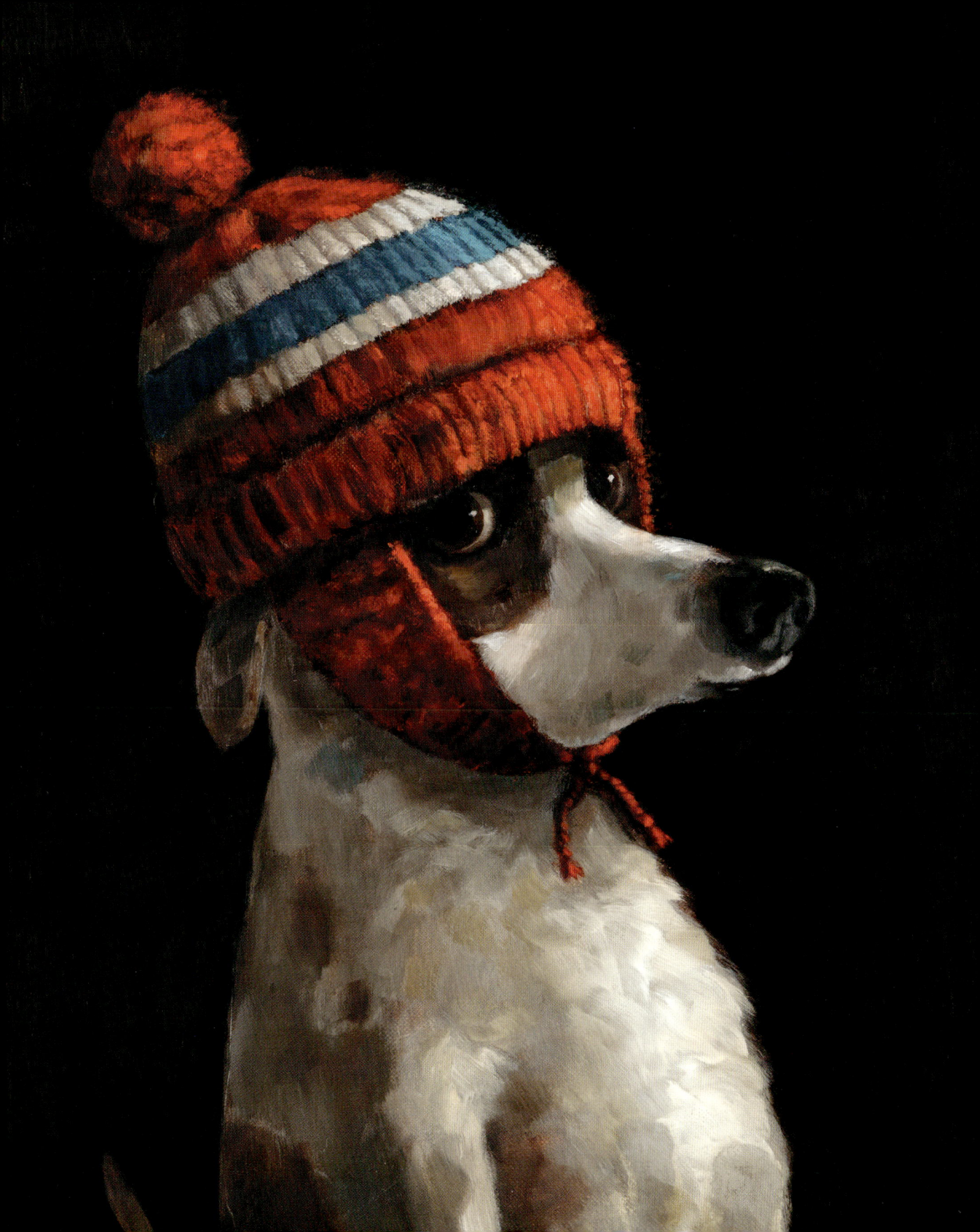

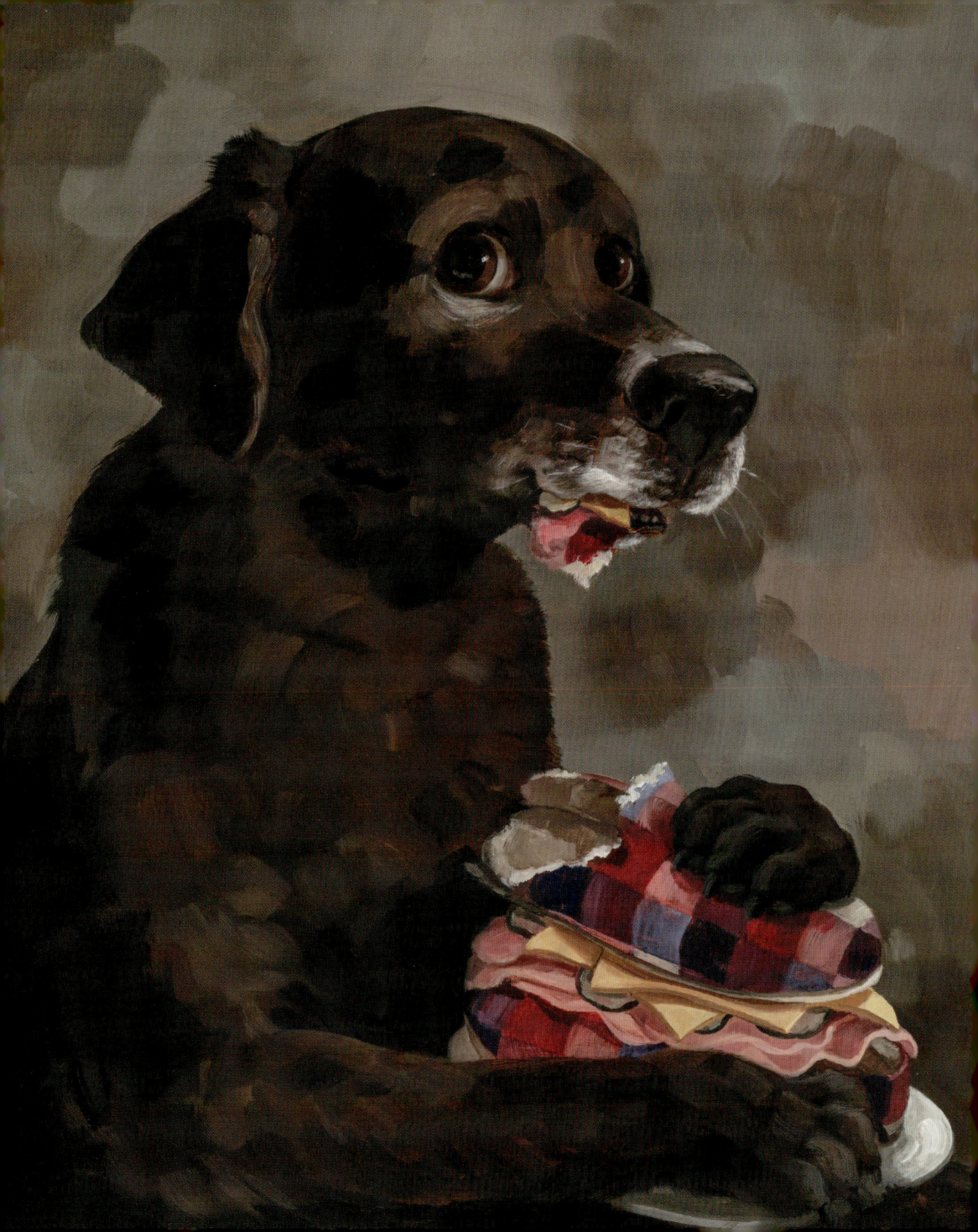

HAM, CHEESE, AND PICKLE
SLIPPER SANDWICH

With extra slipper, please

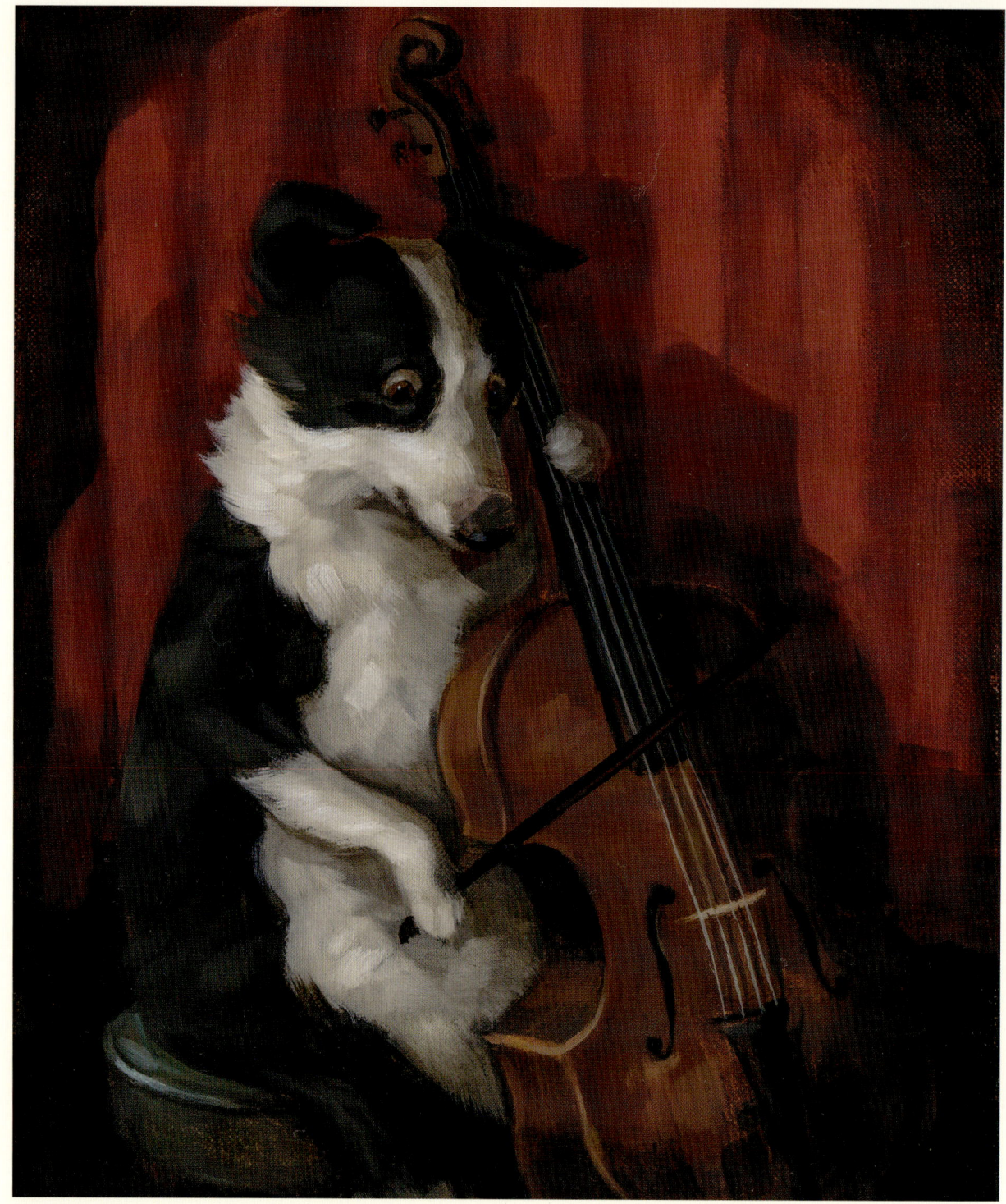

MEG | She fell in love with the cello

DALMATIAN | He's on first violin

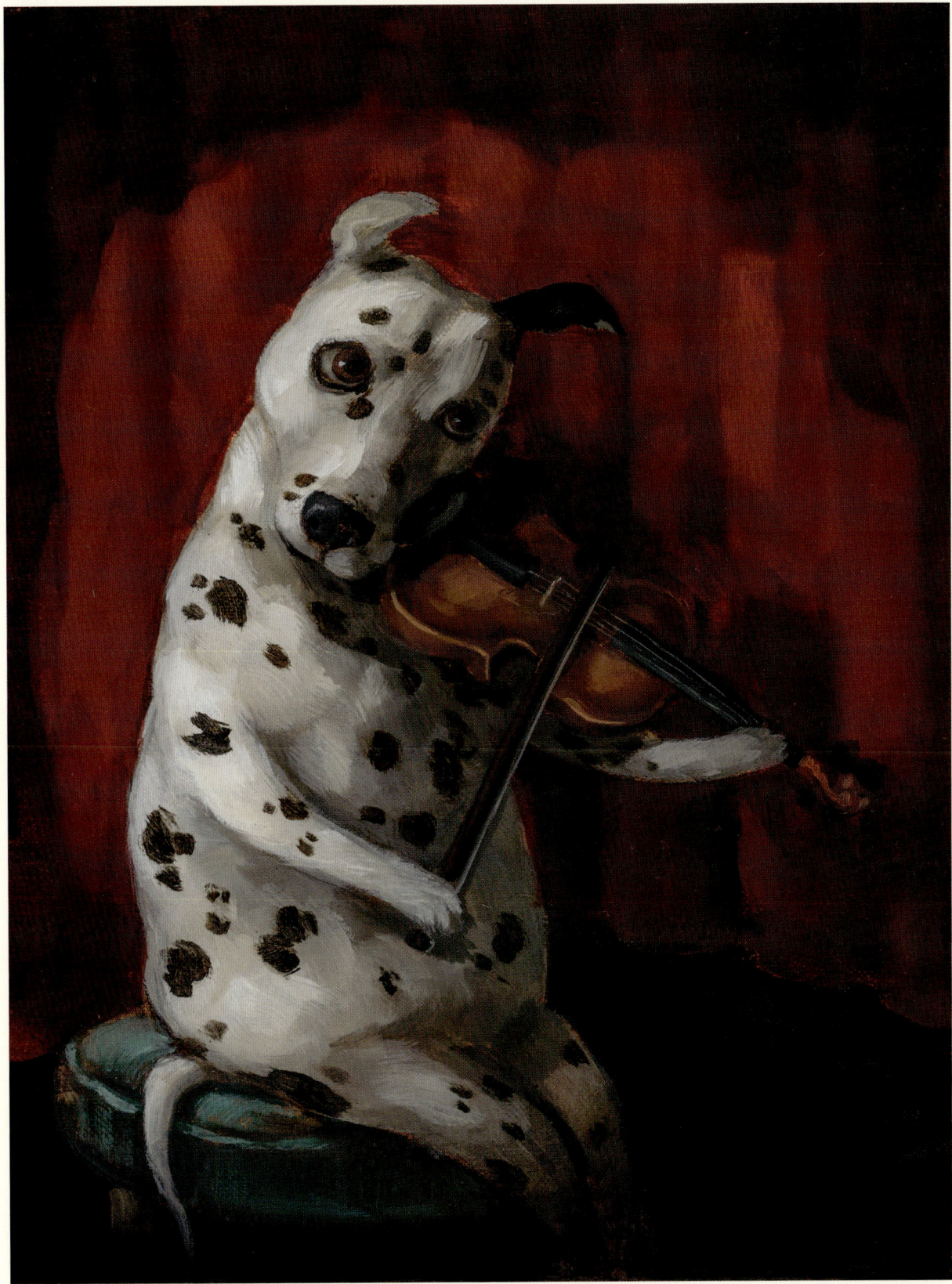

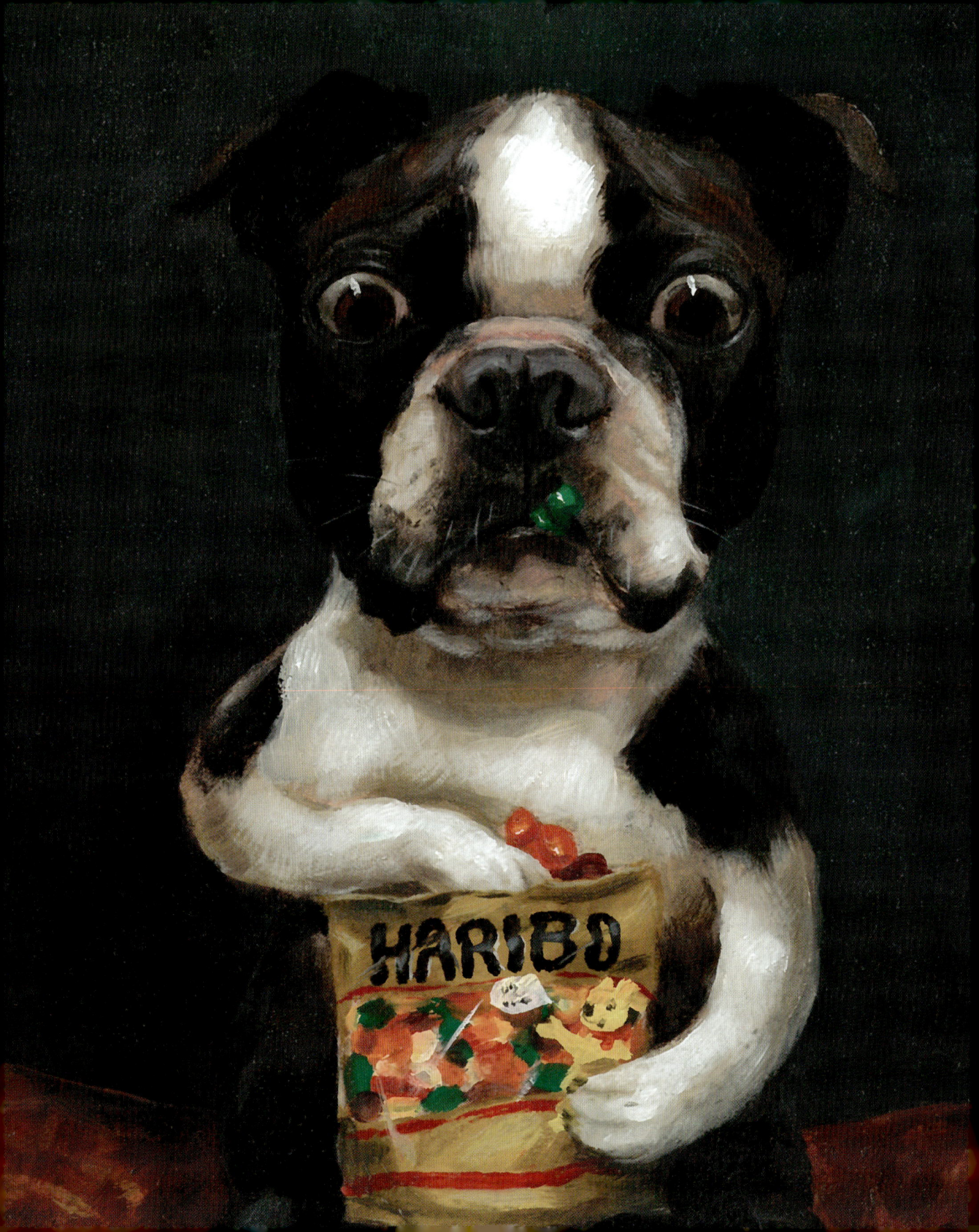

DAVE

He loves the green ones the best

**I DON'T KNOW ANYTHING
ABOUT ANY DONUT**

"And that's all I'm saying
on the matter"

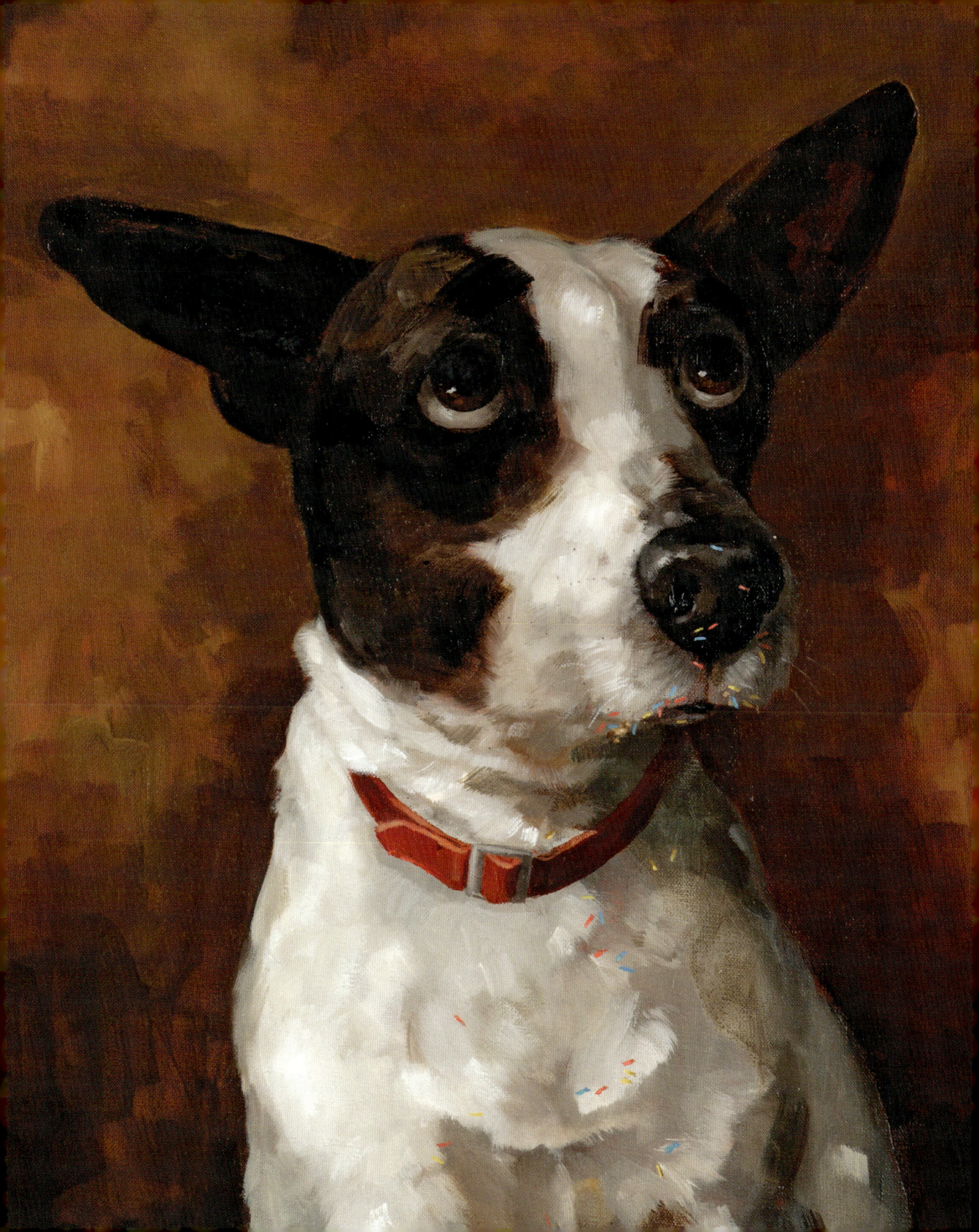

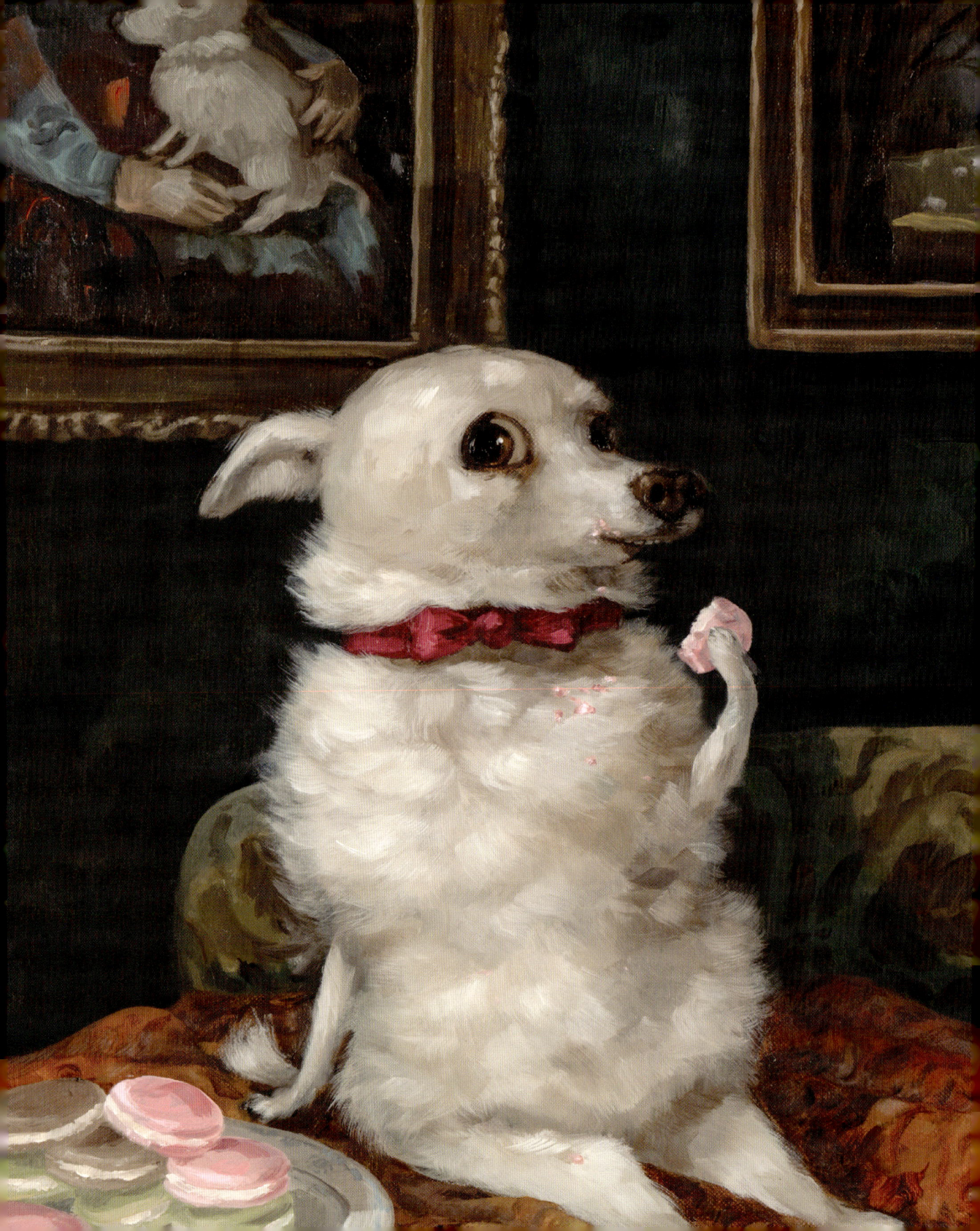

MACARONS FOR JOSEPHINE

Josephine lives in a manor fit for a queen. Surrounded by luxurious textiles and feather-filled cushions, she subsists on a diet of macarons and Champagne. If she does not get the raspberry flavor, which is her favourite, or if her Champagne is not chilled to perfection, she can become quite nippy.

She likes the company of other dogs but only the fancy, well-bred kinds—with double-barreled names.

I LOVE MY BALL

"Well, any ball, really;
this is my 154th"

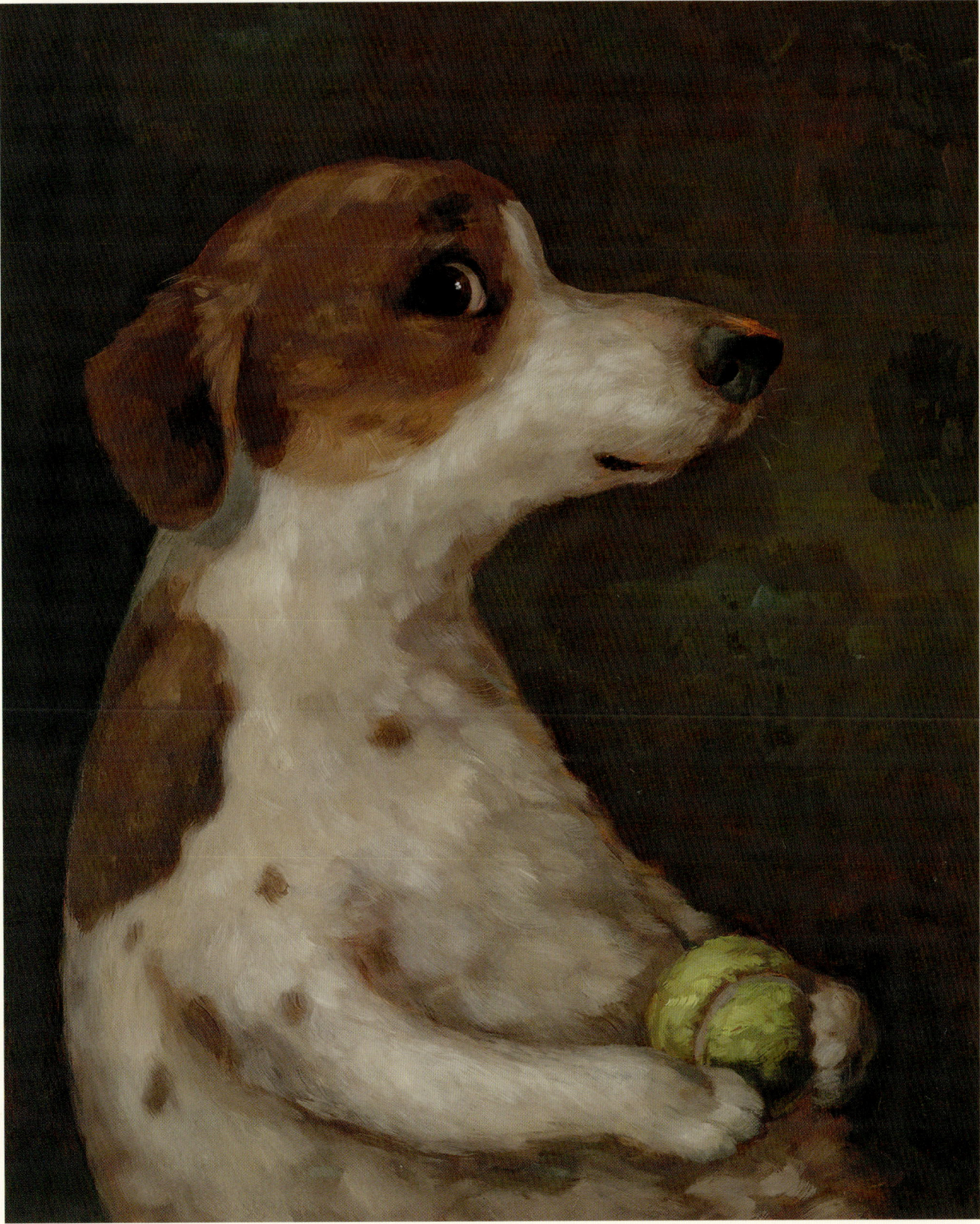

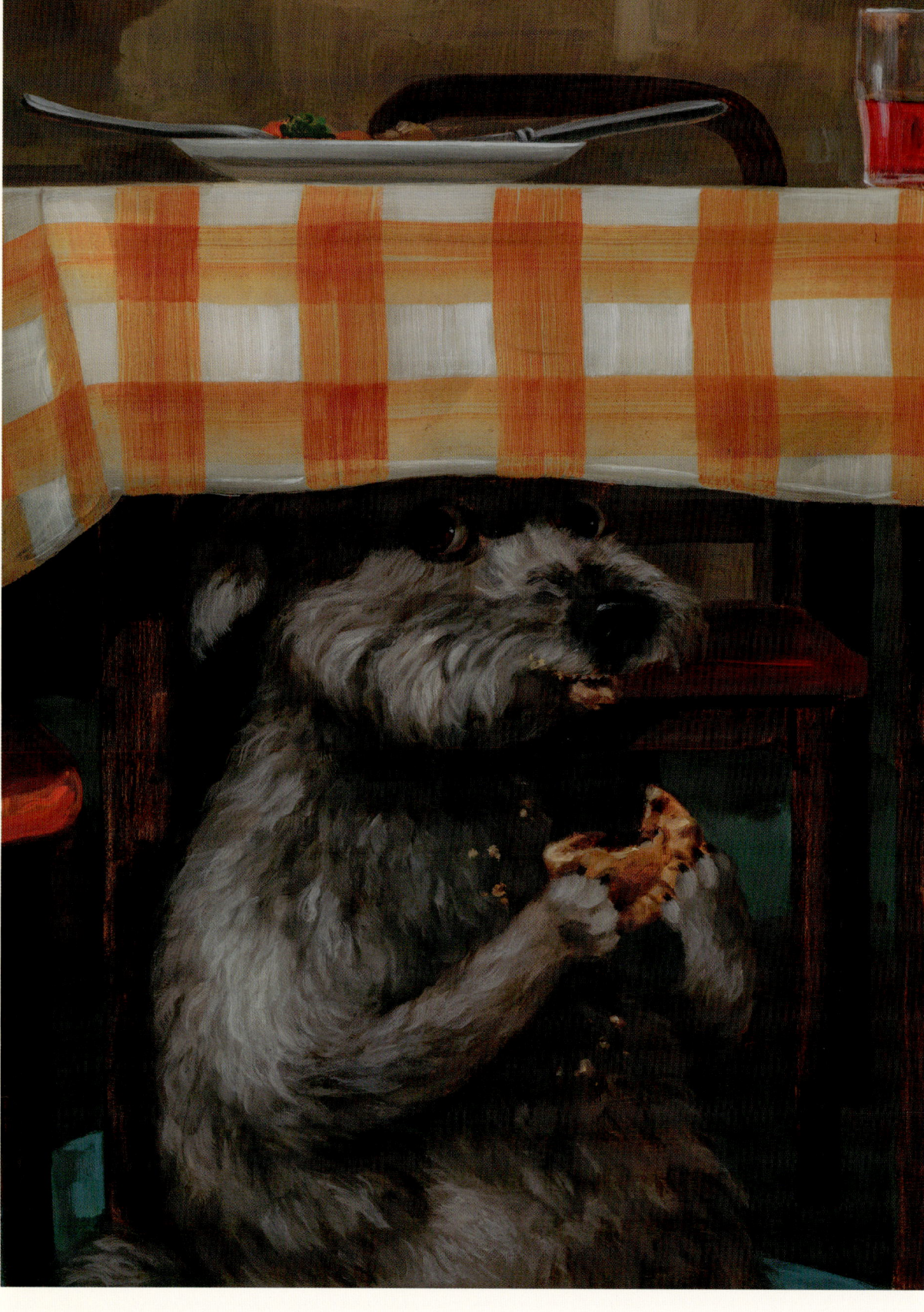

UNDER THE TABLE BUFFET

"Right place, right time" is this
pup's motto

CHOOSE BISCUITS

Of any kind

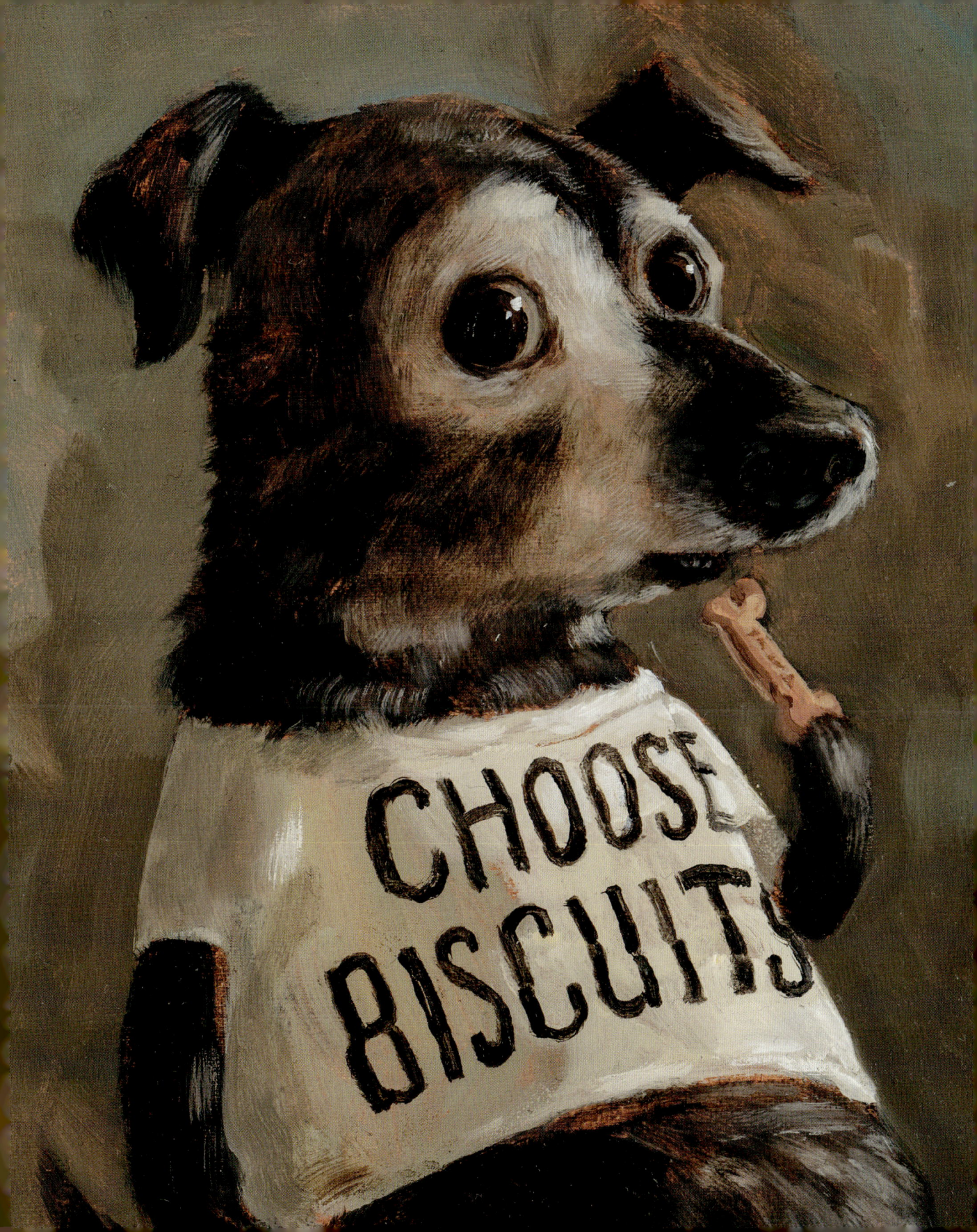

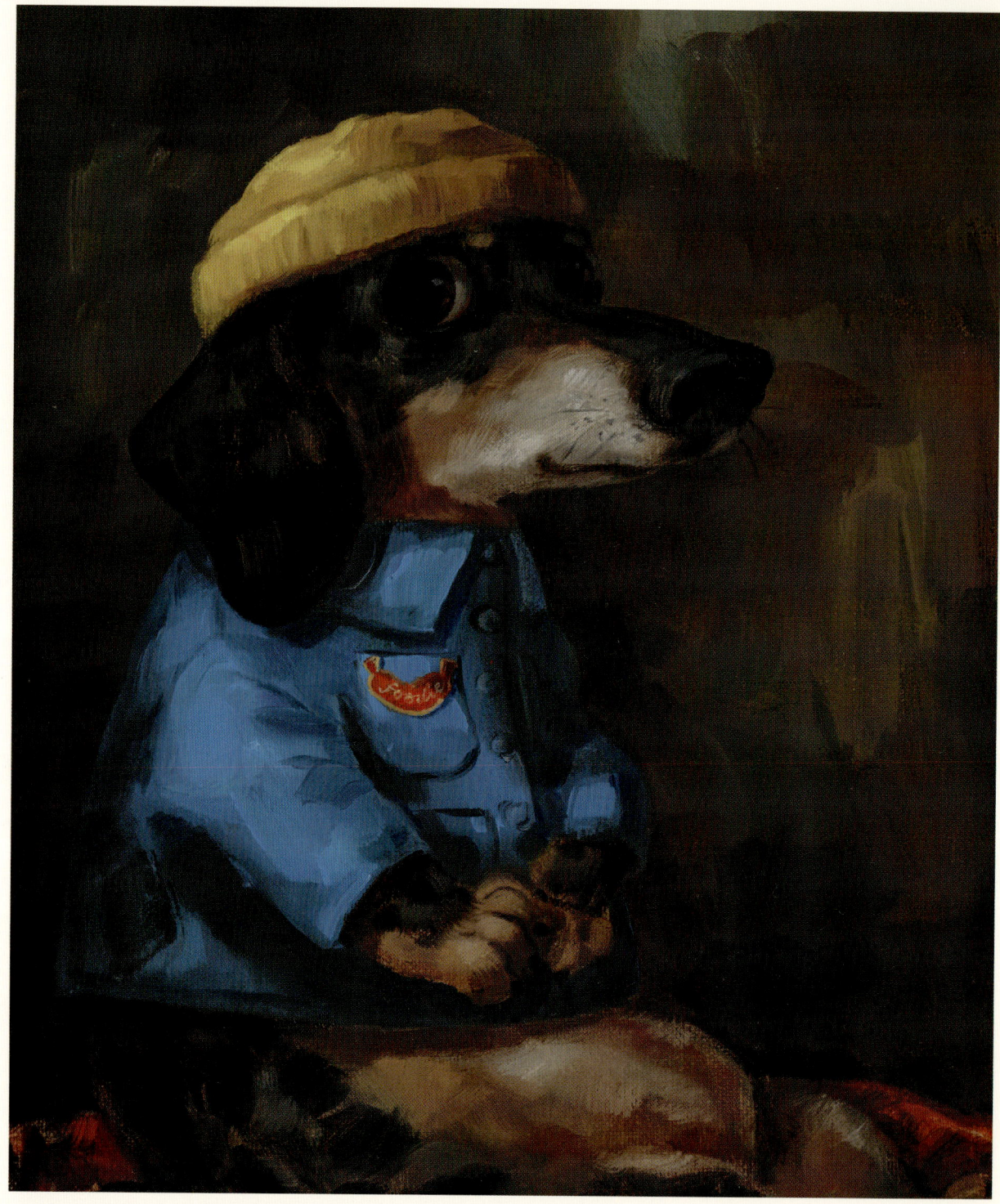

LITTLE RUDY | He's a foodie

LITTLE SUE | Rock chick

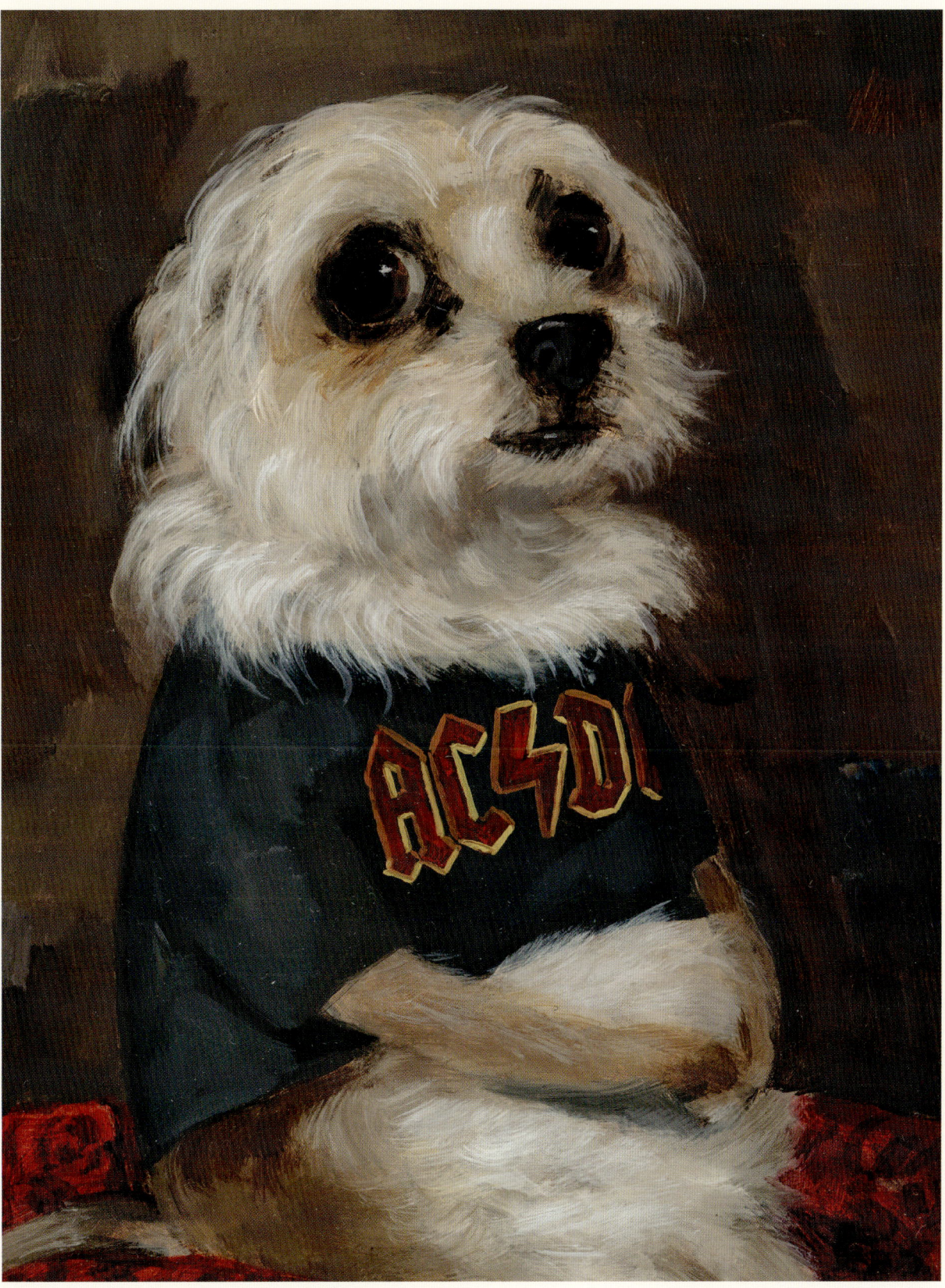

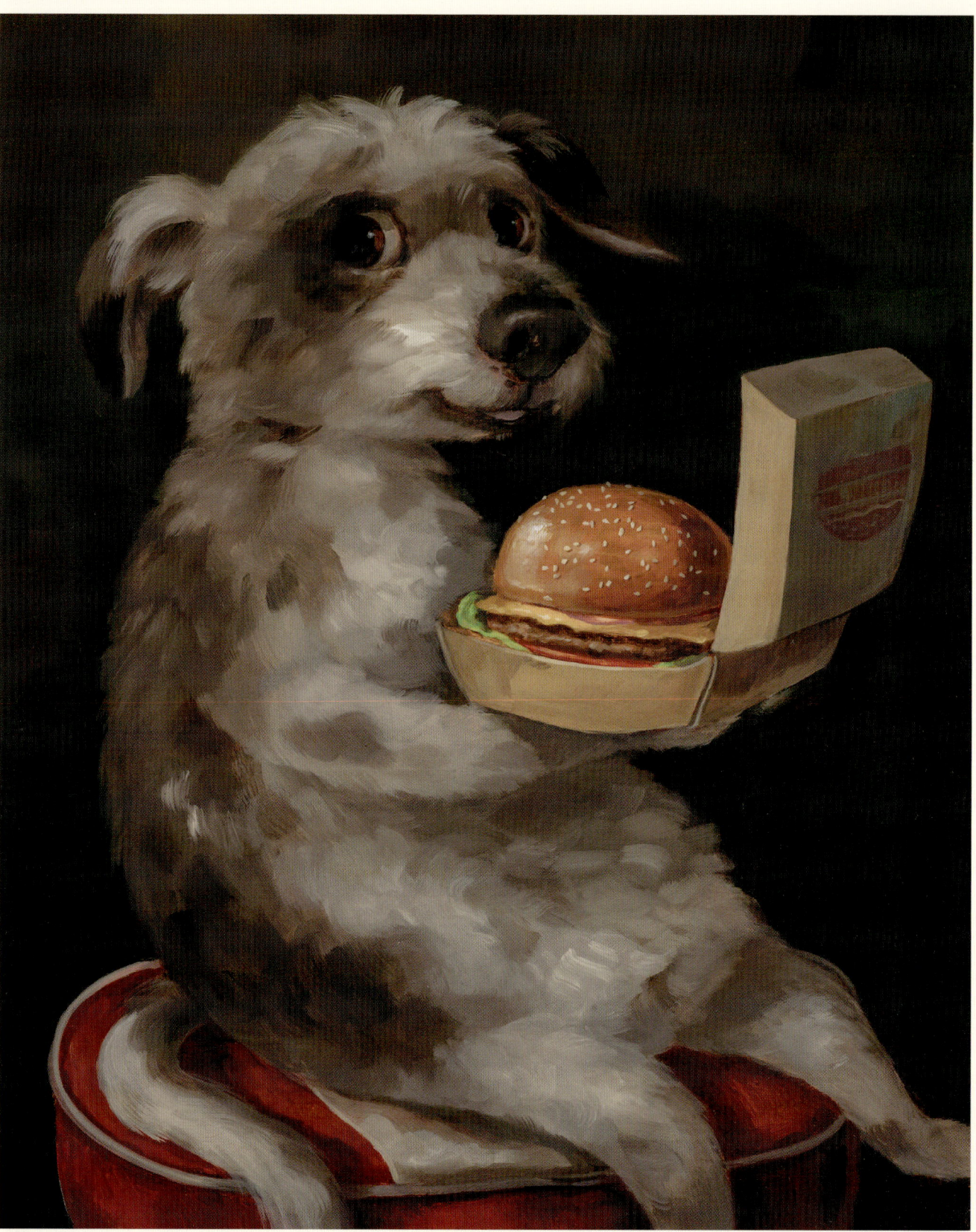

LEFT HOLDING THE BURGER

The ultimate test of trust

FOUND A FRIEND

"I found you and I'm not letting you go . . . whether you like it or not"

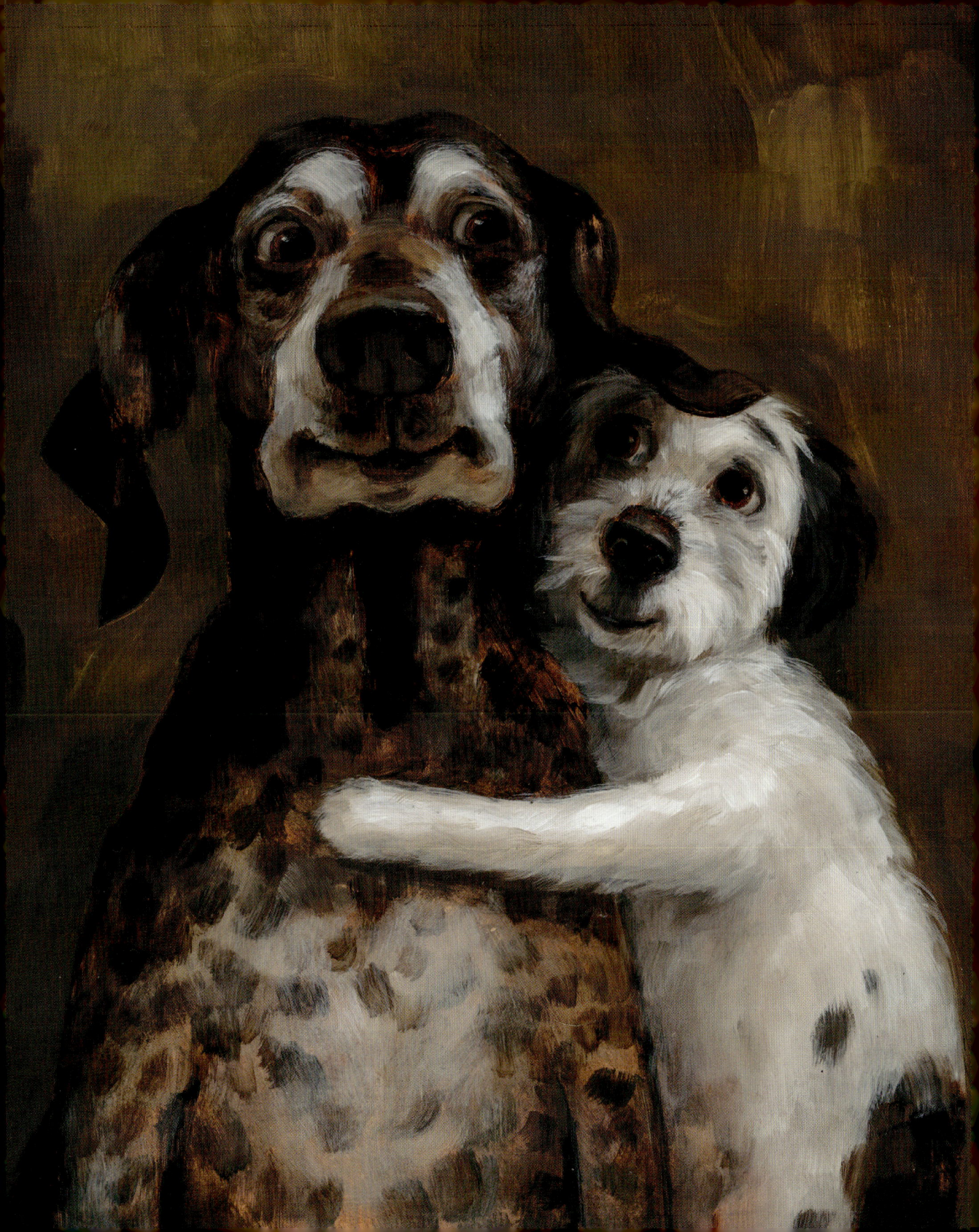

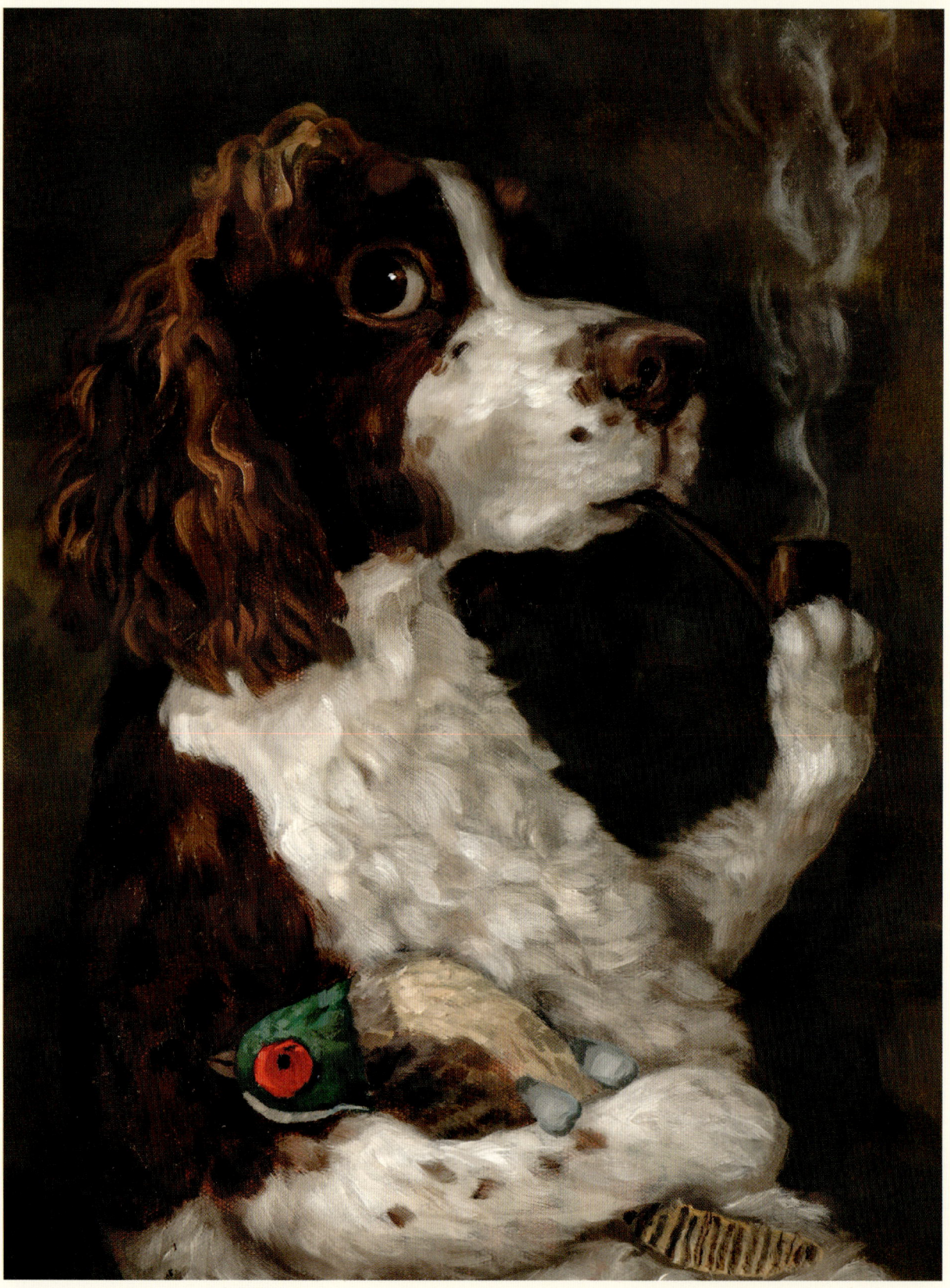

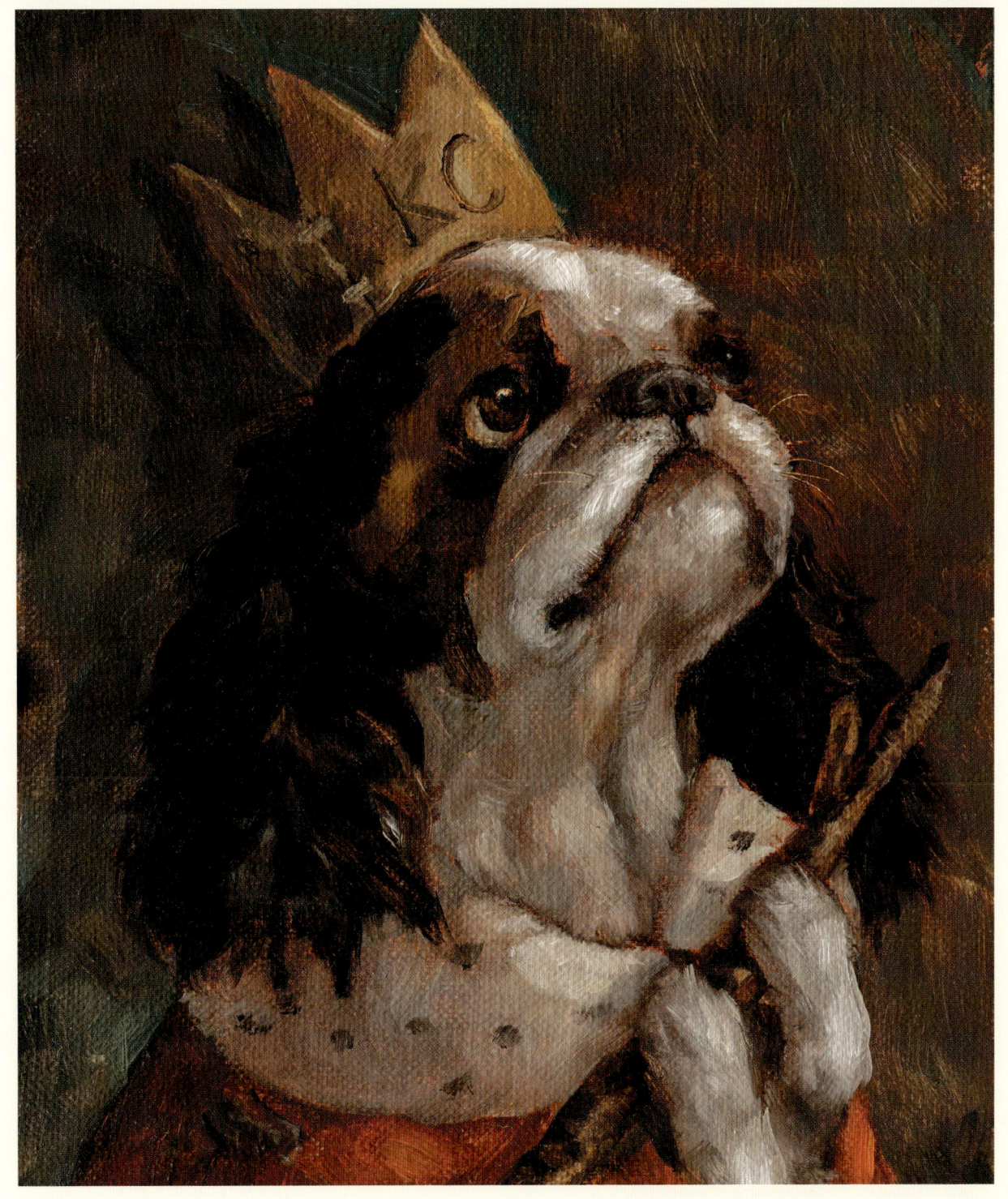

KING CHARLES | Coronation ready!

DANIEL | He loves a pipe after an exciting
day of flushing toy pheasants

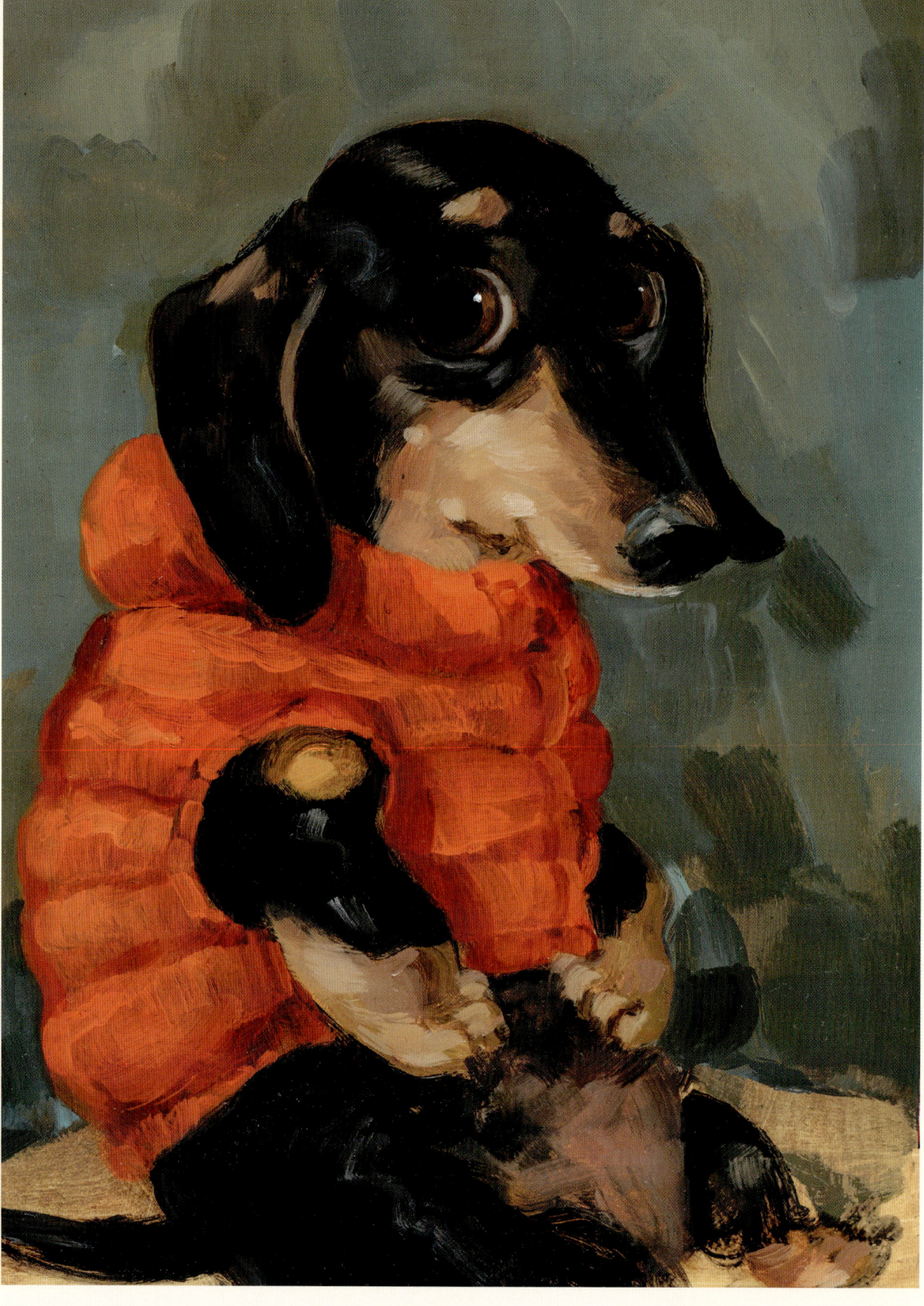

PUPPY IN A PUFFER

She's ready to step out for
the first time

PATSY

Hey, Patsy, fetch! Patsy, sit! Patsy, stay!

She wasn't doing any of that good dog stuff until she'd had her coffee.

She was forty-nine (in dog years) and past the age of trying to impress.

Patsy had been around the block. So many times. Always with her humans to their favourite coffee shop. Every day for the past seven years. It's no wonder she developed a taste for it.

"And the usual for Patsy?" the barista would say. "I'll make hers first."

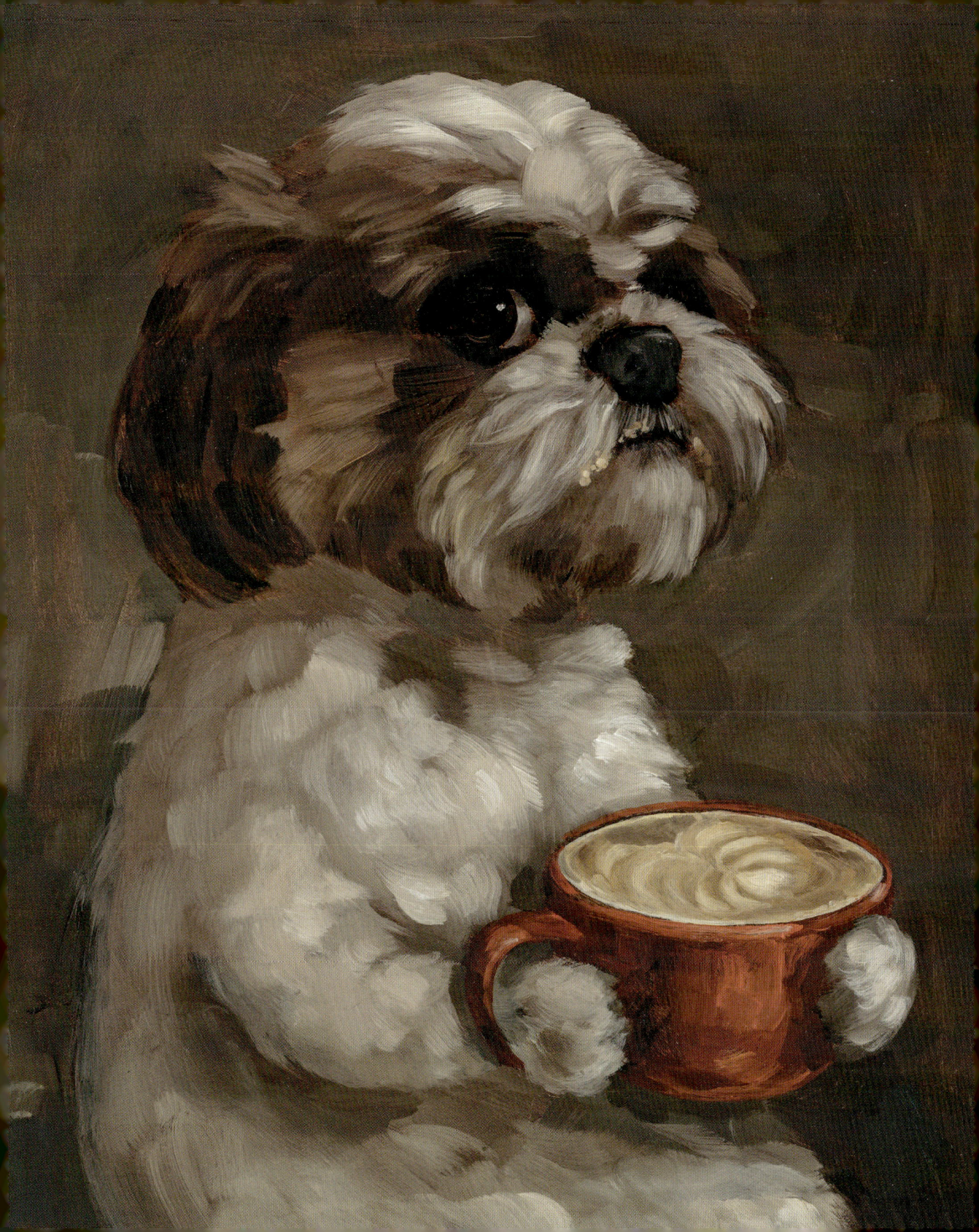

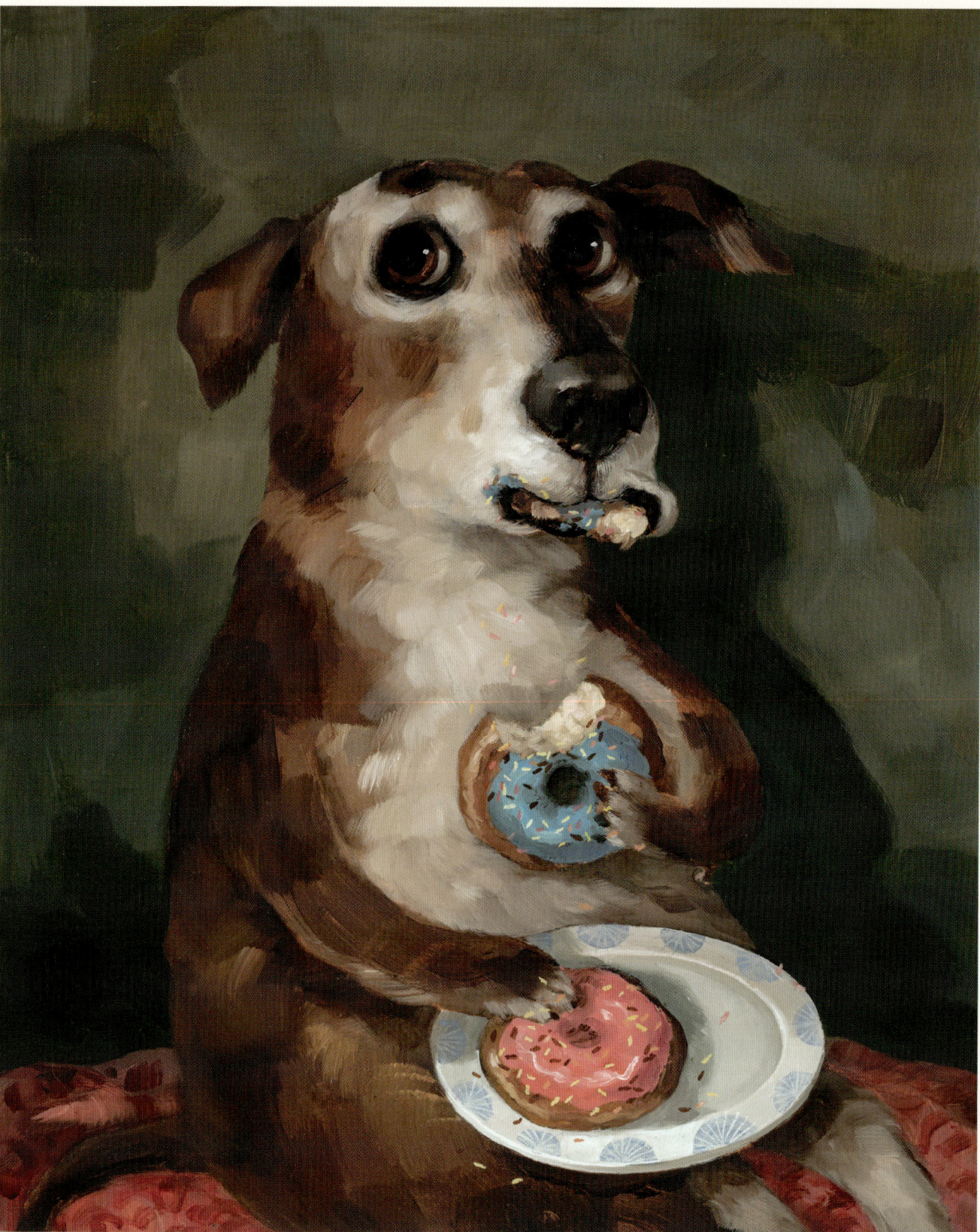

ONE IS NEVER ENOUGH

The universal rule of donuts

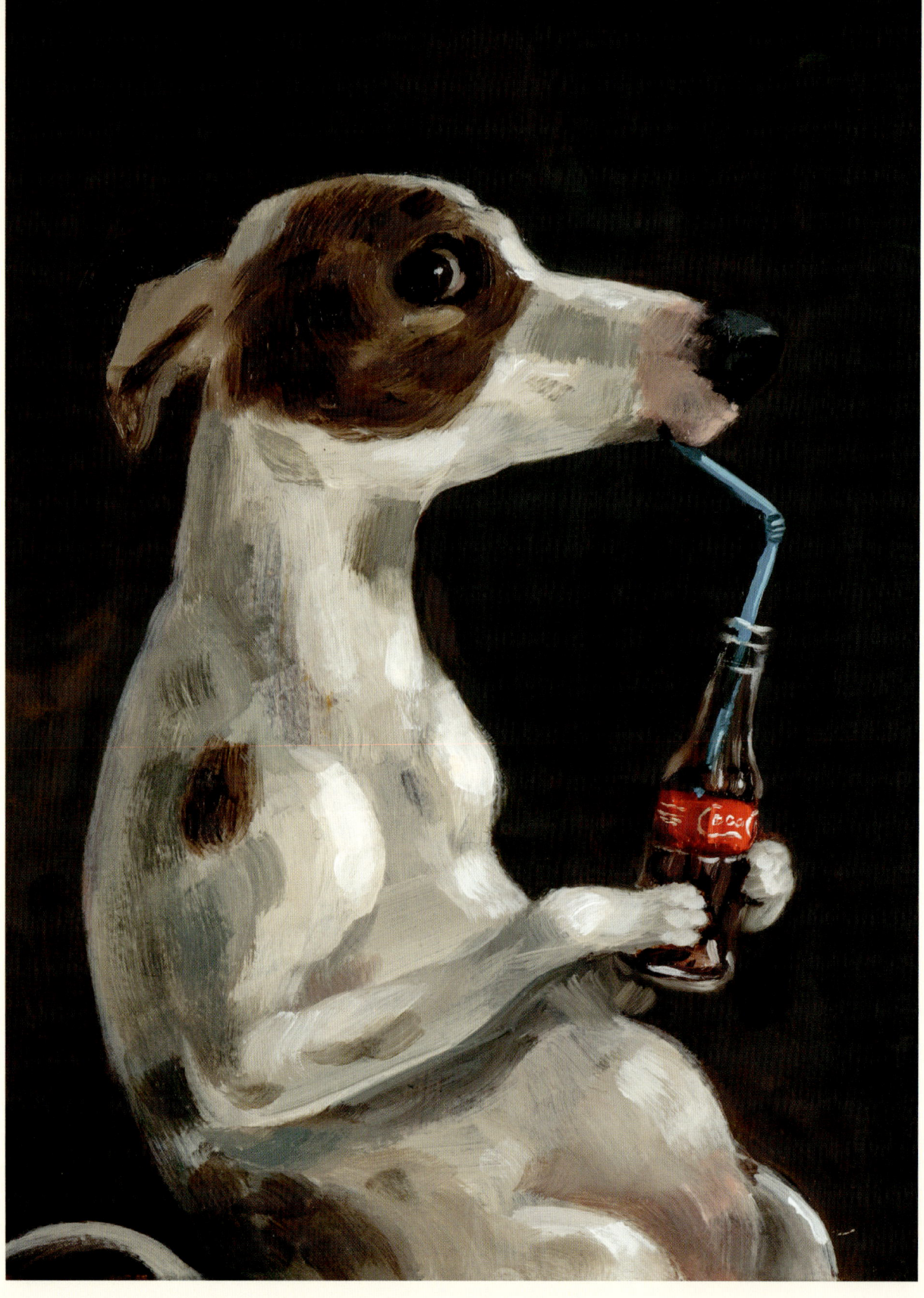

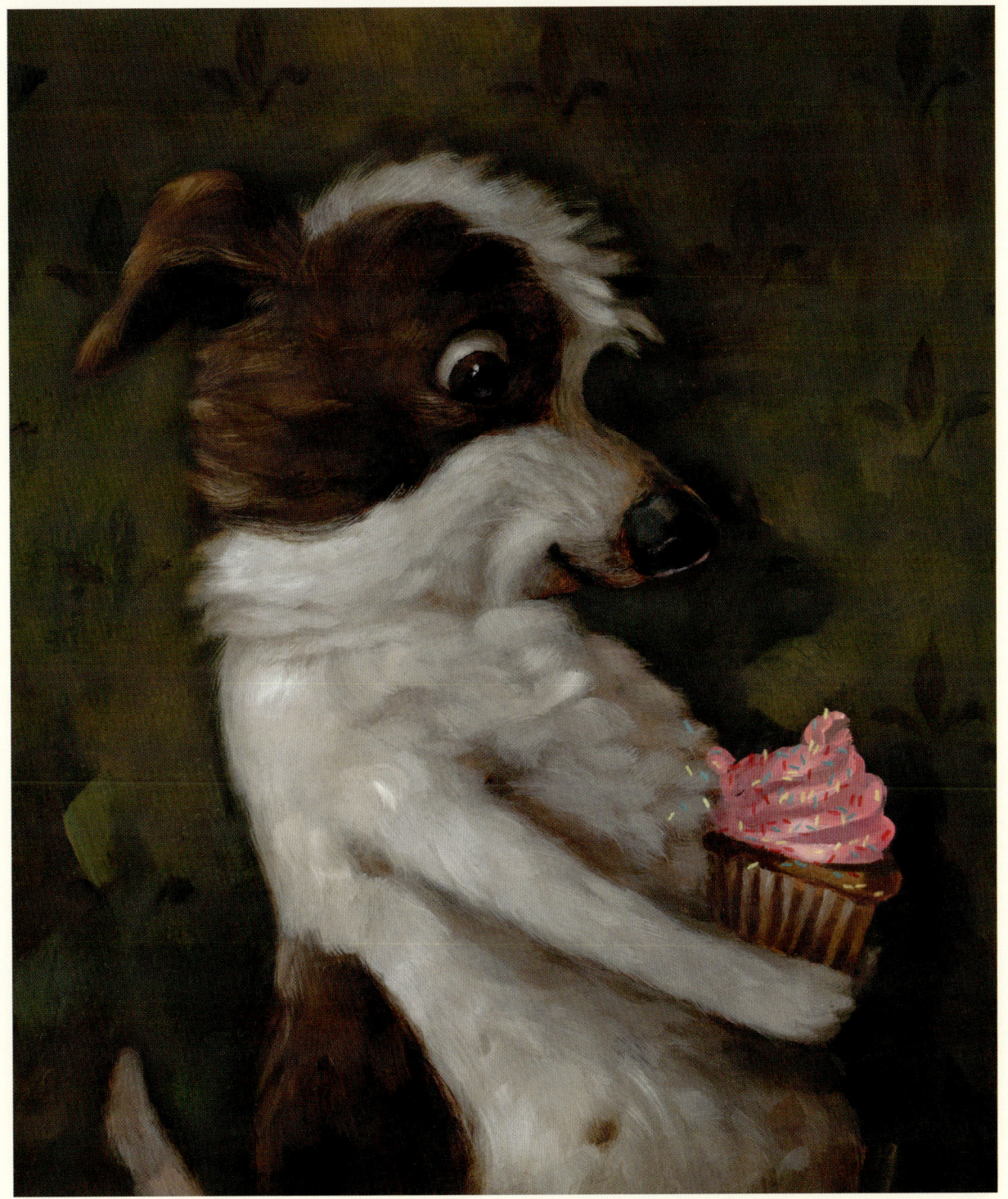

HAPPY BIRTHDAY TO ME | A cupcake for tea

COLA WHIPPET | He's gonna get the zoomies

HE IS LOST WITHOUT LITTLE DONKEY

His best friend
His "wing donkey"
His little donkey sister from another mister
His emotional support donkey
His little donkey confidant

He kept her safe in his shirt pocket.

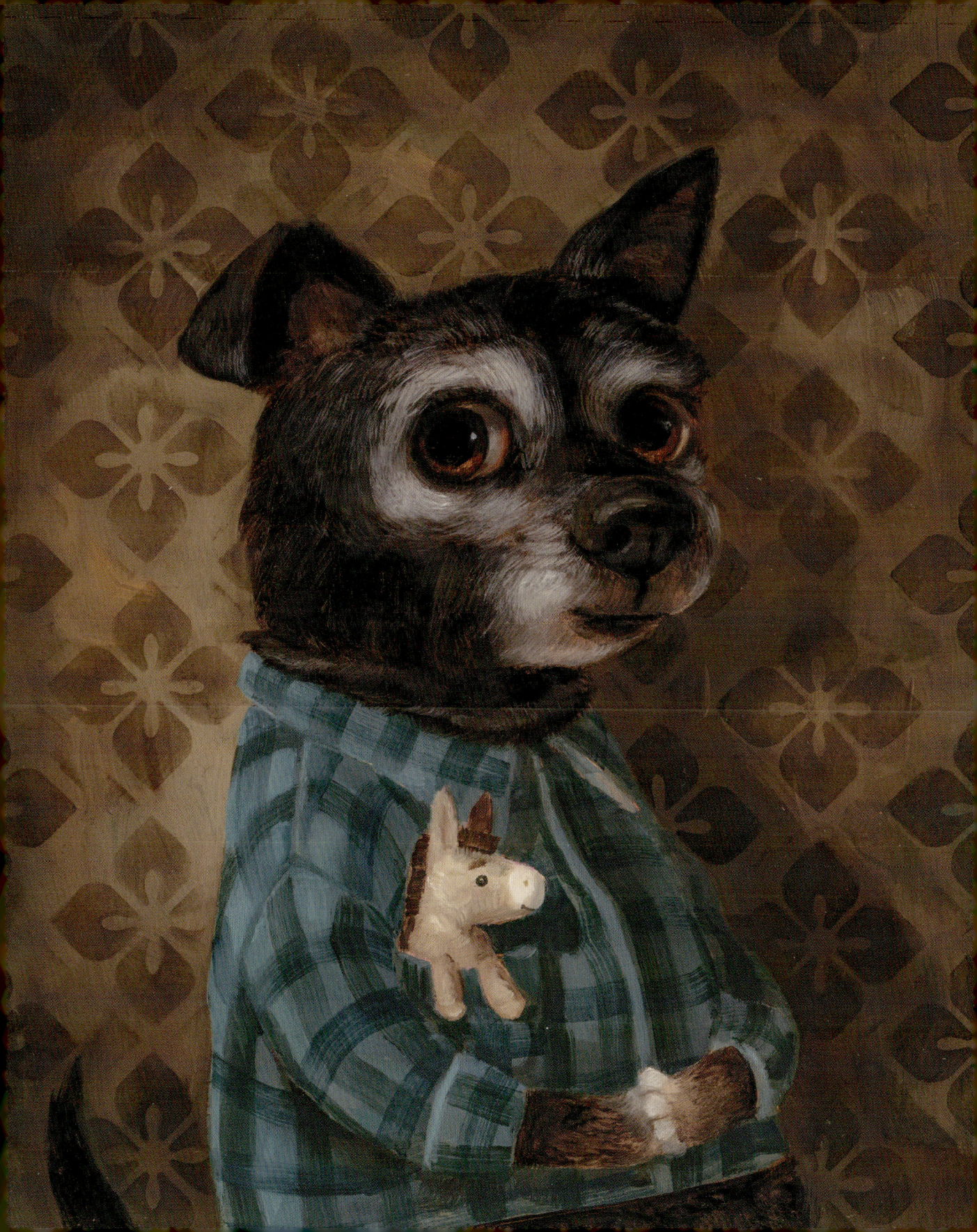

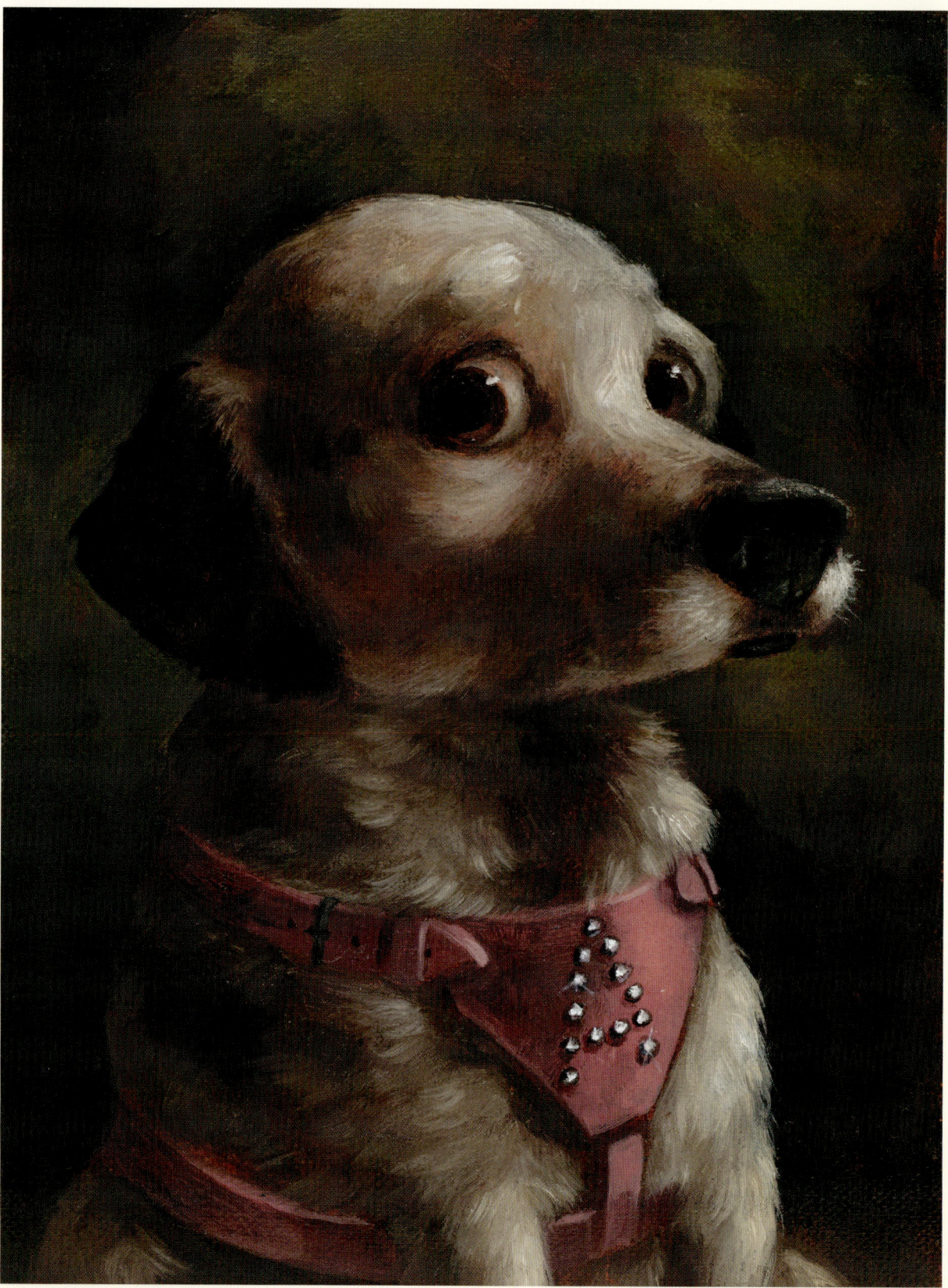

ALAN

He looks a million dollars
in his new harness

ME TIME

"When most of your day is spent people-pleasing,
you really need to make sure you get a little me time,"
said this little princess.

According to this pup, it's pretty full-on being a dog.

"I've got to be cute twenty-four/seven . . . I've got to be
available for snuggles at any moment, and this happens
a lot, a result of being so cute . . . I have to listen to her
songs about me for the millionth time . . . I have to NOT
chew a lot of things. This is the most exhausting!

"It's important I have a little time to myself every now
and again."

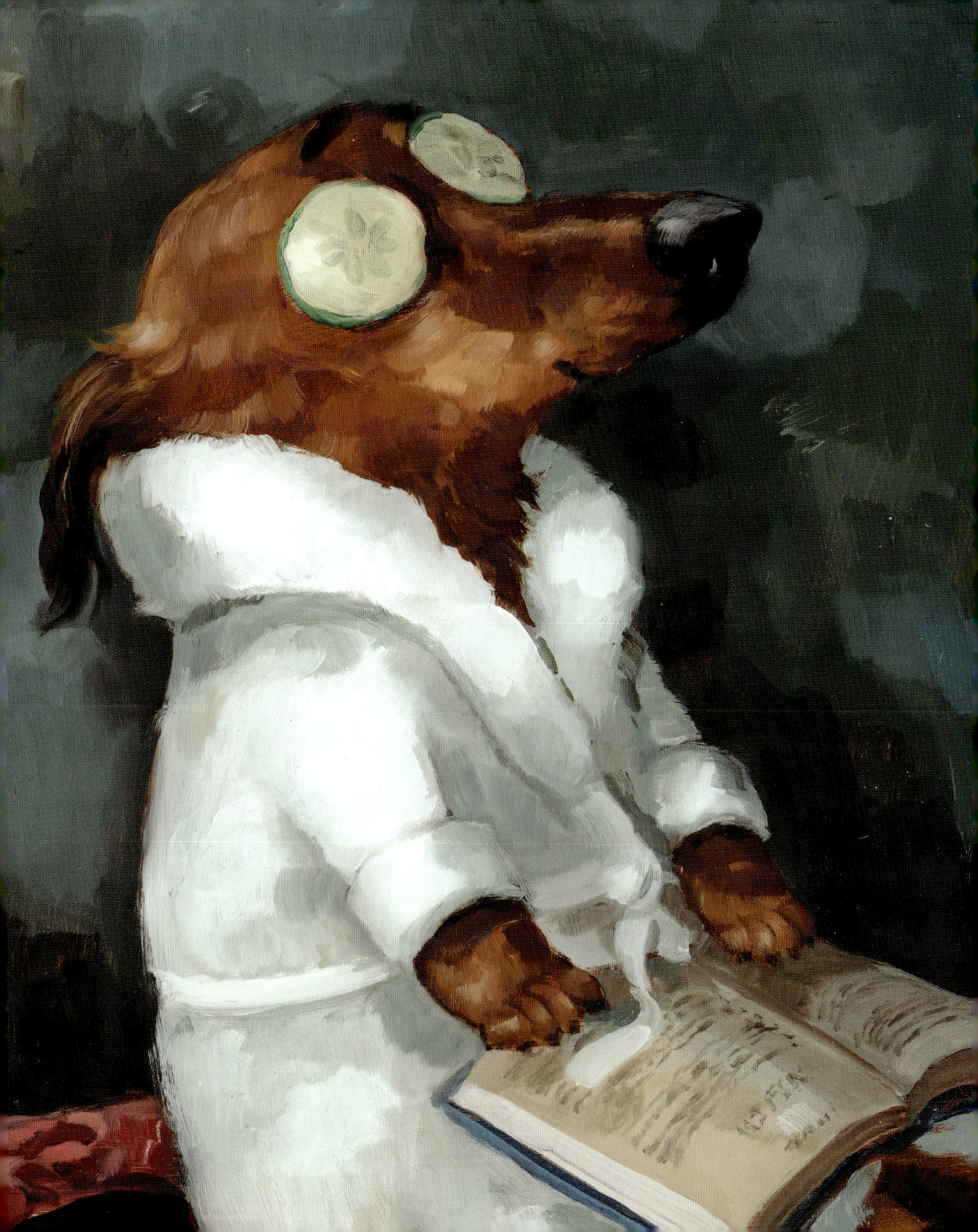

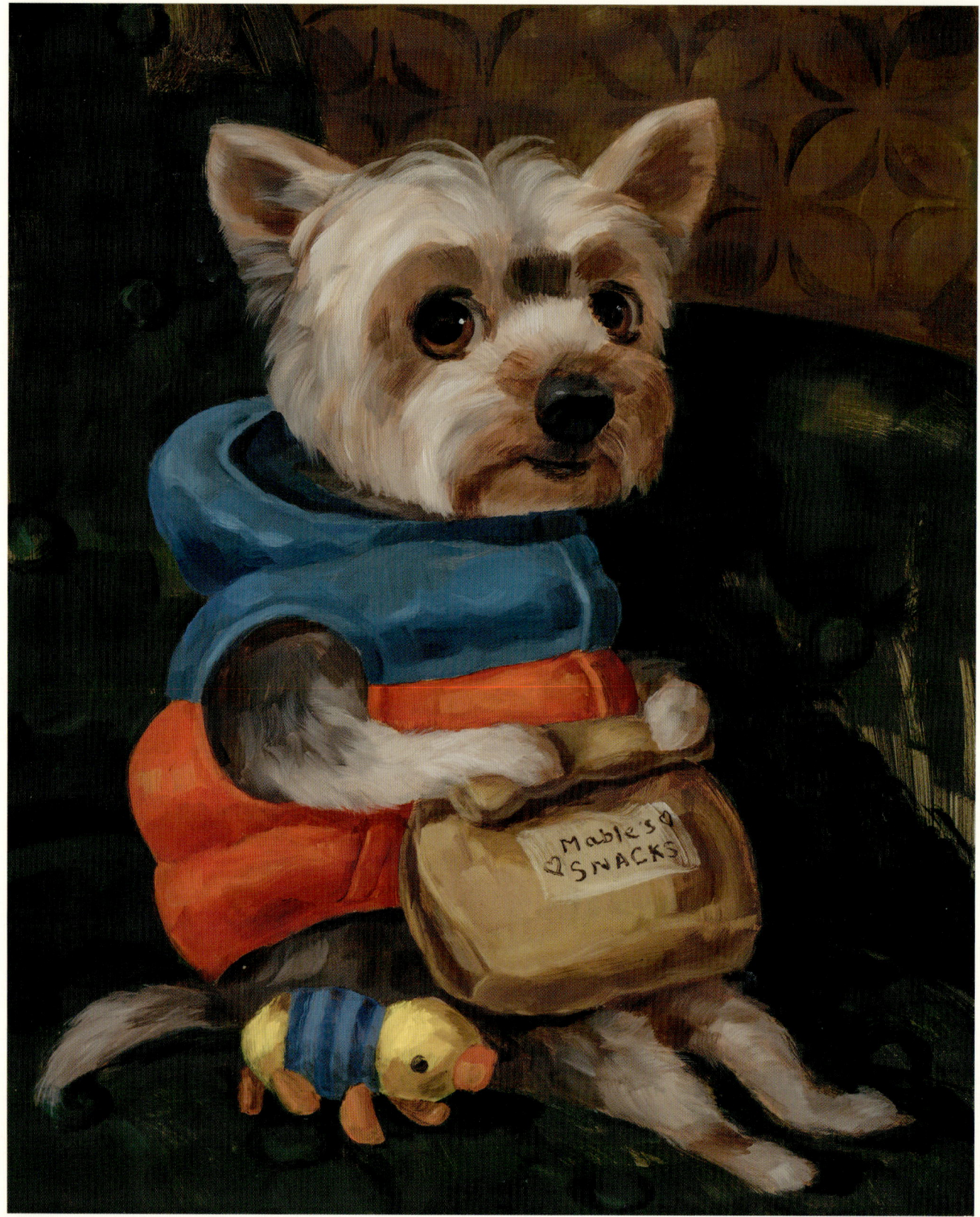

MABLE

She is ready for puppy class

DOG IN A GILET

He never saw himself as "one of those dogs" who wore clothes. . . . What would his friends at the dog park think?

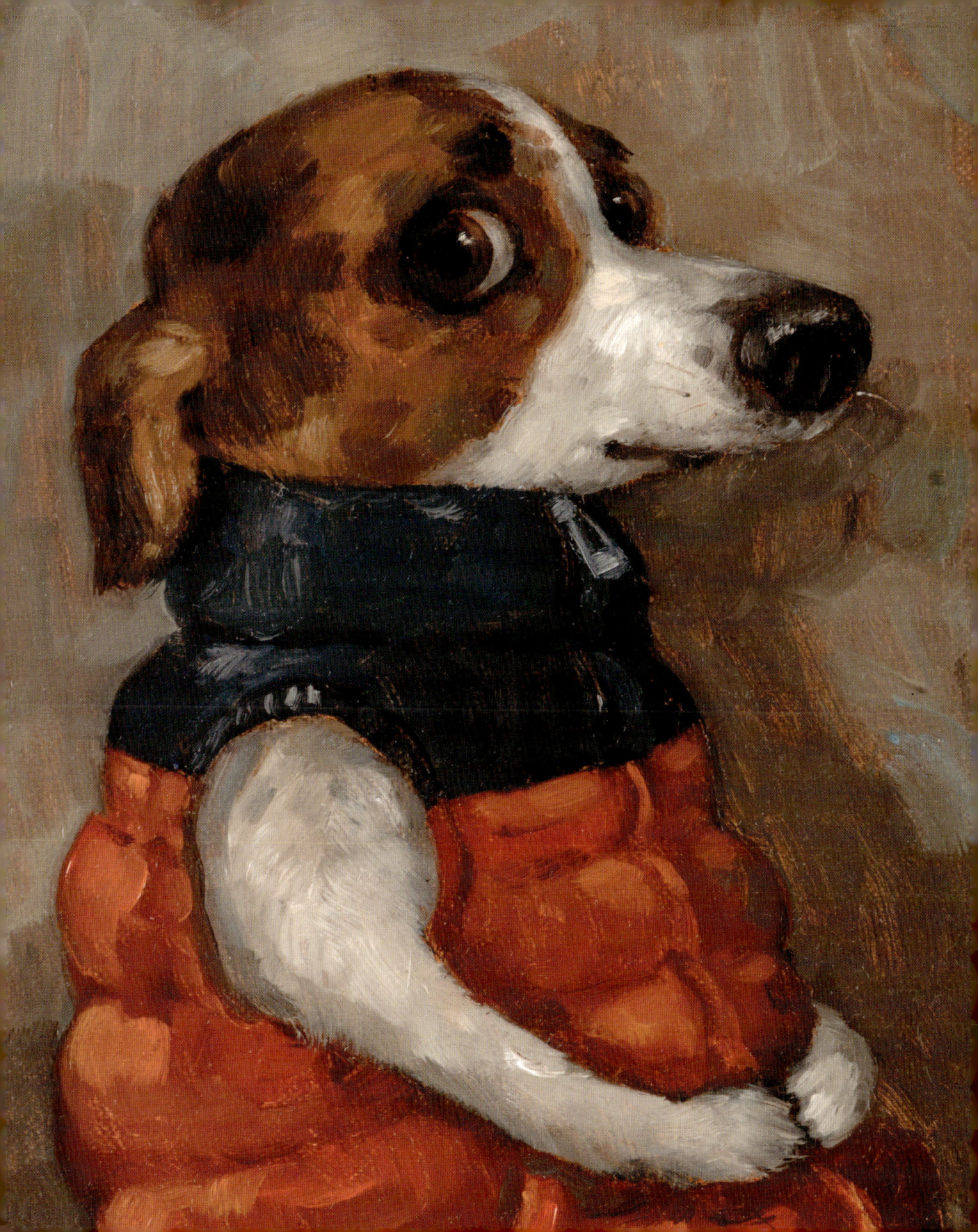

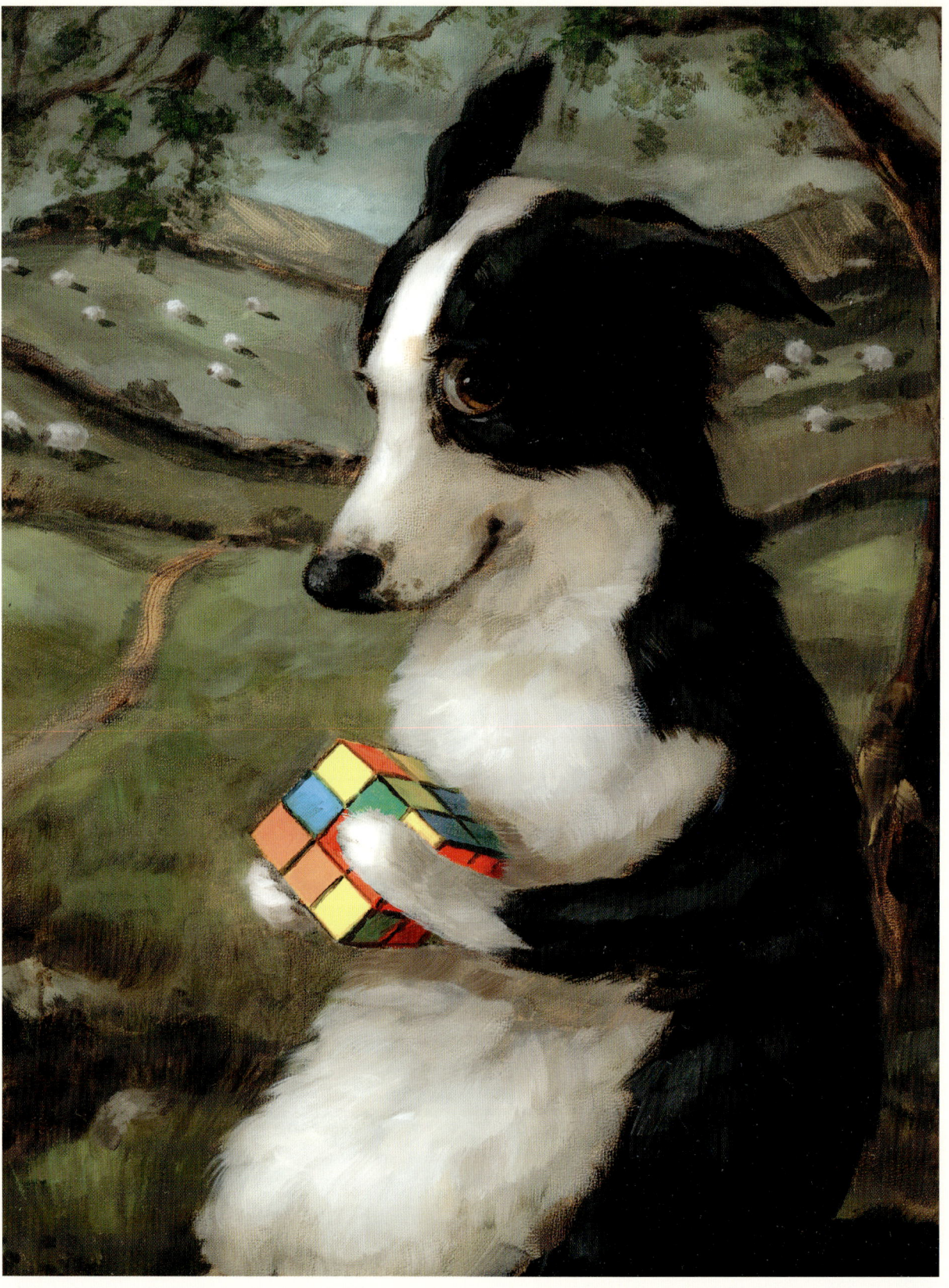

PIP

The truth is, she's a bit scared of sheep . . . but she keeps her collie mind busy with a Rubik's Cube

TERRIER IN CYCLING CAP

Always along for the ride

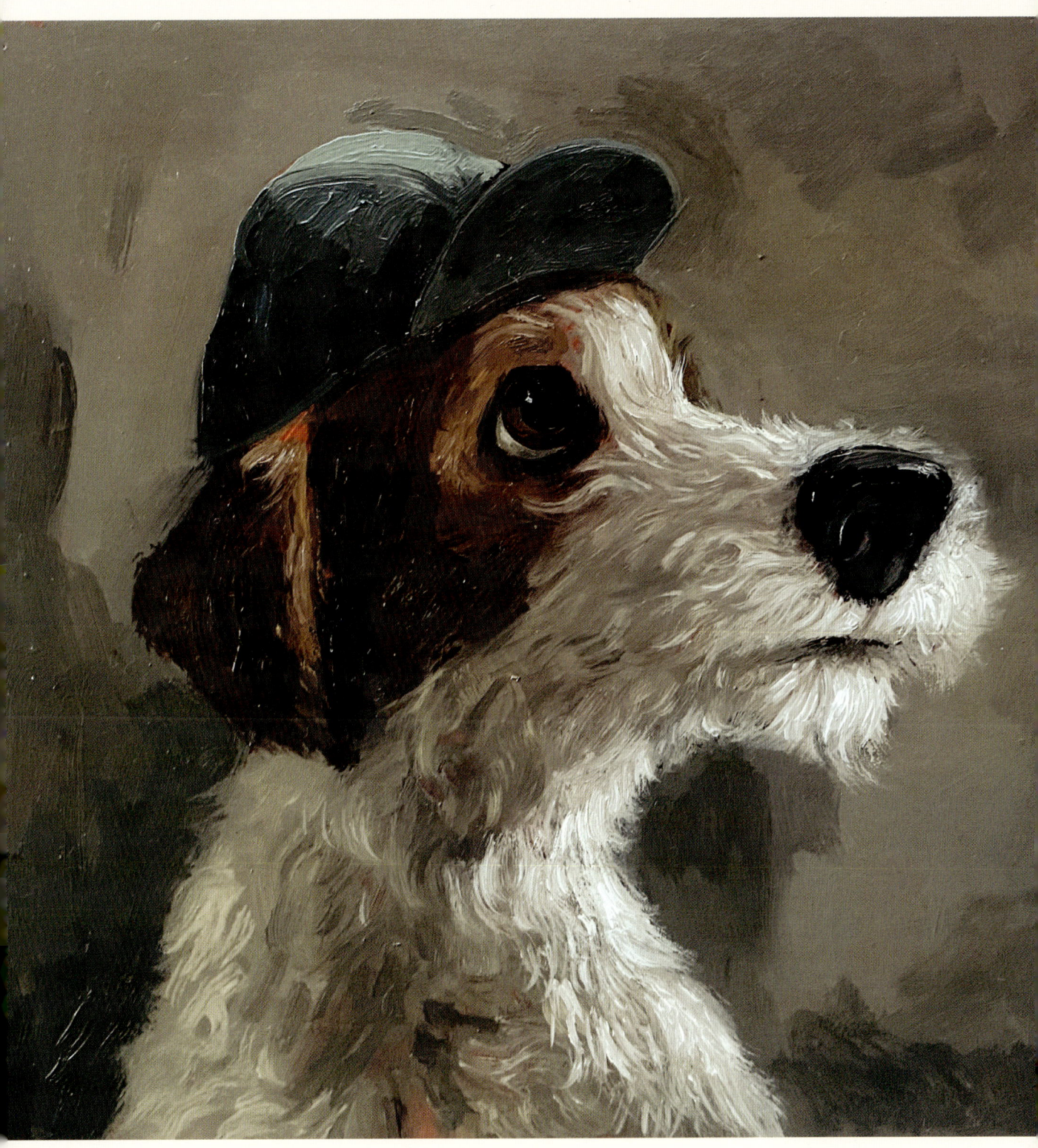

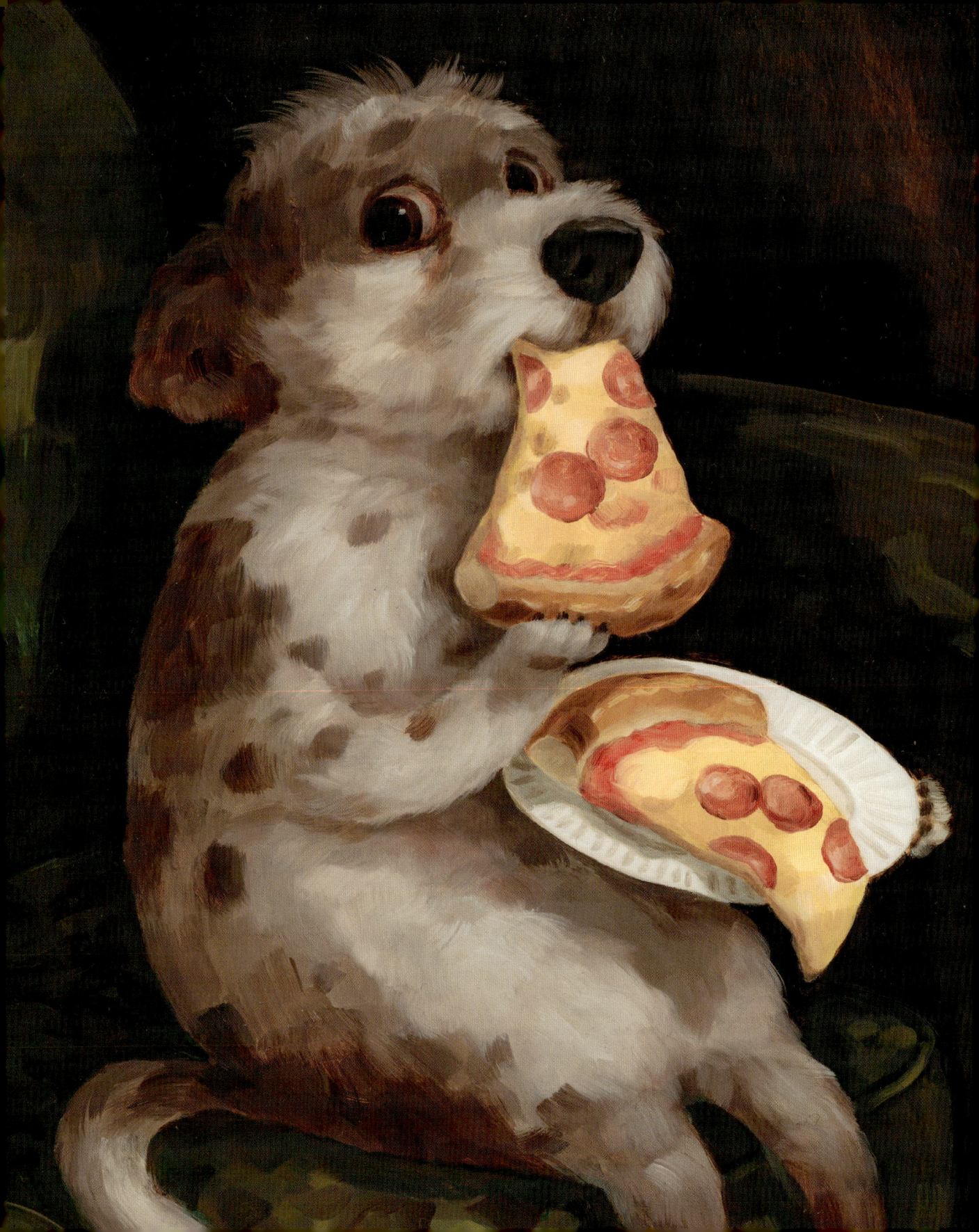

ONE SLICE IS NICE
_____

. . . two is better

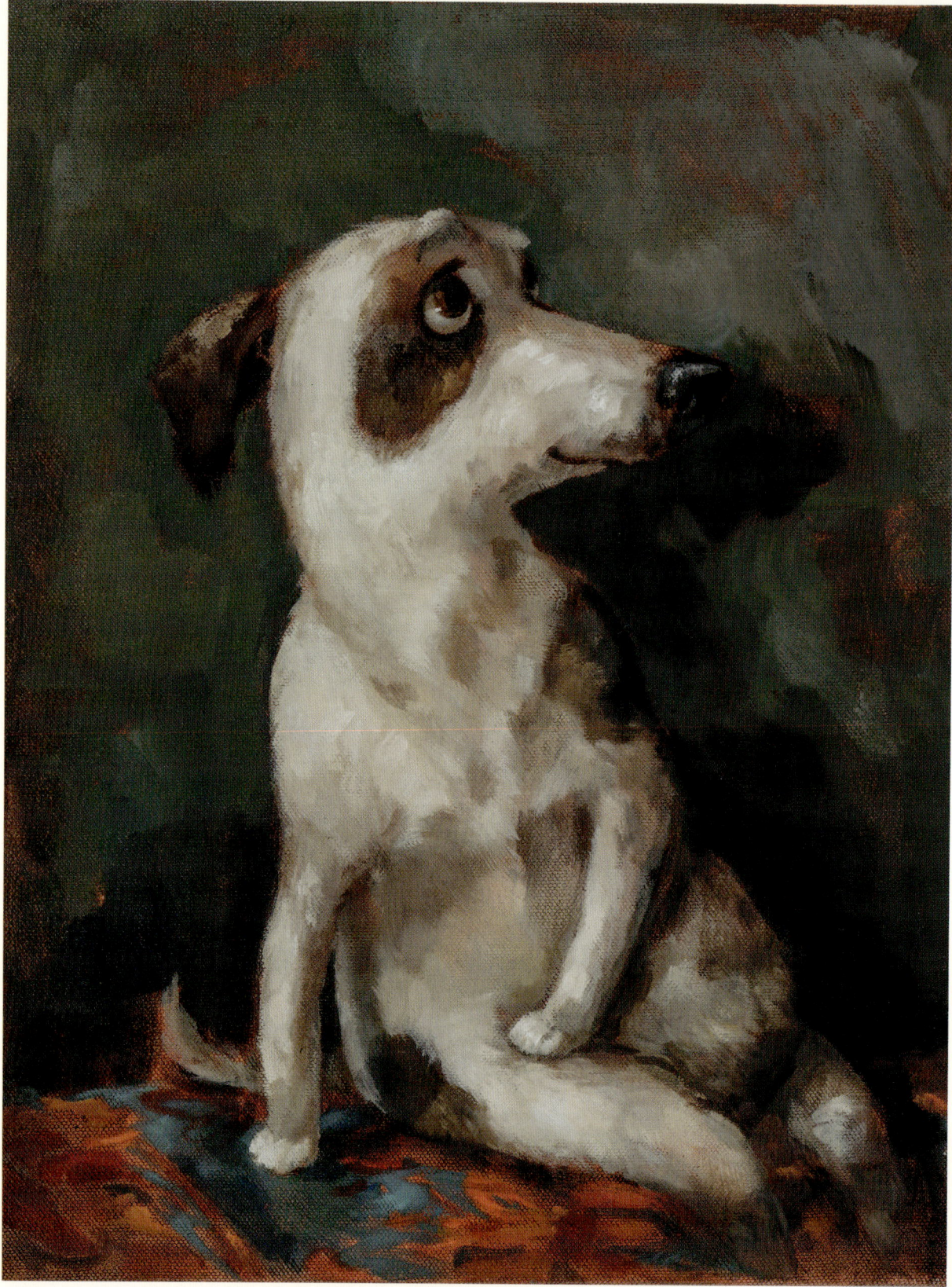

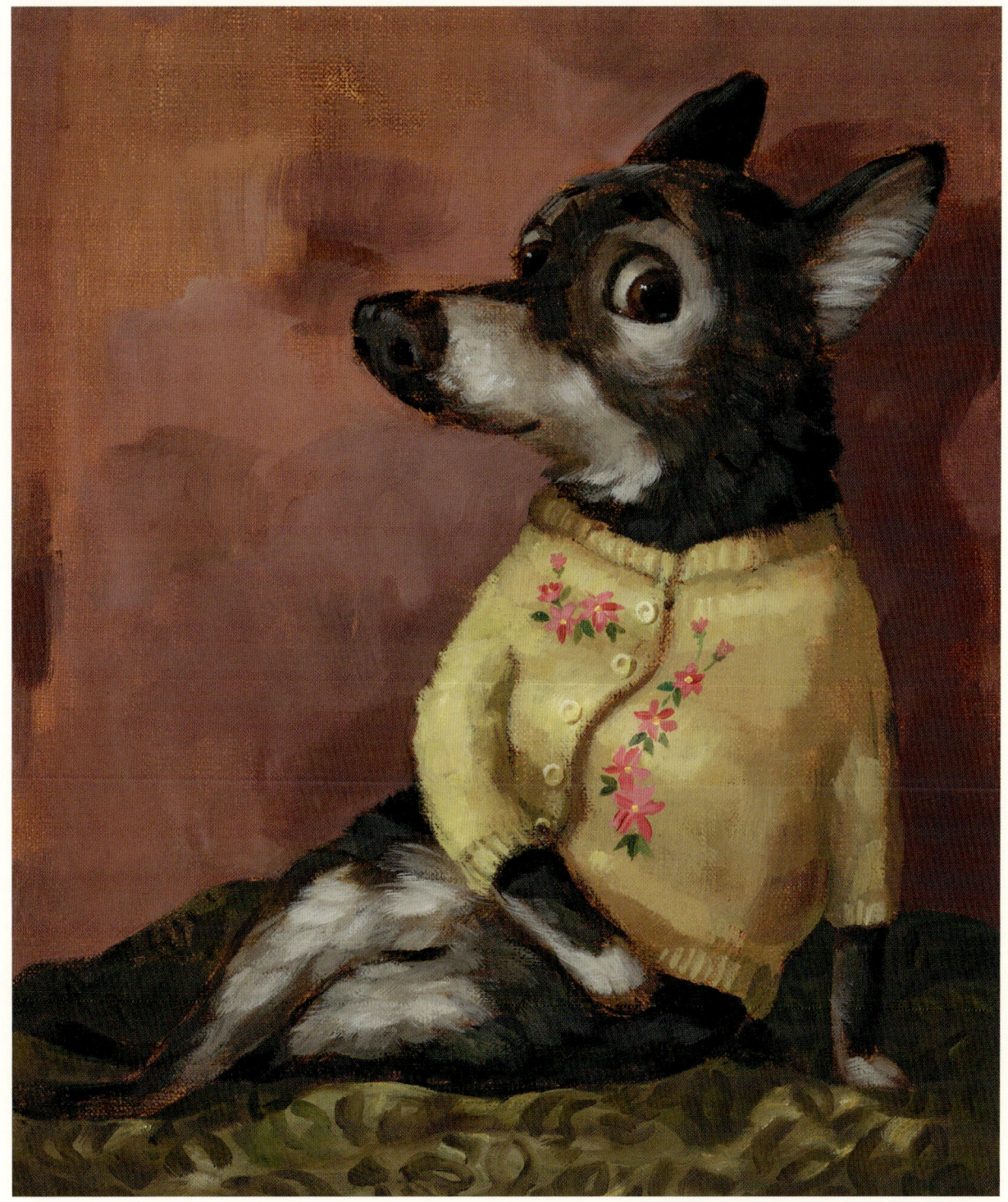

DEBBIE | She loves her new cardigan

DEMURE DOG | Reserved, modest, and shy

ONE FOR NOW, A COUPLE FOR LATER

Thoughts of snacks and where the next one was coming from were a big part of this little dog's daily concerns.

He knew that when the humans had people over for a cuppa, the biscuits came out. The fancy ones, in the selection box, and they would be arranged on one of the best plates. When finally the guests were leaving and goodbyes were being said at the door, there was a small window of opportunity, and he took it! It would be rude not to, he thought. One for now. A couple for later!

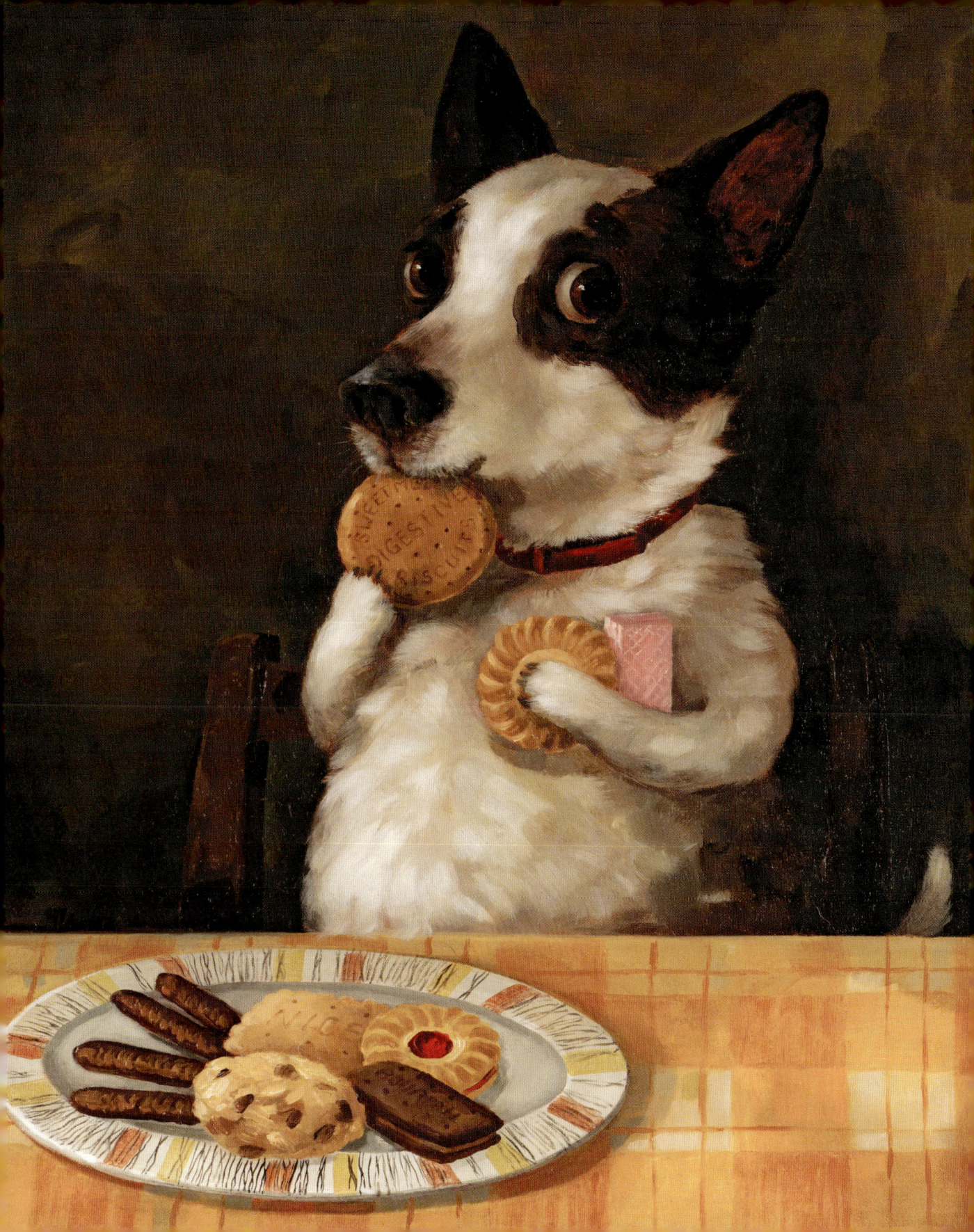

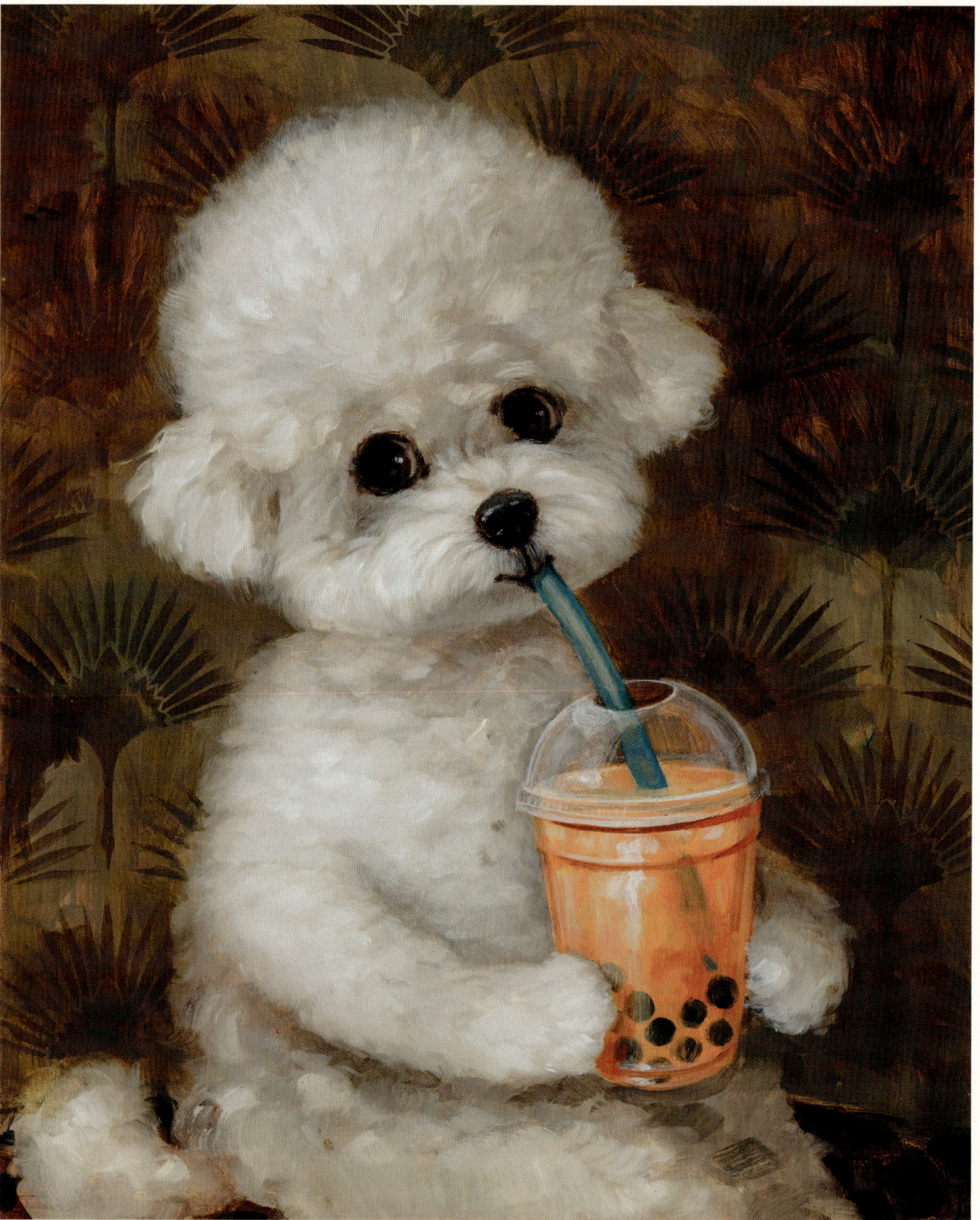

YUKI

She knows the best treats
come with a straw

BARK'TERYX

She's ready for a day in the fells

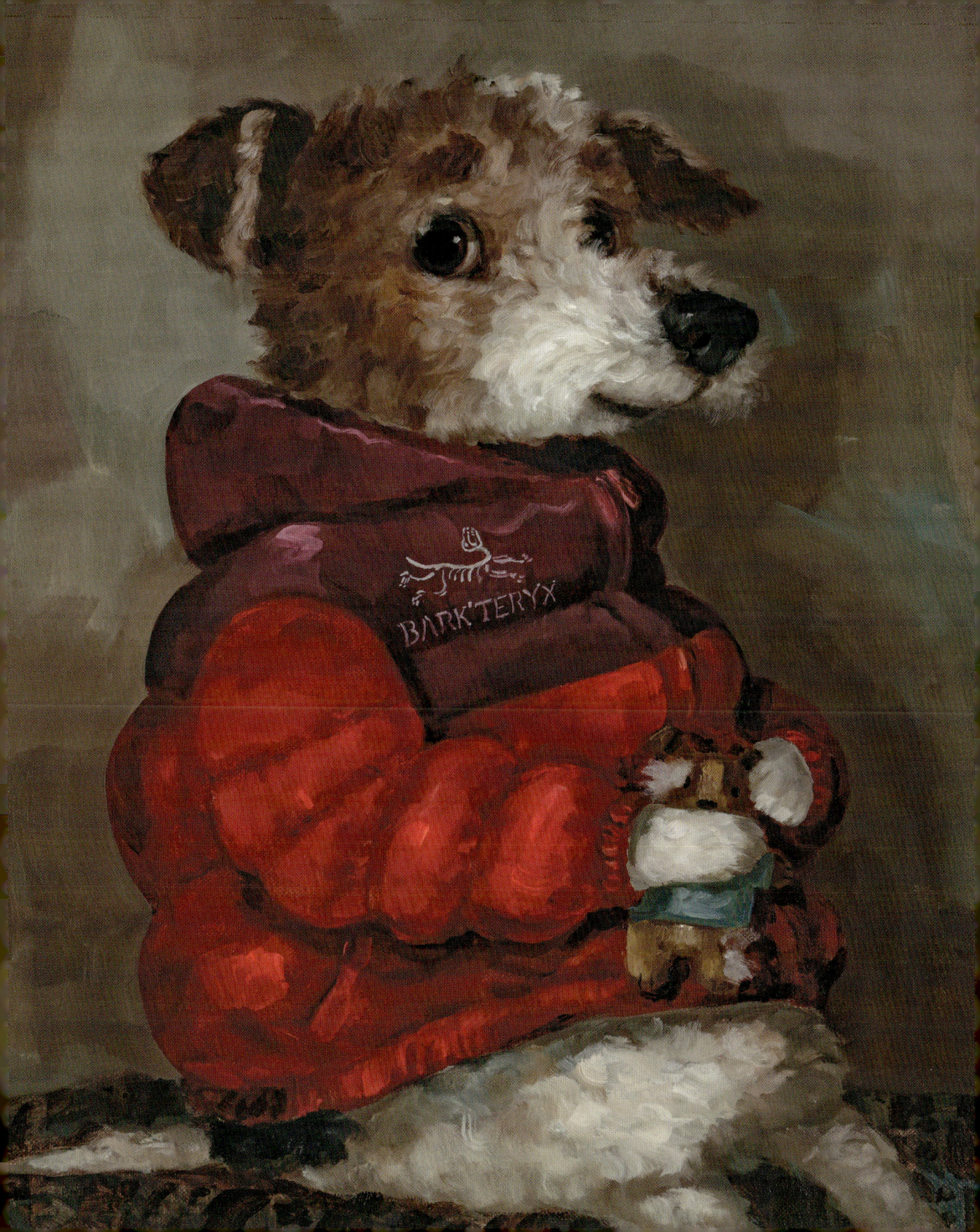

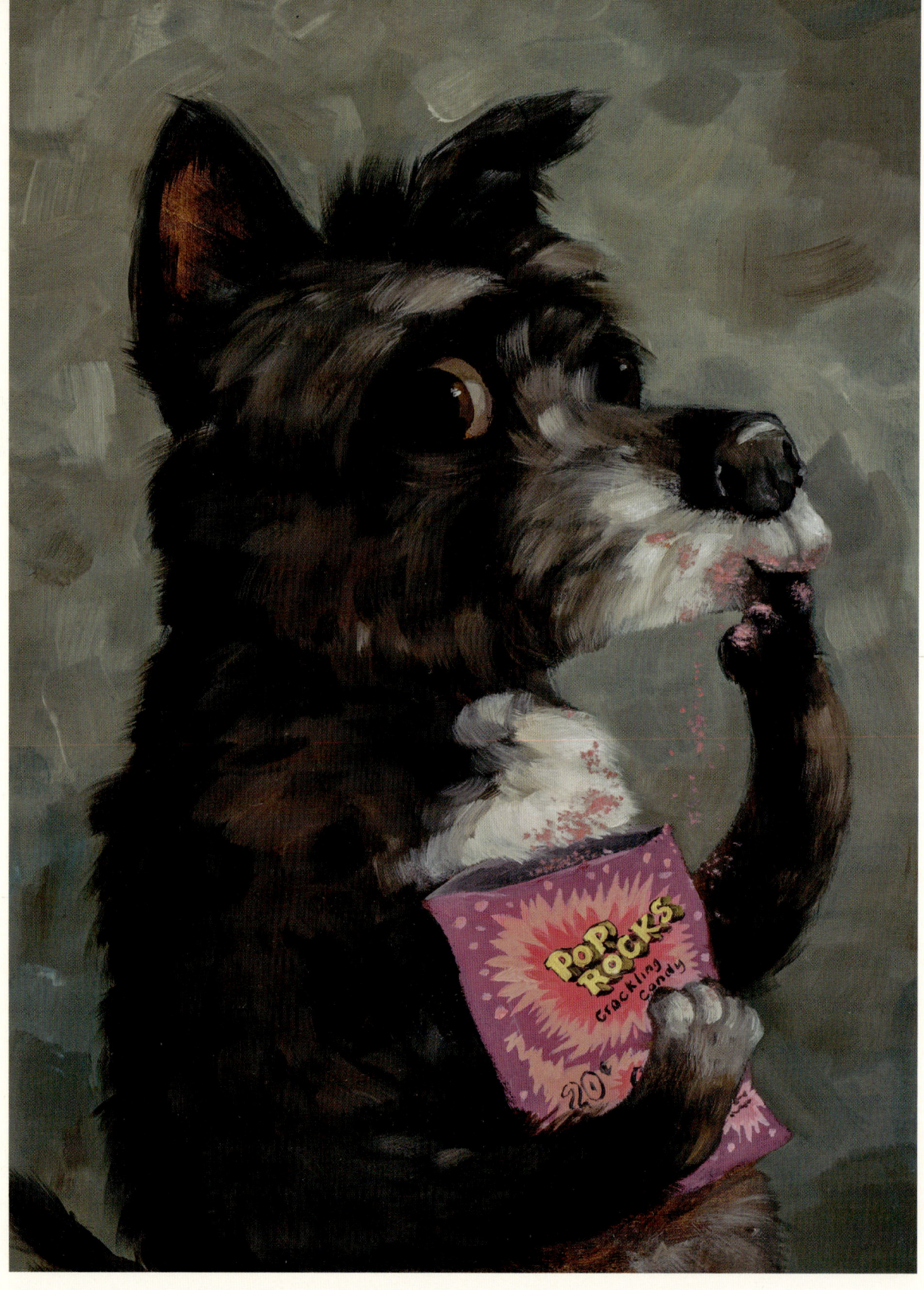

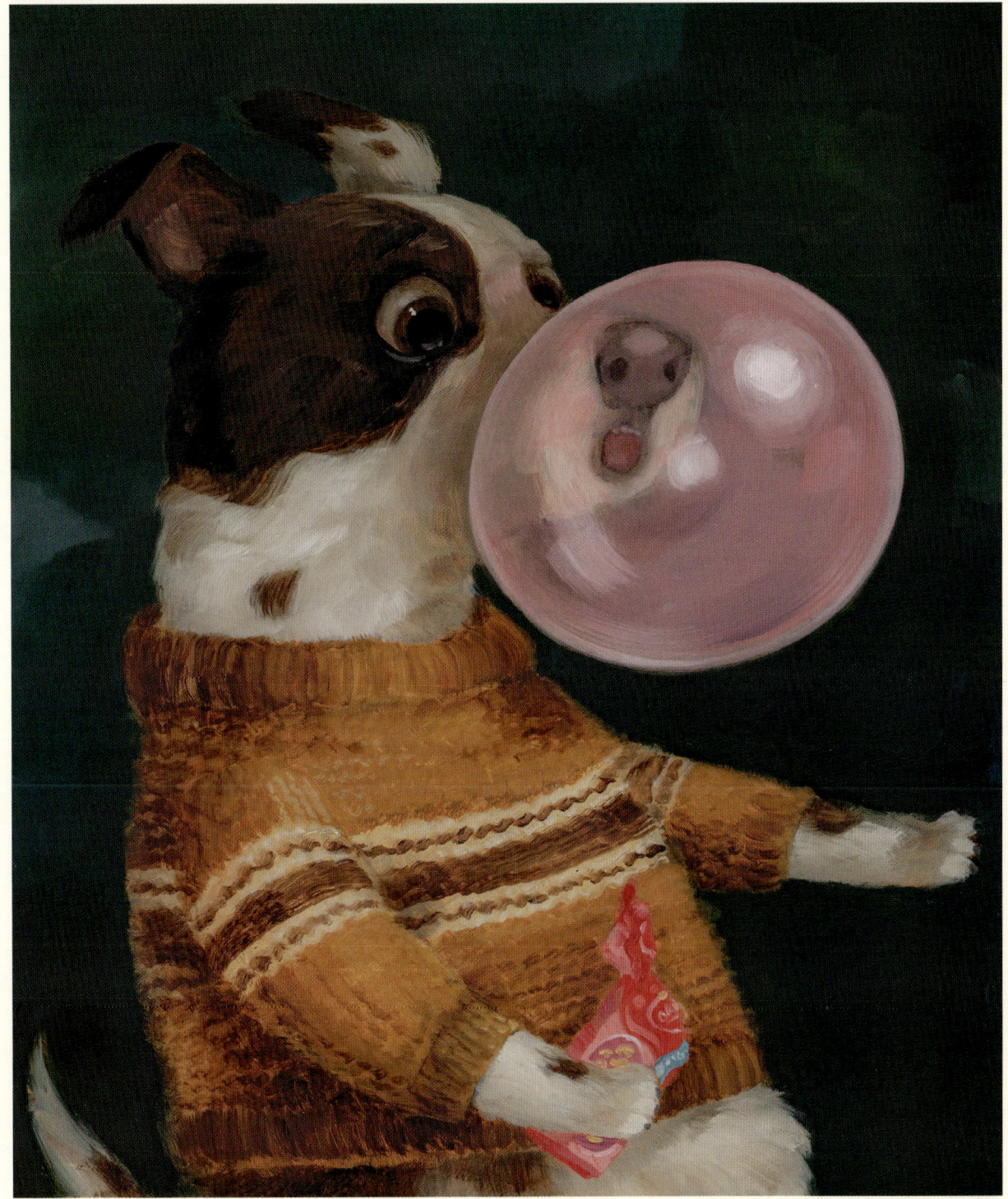

I DID A GOOD ONE | . . . finally!

POP ROCKS PETE | He couldn't stop

GOOD BOY

Some of the things that make him a good boy:

He sits patiently for his dinner.

He's friendly to other dogs at the park.

He doesn't lick his privates in company.

He always fetches the ball.

He likes to visit the local tennis club, where he is a big hit with all the players. He takes his job seriously and never misses a ball. He loves to follow the rules, as he knows well that tennis is a gentleman's sport. Often he dreams of being the best ball boy at Wimbledon— one can only dream.

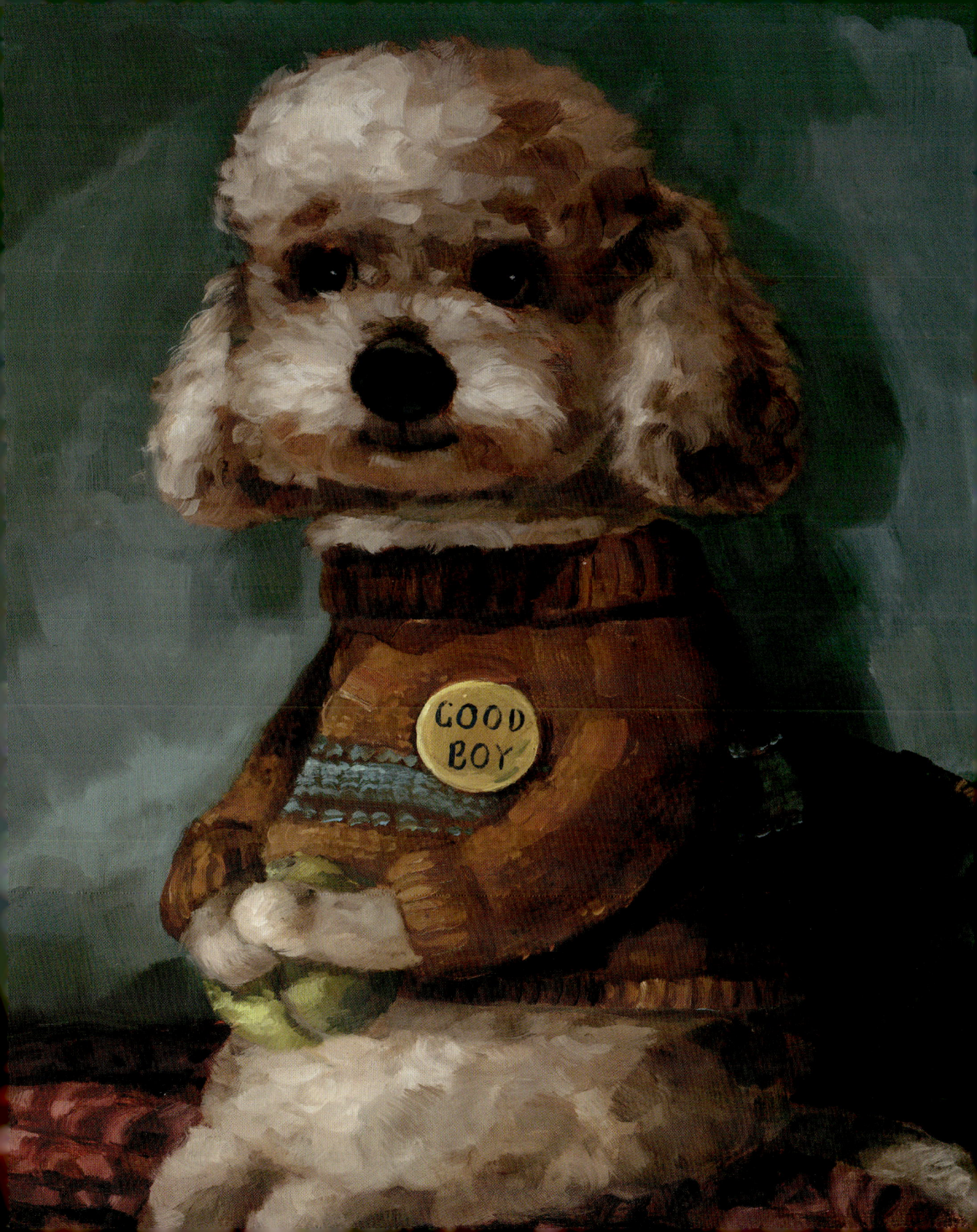

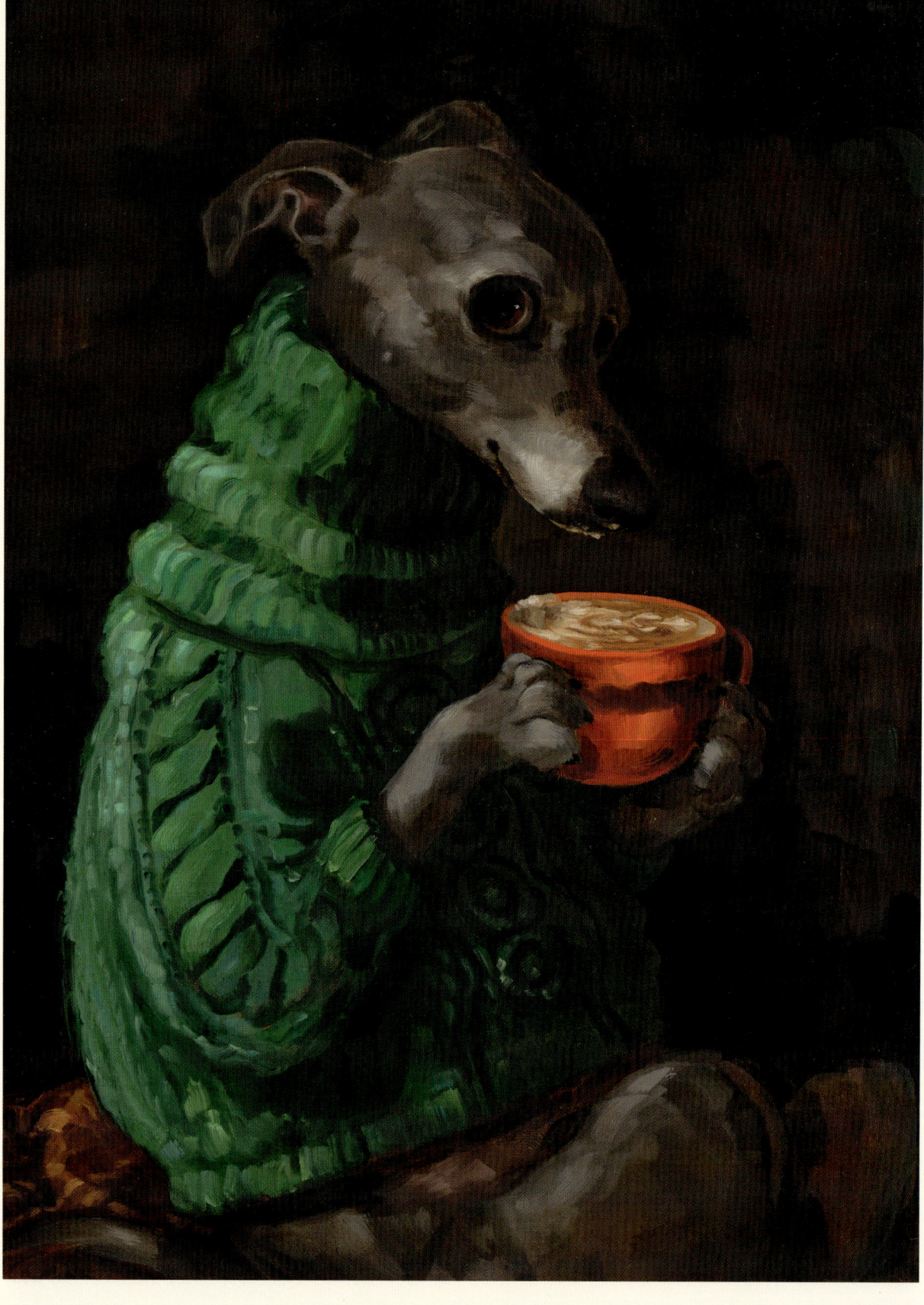

WENDY

She loves her skinny latte

PIP

He loves the story of *Balto*

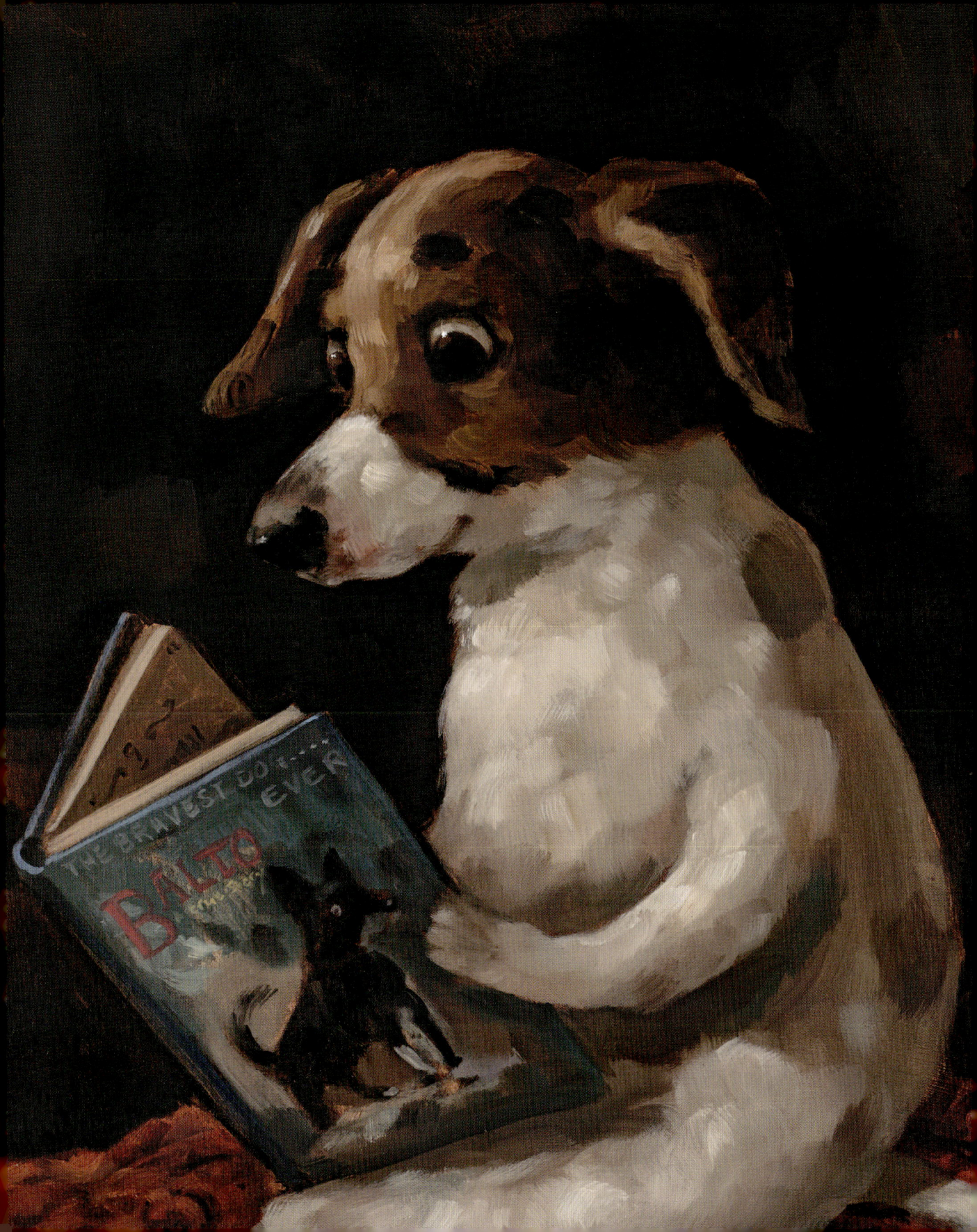

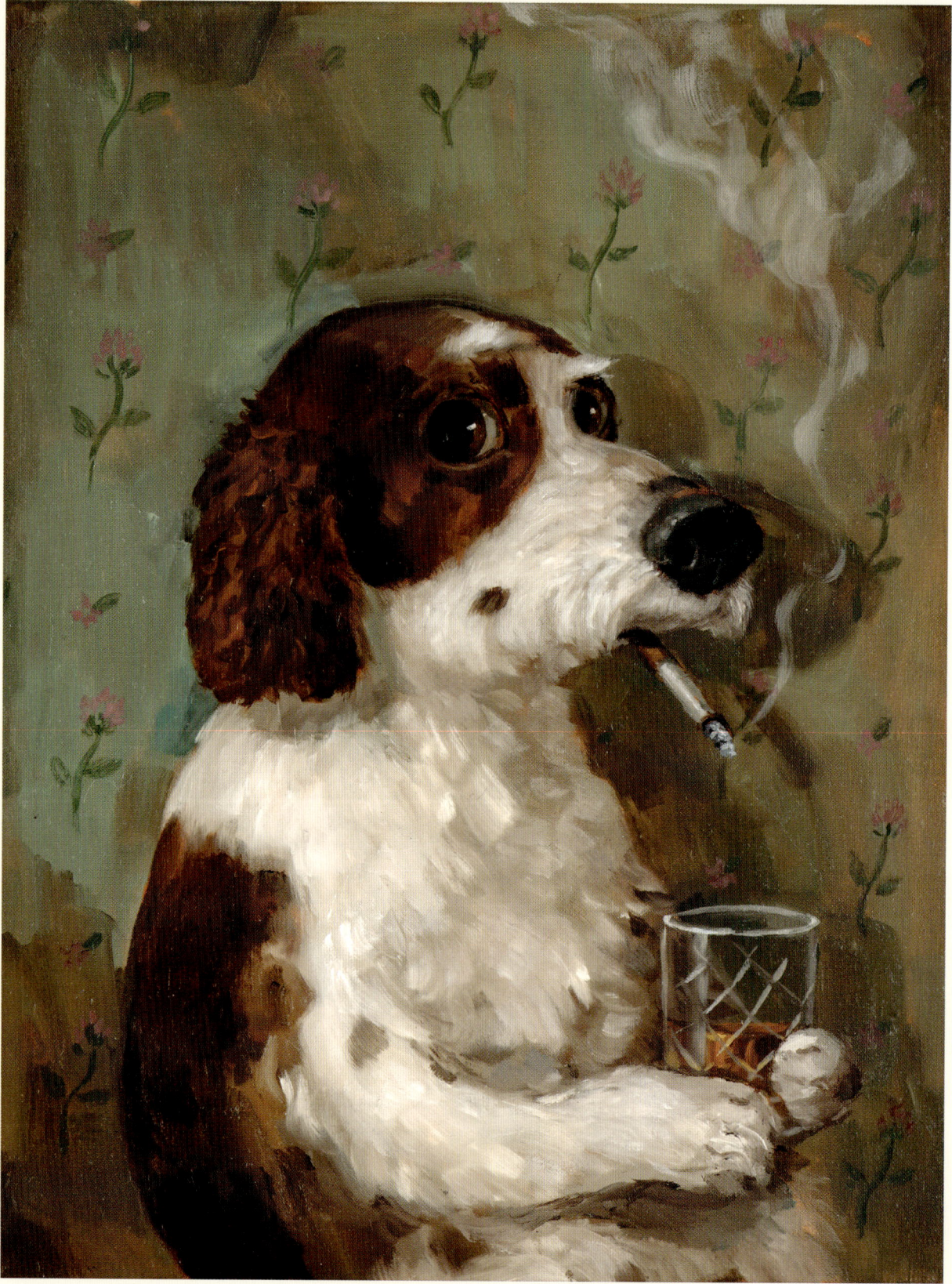

OUR RESCUE . . .

. . . came with a few bad habits

IVY

This sassy little pup has to have
her fish at 5:00 p.m. on the dot . . .
or there is trouble

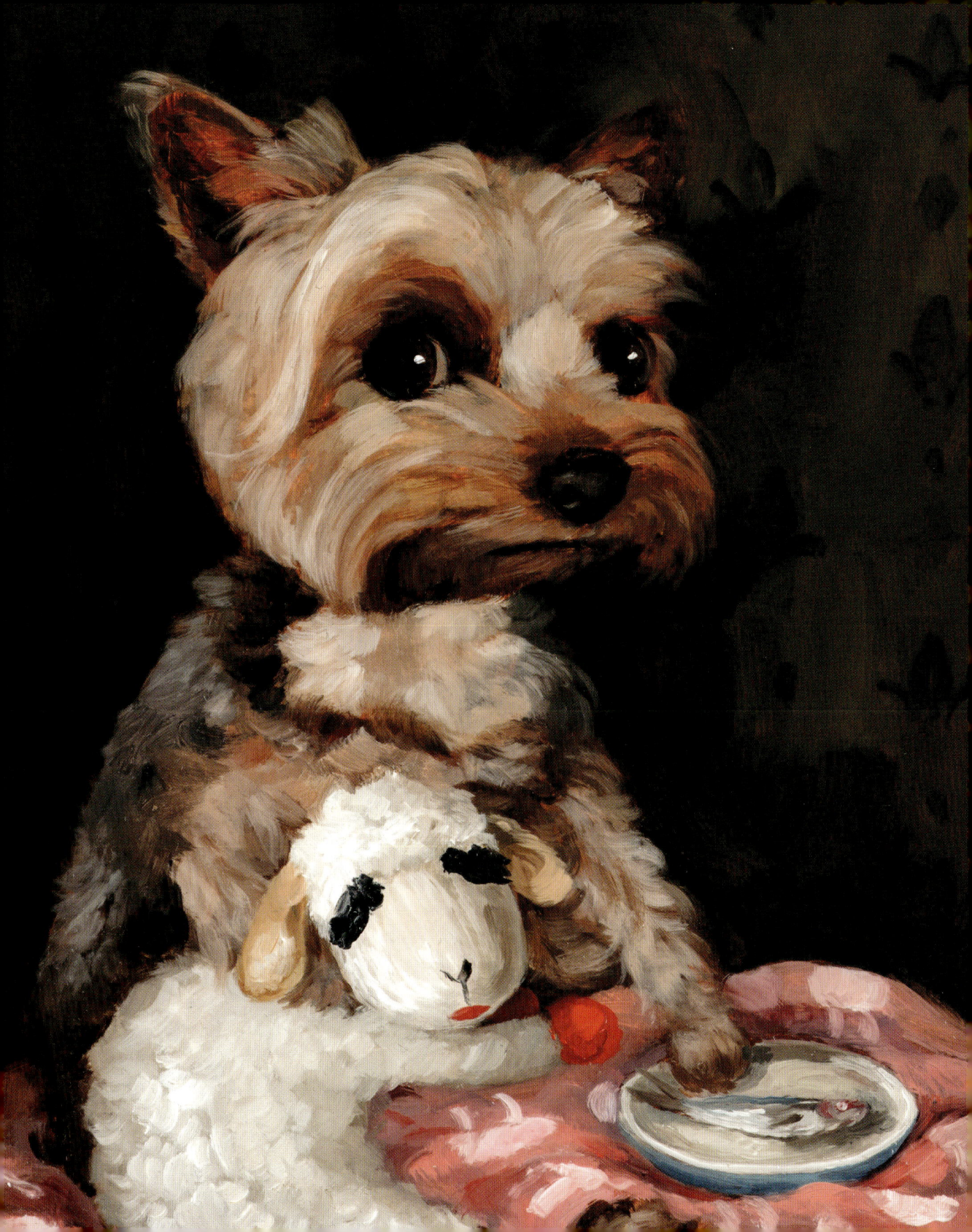

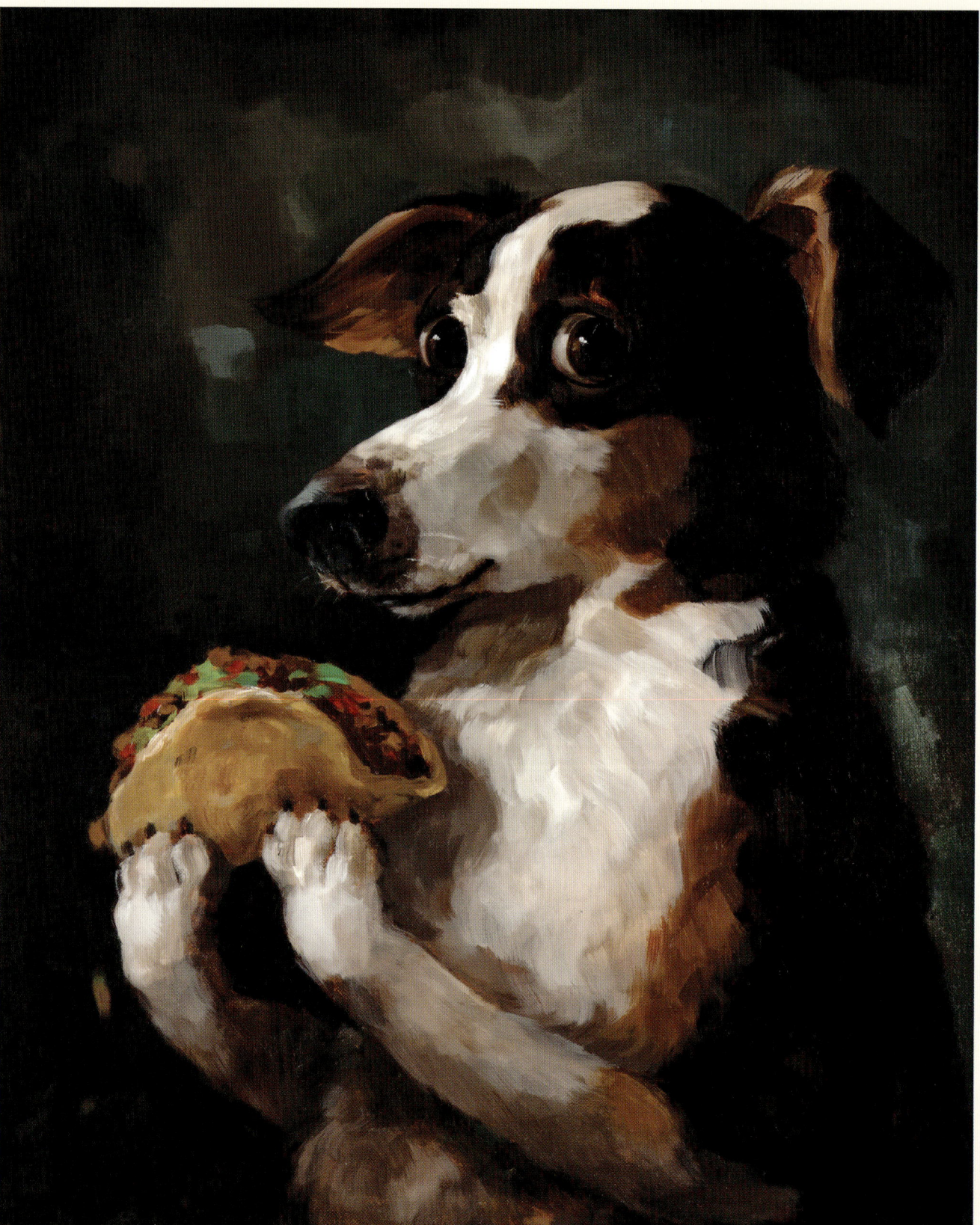

TACO TESTER

A job he takes very seriously

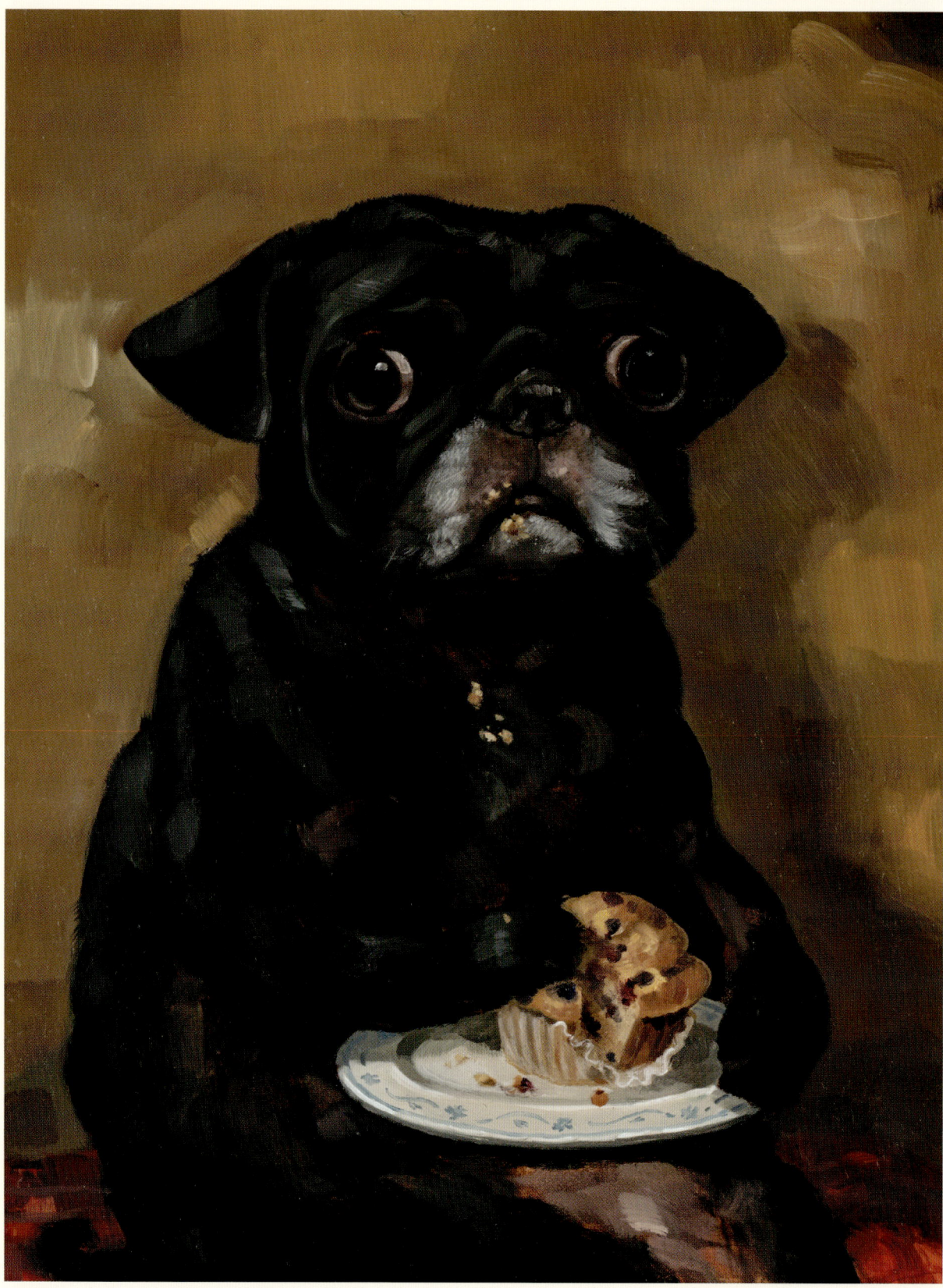

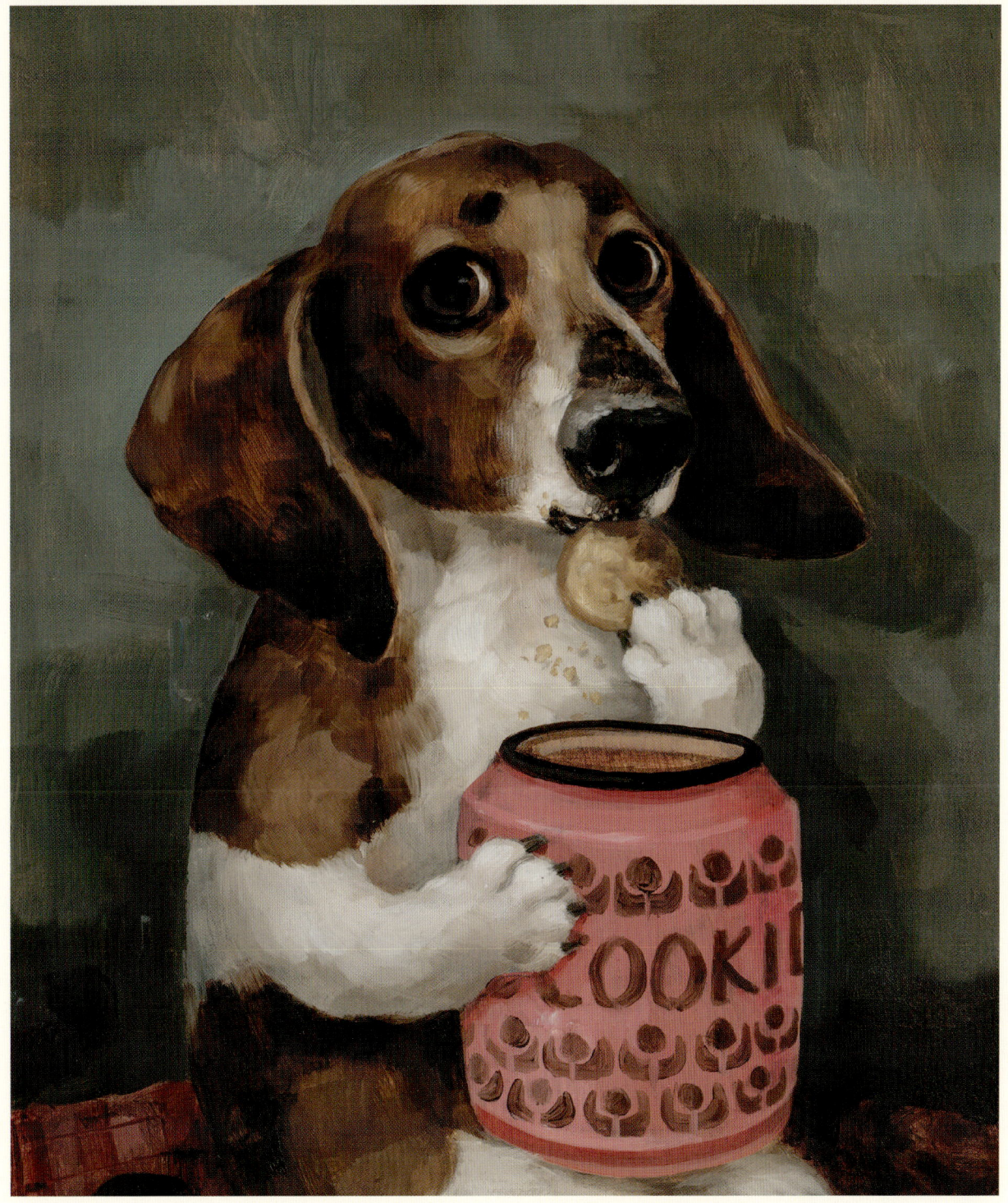

BRUNO ATE COOKIES | Seven and counting

PUG MUFFIN | (noun): A pug who loves muffins

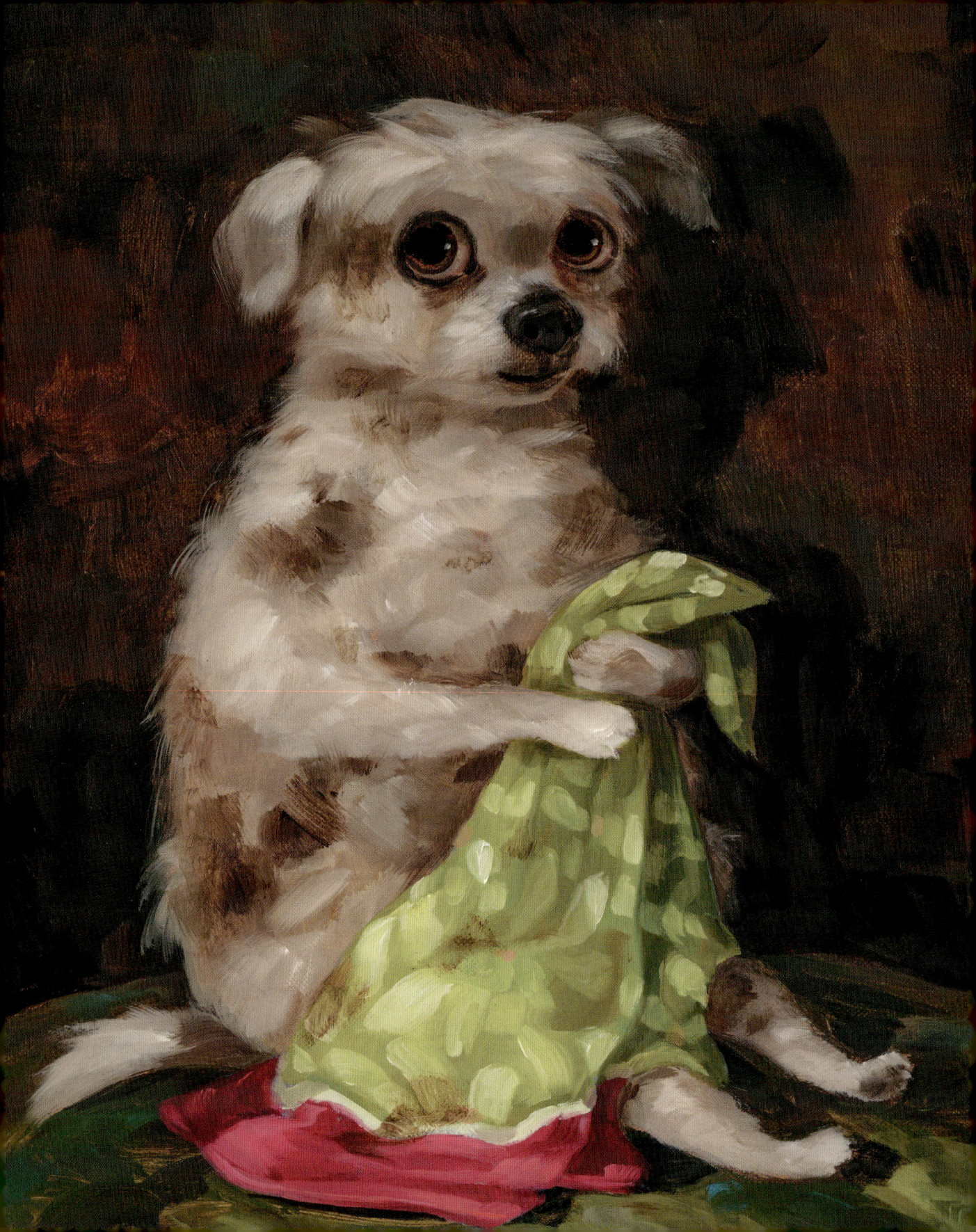

DIRTY AUDREY

After thirteen years (ninety-one in dog years), one would expect a dog's sense of smell to be less keen than it once was. Yet as time passes by, Audrey's ability to sniff out the good stuff has become only more attuned. She is at the top of her game—a specialist in her field (at least in the field at the back of her home).

Audrey is an expert fox-poo locator!

And what does she do when she finds some? Well, this portrait says it all.

TACO LOVER

She likes it hot!

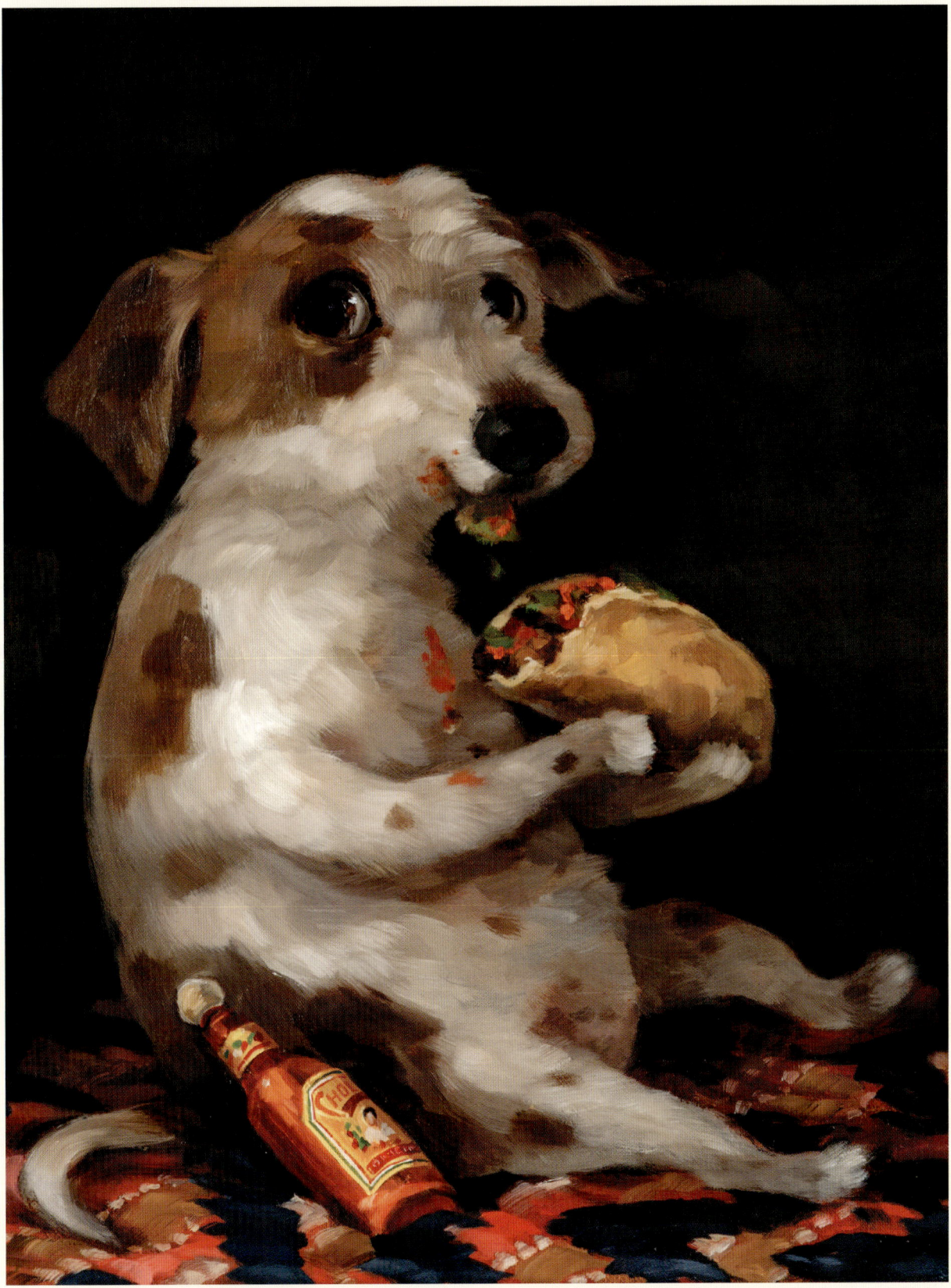

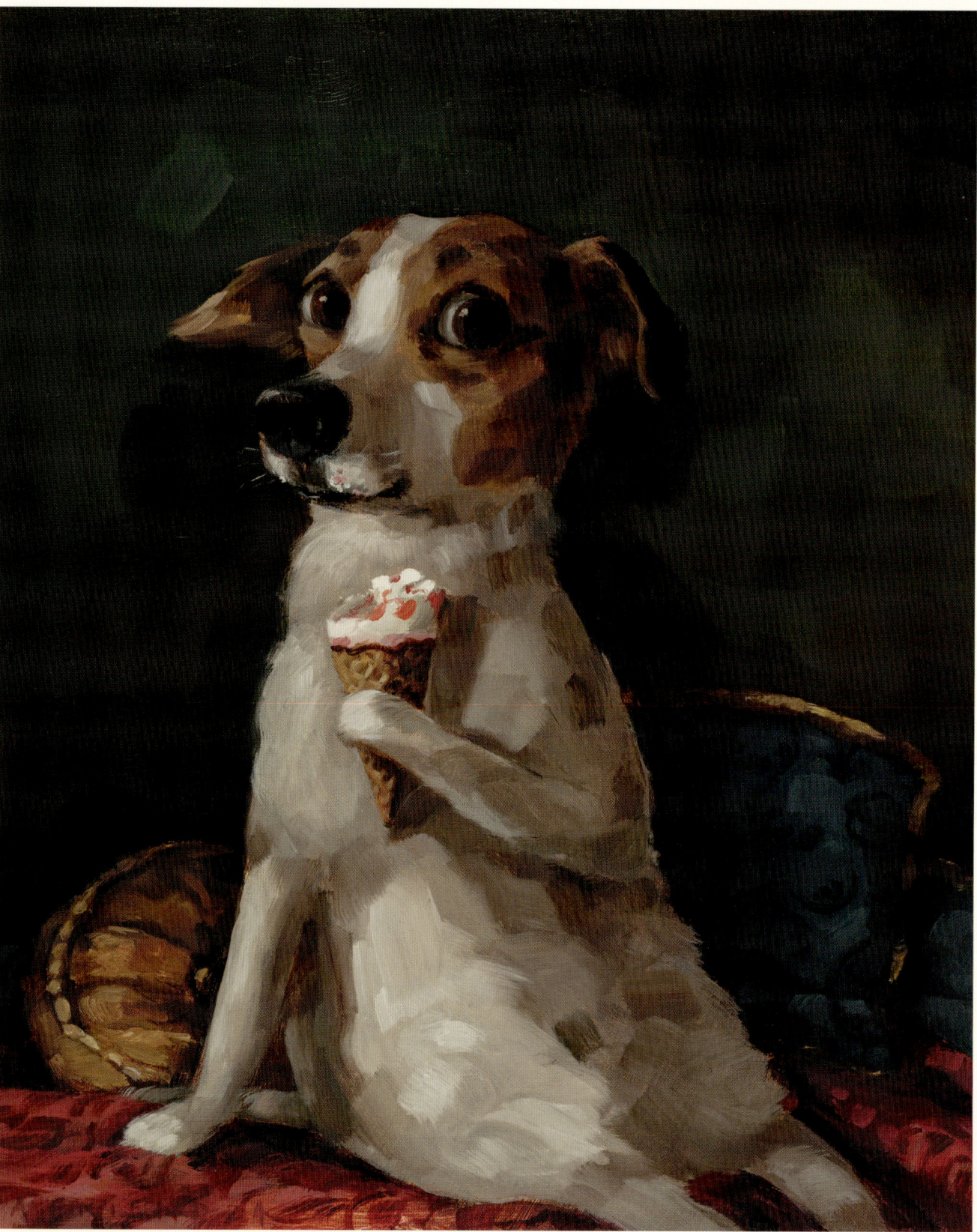

JUST ONE CORNETTO

"Give it to me!"

ROY AND RITA

"It's complicated" says everything about these two. Their relationship began as an unlikely one. No one was expecting them to get along. Yet Roy's soft and gentle manner led to their sharing warm dinners and sitting together on his favourite chair.

The problem is, Rita has sass, double helpings of it, and her mood can change at the drop of a piece of kibble. No one dares to think what is going on in Roy's head here. He adores her but is mildly terrified of her in equal measure. He probably knows he needs to let Rita be Rita, but his eyes say it all.

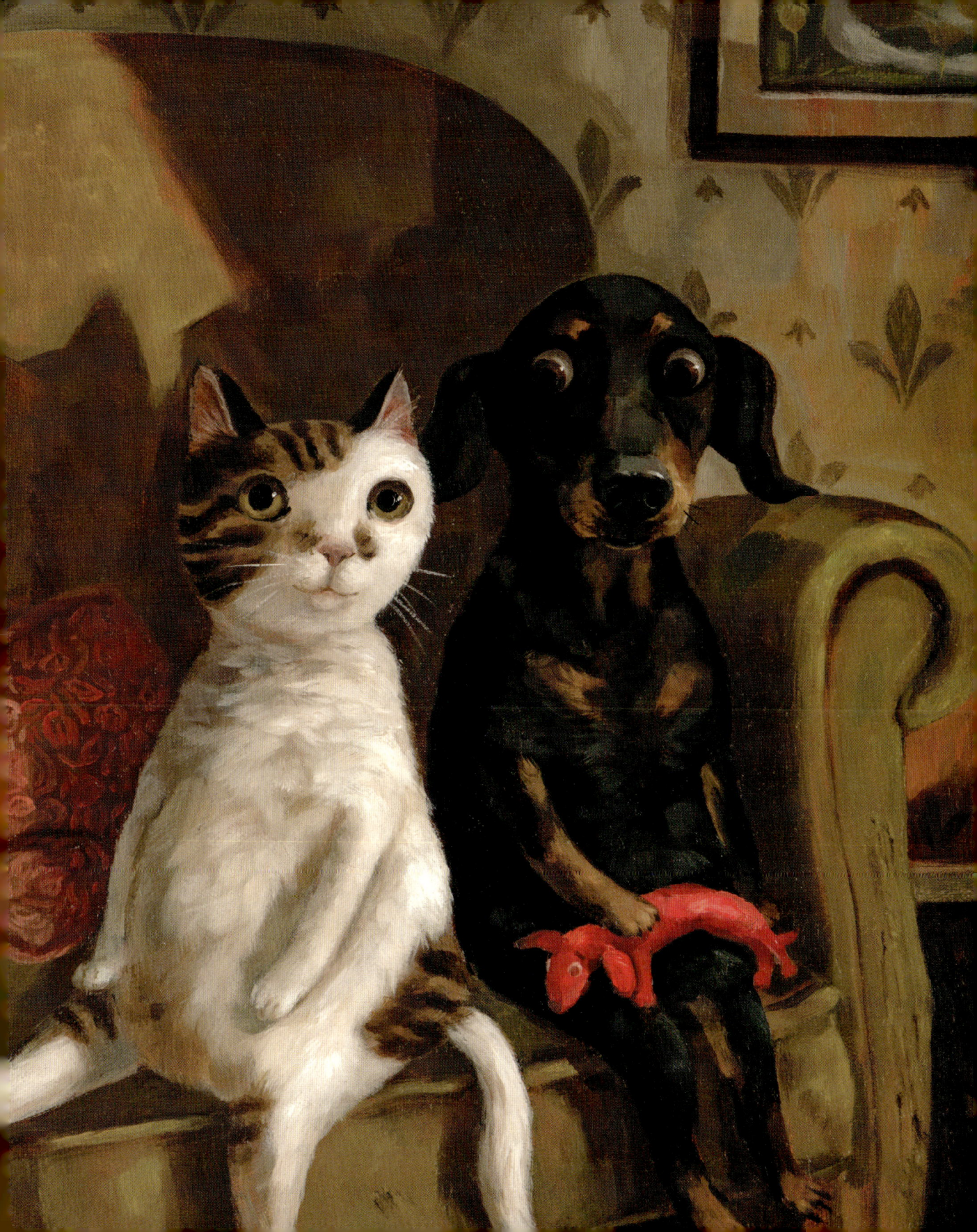

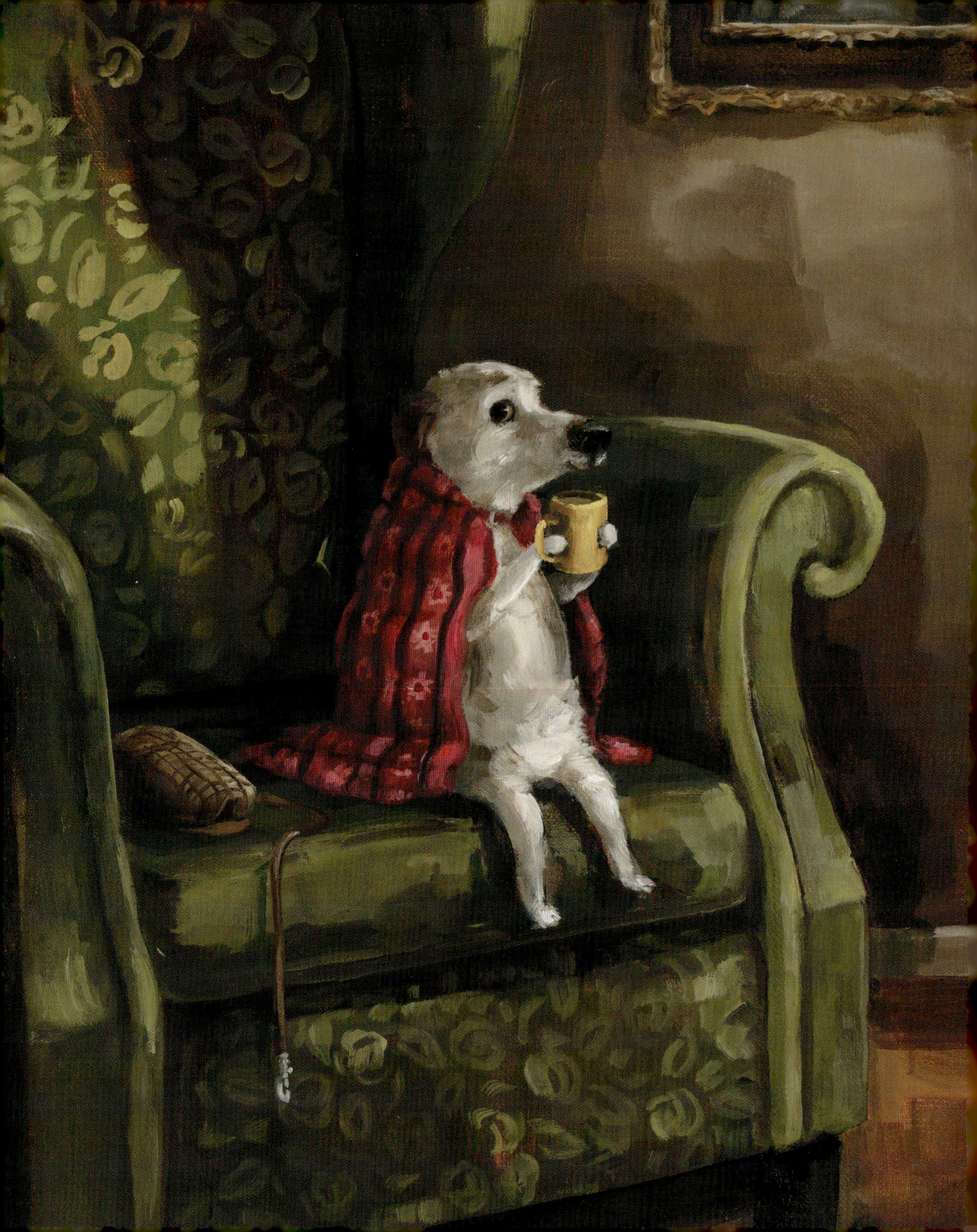

**ERNEST HAD BEEN
ON HIS WALK**

He's back and all cosy with
a mug of something warm and
his favourite blanket

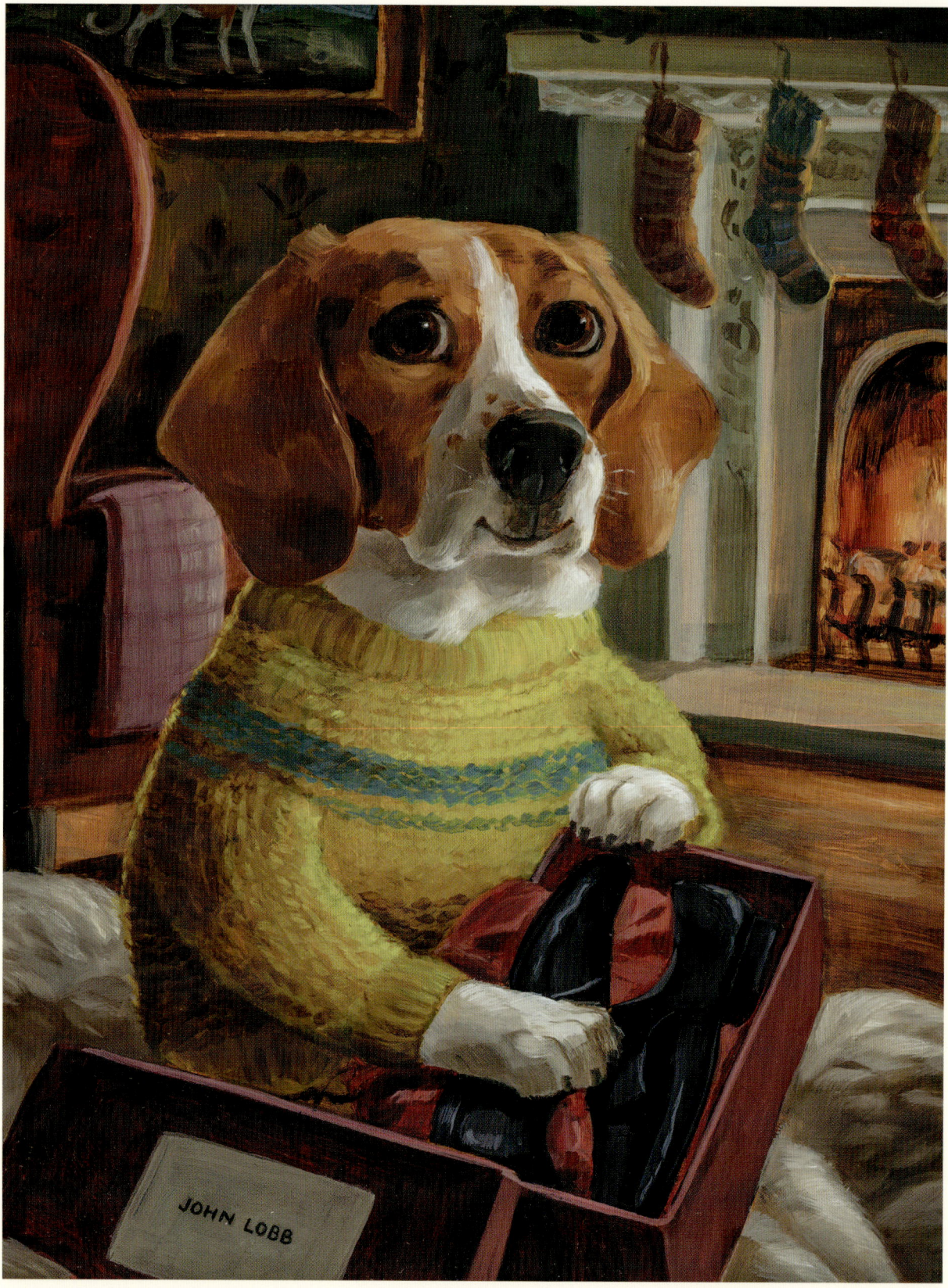

JOHN LOBB

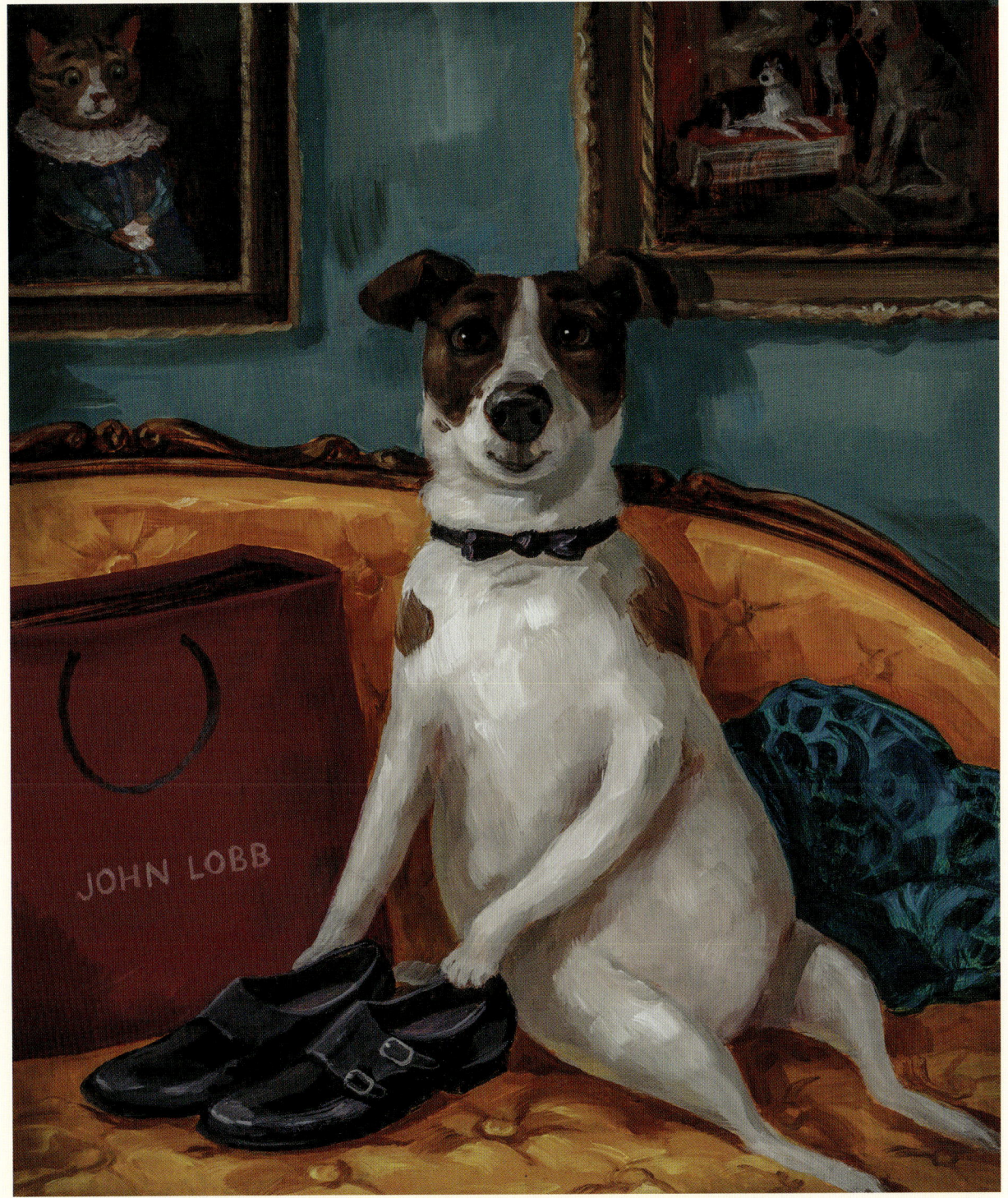

VICTOR | He is a dapper chap

OSCAR | Wilde about these shoes

PAUL
———
Sometimes Pawl

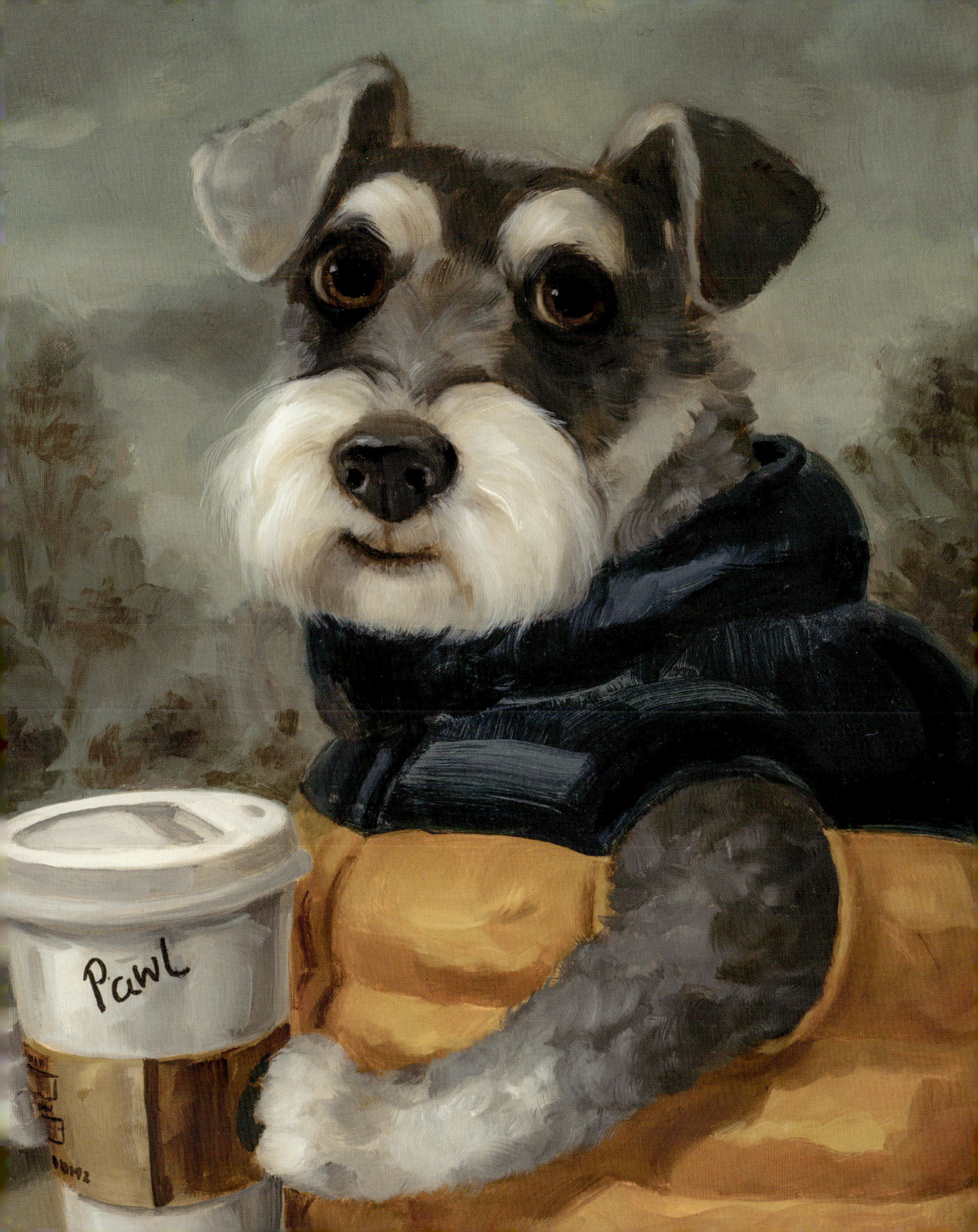

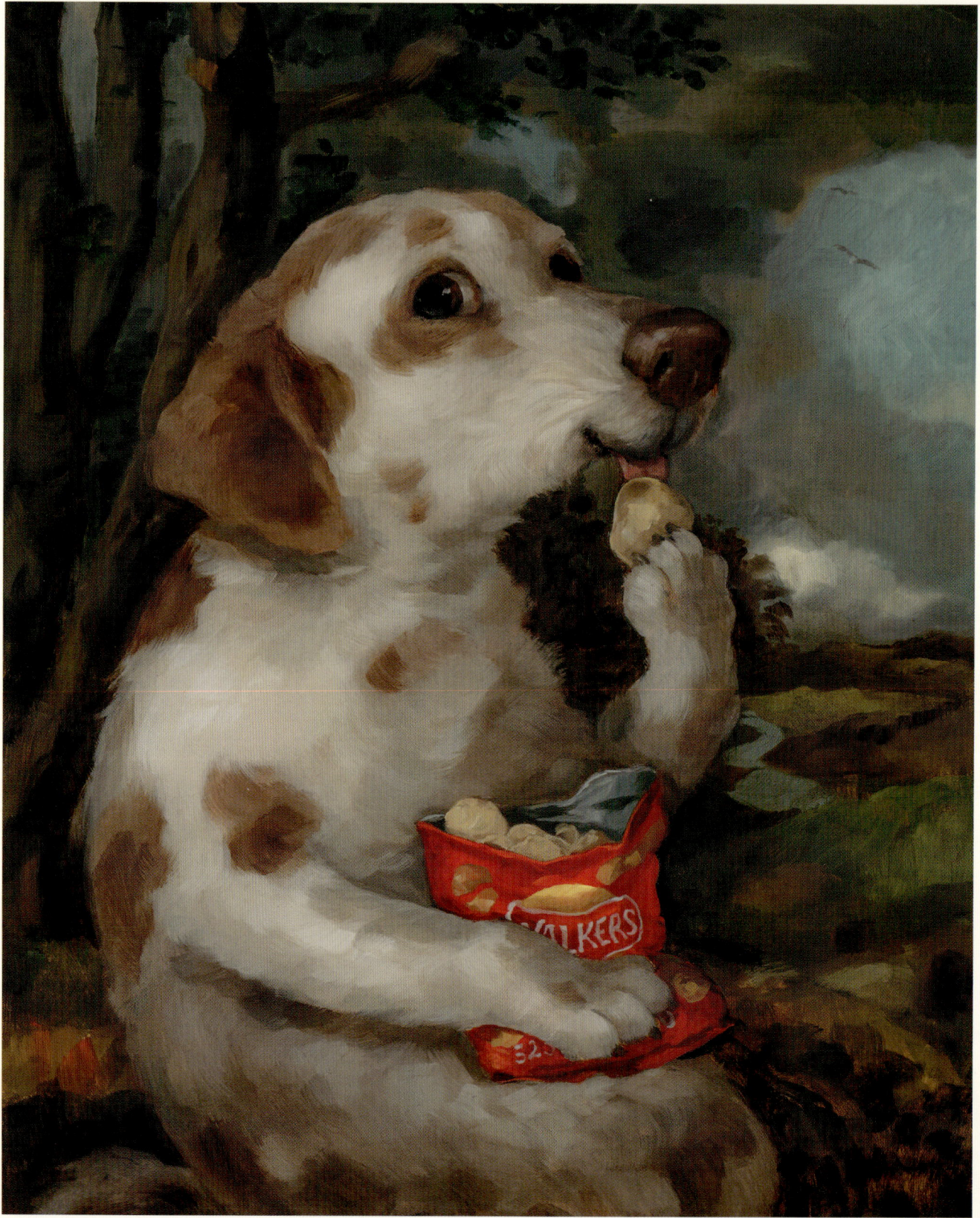

HE FOUND THEM IN A BUSH

It was a full packet too

DOUGLAS MADE A PORTRAIT
OF HIS BEST FRIEND PAUL

Douglas was a sensitive chap. At just three years old he had managed to get himself a whole list of worries: sheep, men with hats, red cars, sparrows, and crisp packets blowing in the wind, to name but a few.

As anyone who has lived with a border collie knows, they have to keep busy. (In Douglas's case, so he wouldn't worry about any of the above.)

Douglas turned his collie mind to other things. His favourite pastime was the Fetch A Sketch. Not easy to operate without thumbs, but he persevered.

Here he is with a very accomplished portrait of his best friend, Paul, also a collie. Douglas only likes other collies.

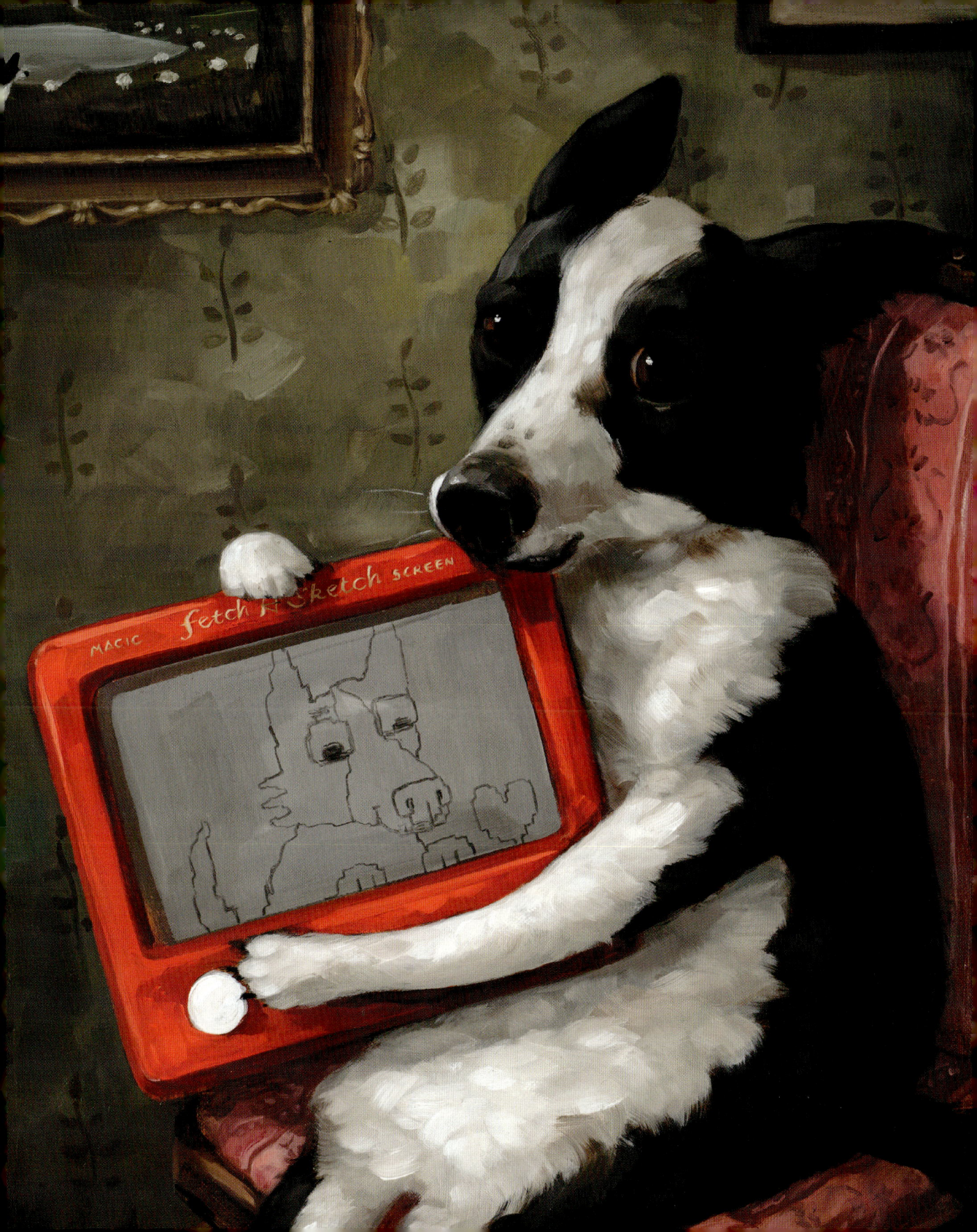

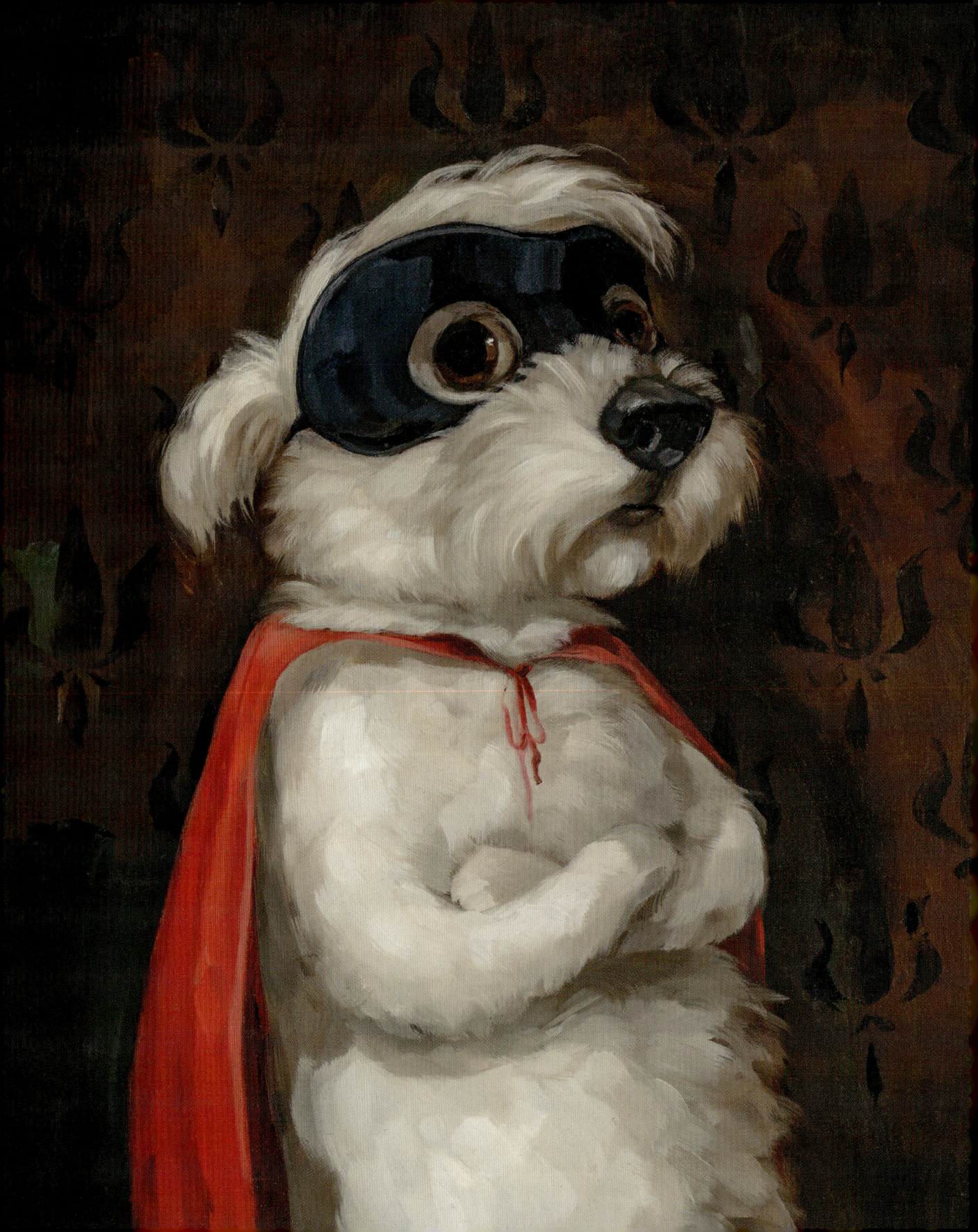

SUPER FRANK

"Being a superhero is a serious
biscuit . . . I mean business"

DACHSHUND IN A CYCLING CAP

He enjoys wearing a cycling cap
as much as he loves the idea of
bicycling . . . the reality is his little
legs won't reach the pedals

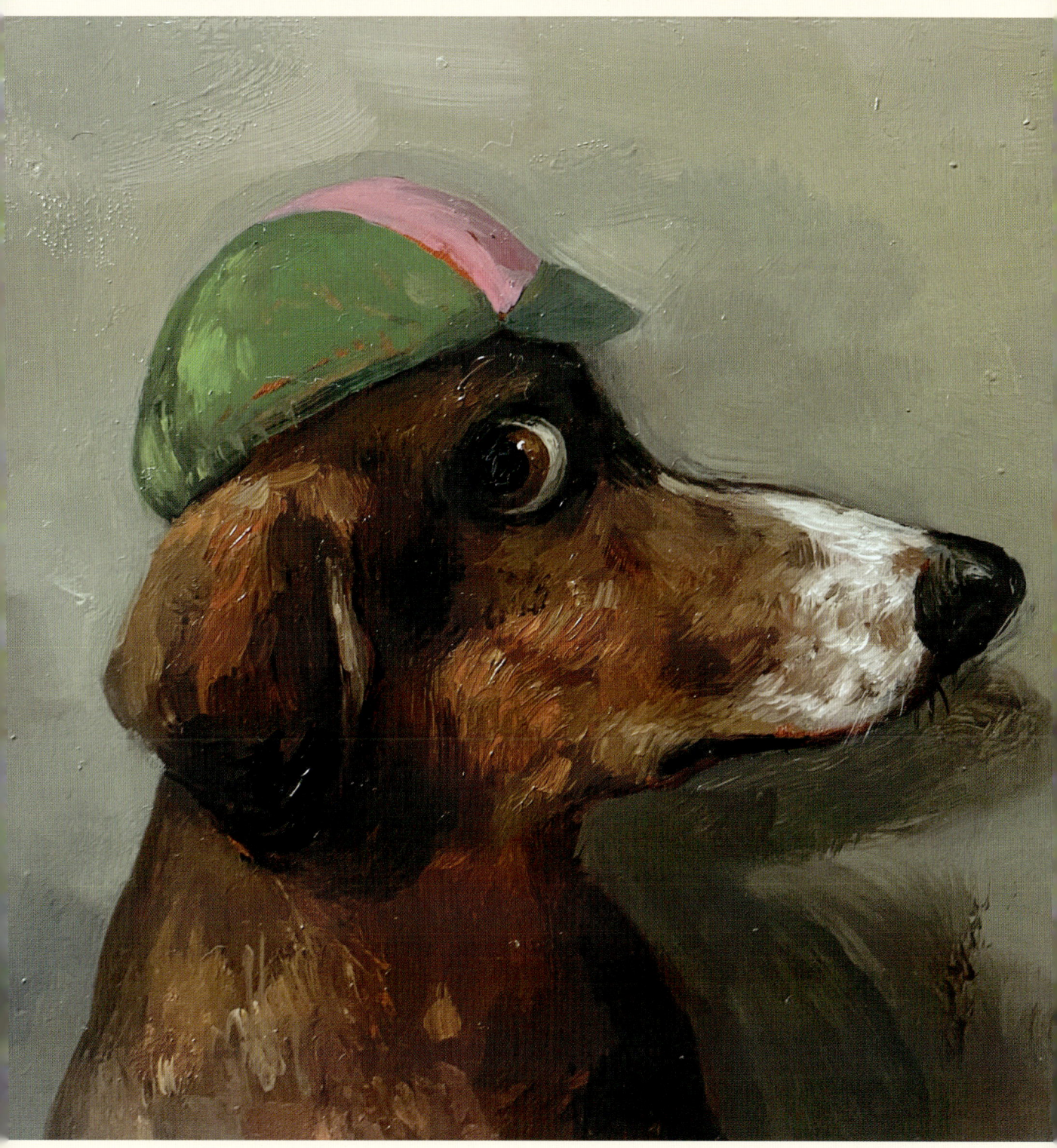

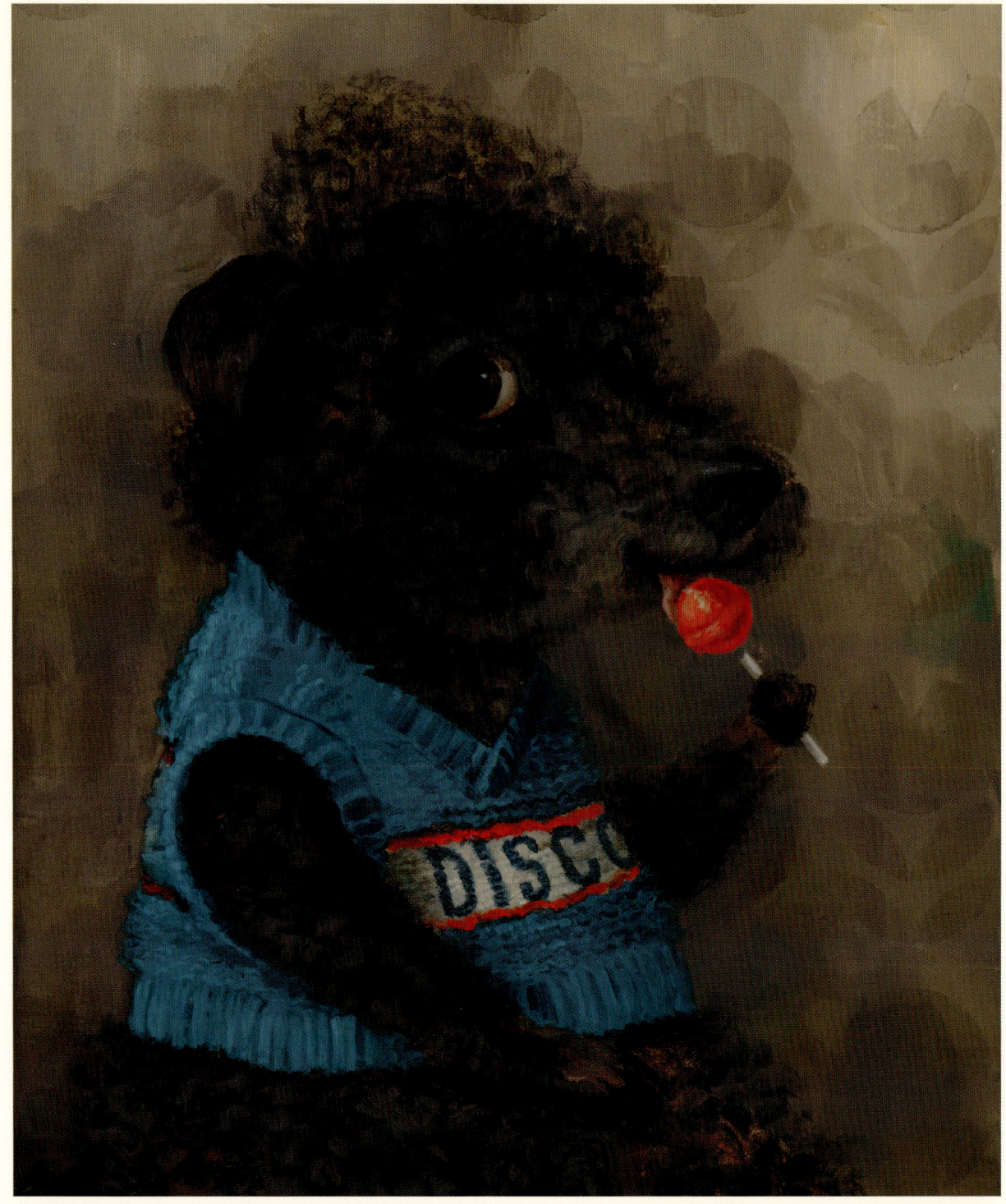

DISCO DAISY | Life is disco and lollipops

CUTE PETE | . . . those eyes!

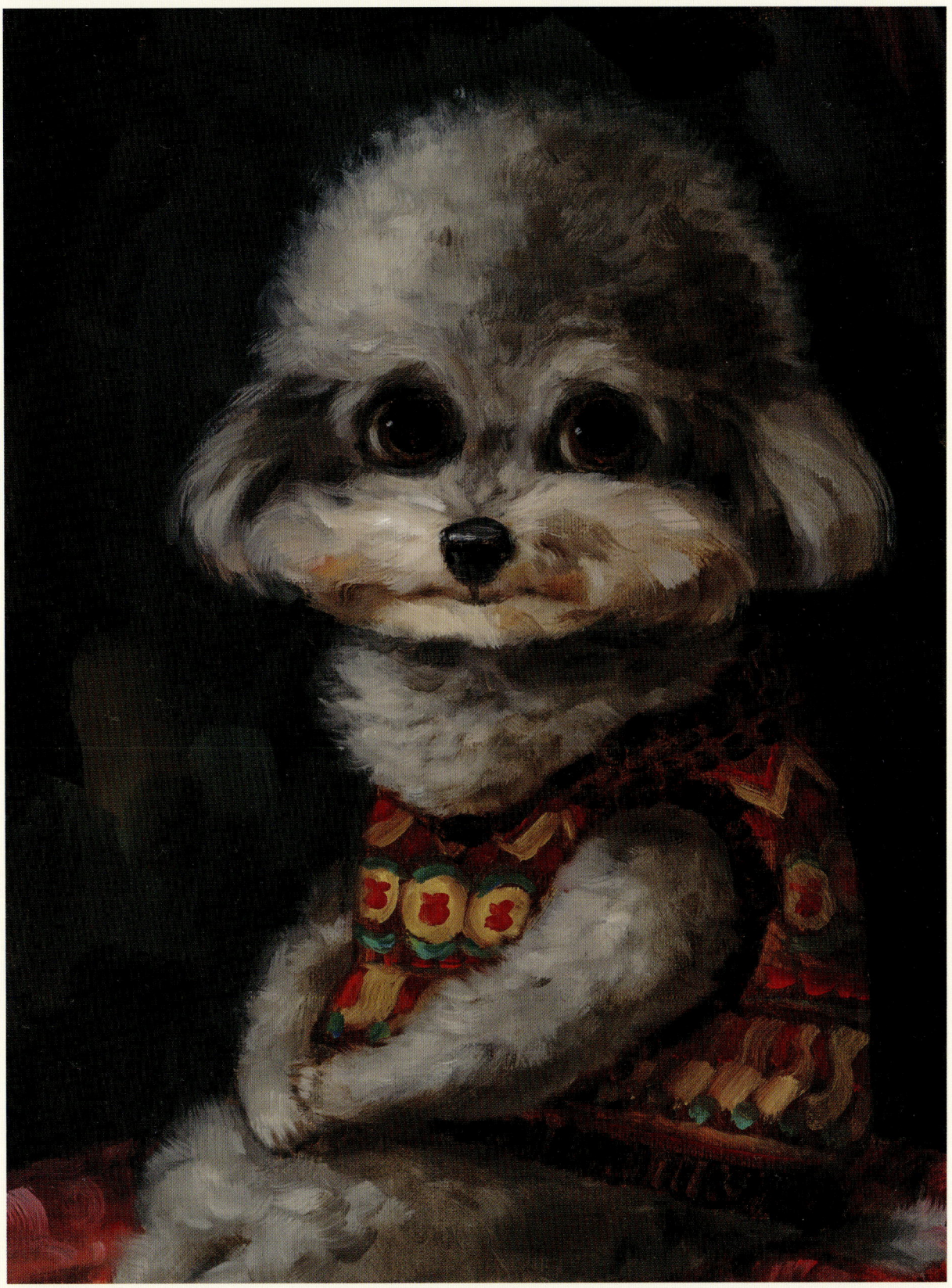

SHE LOVES DOLLY

24 hours a day! Not just 9 to 5

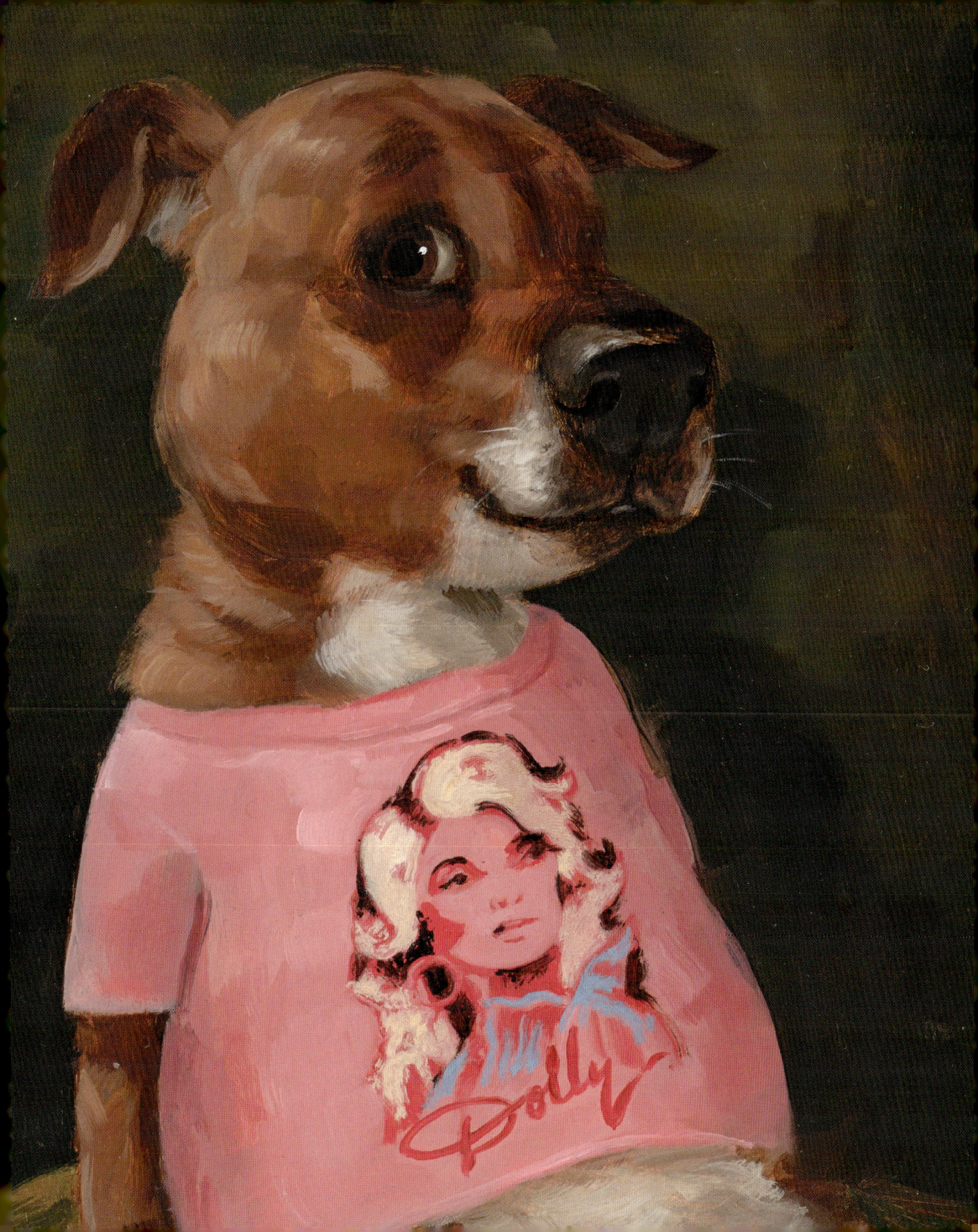

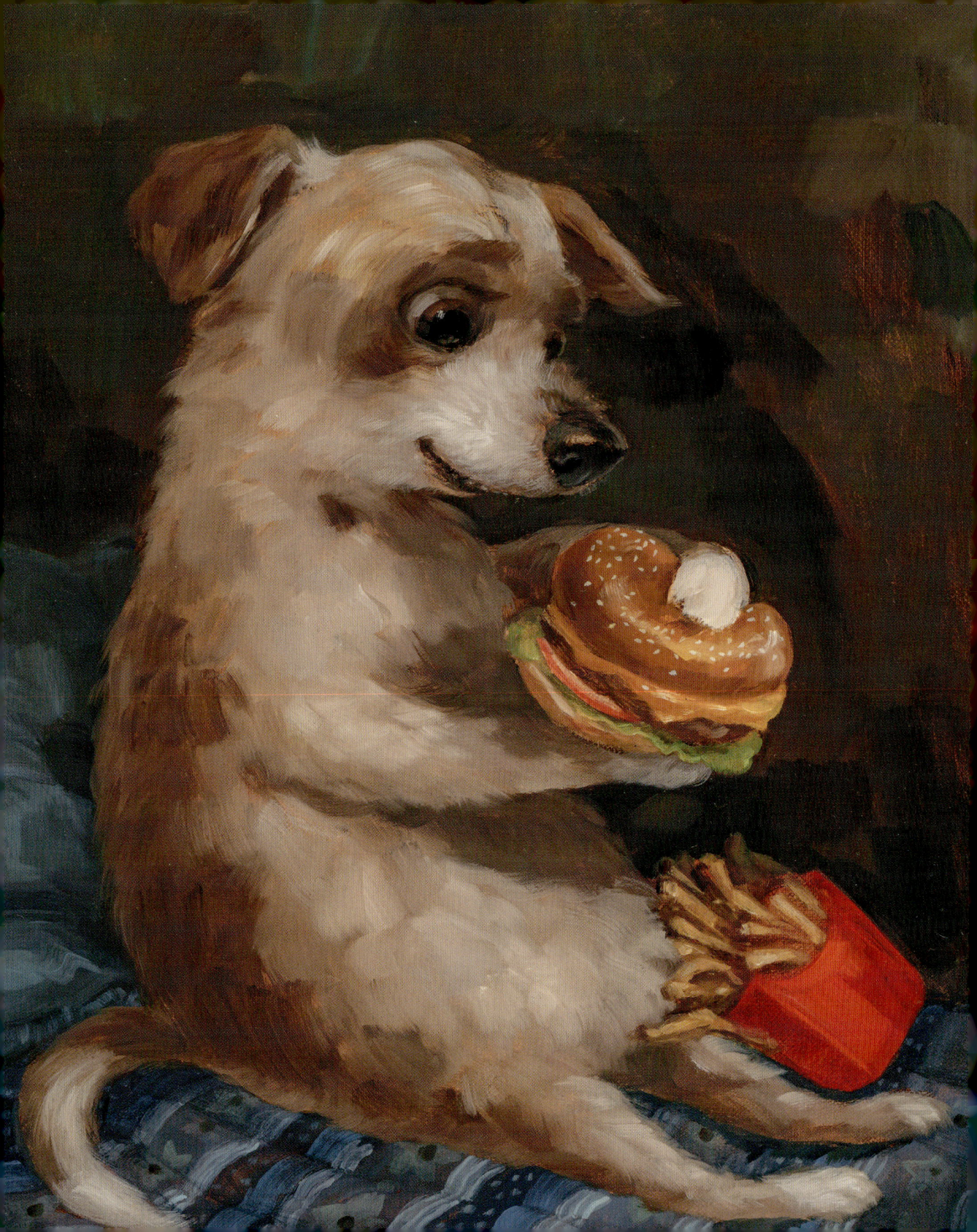

BURGER LOVER

Hold the pickles, please

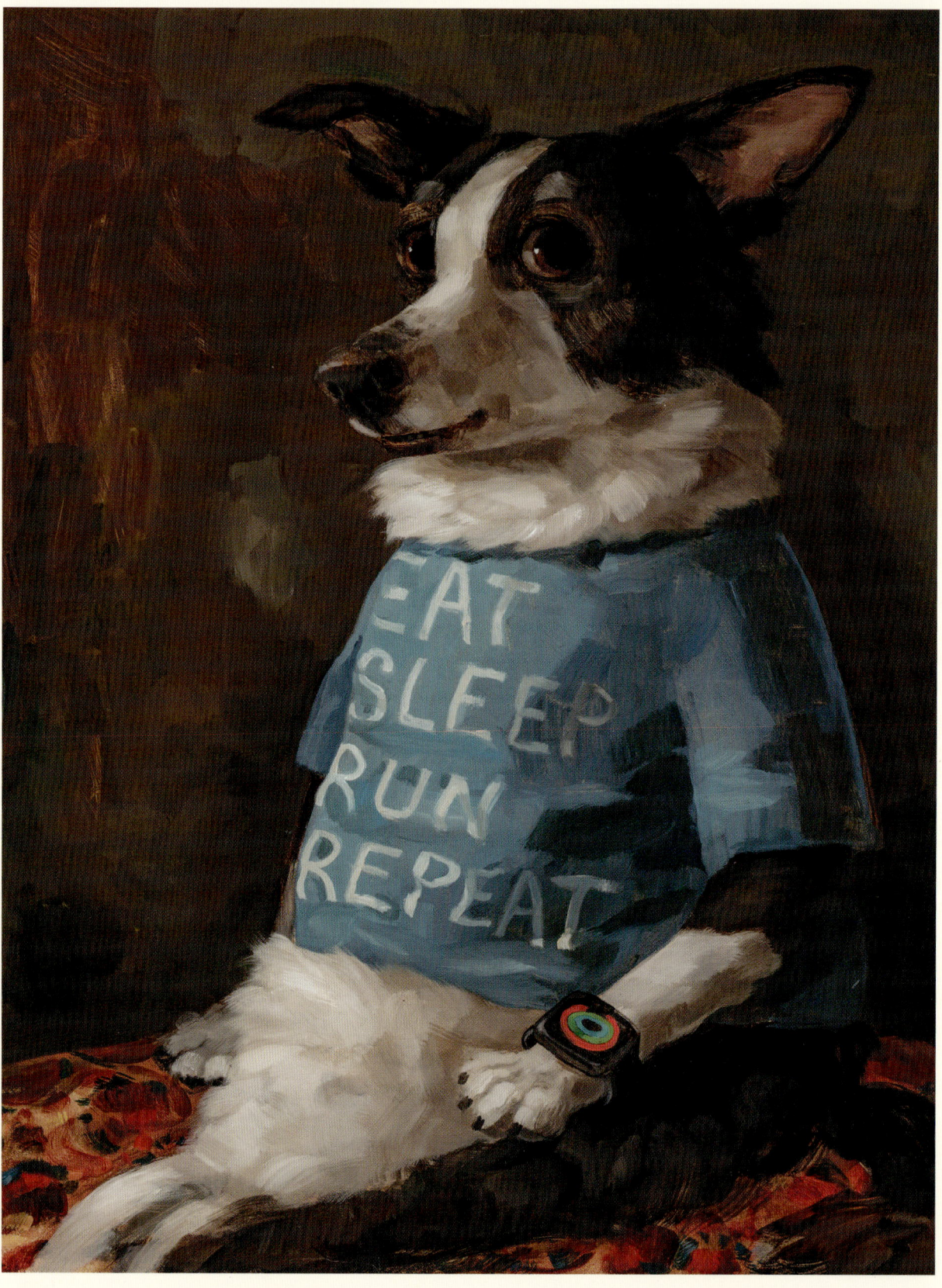

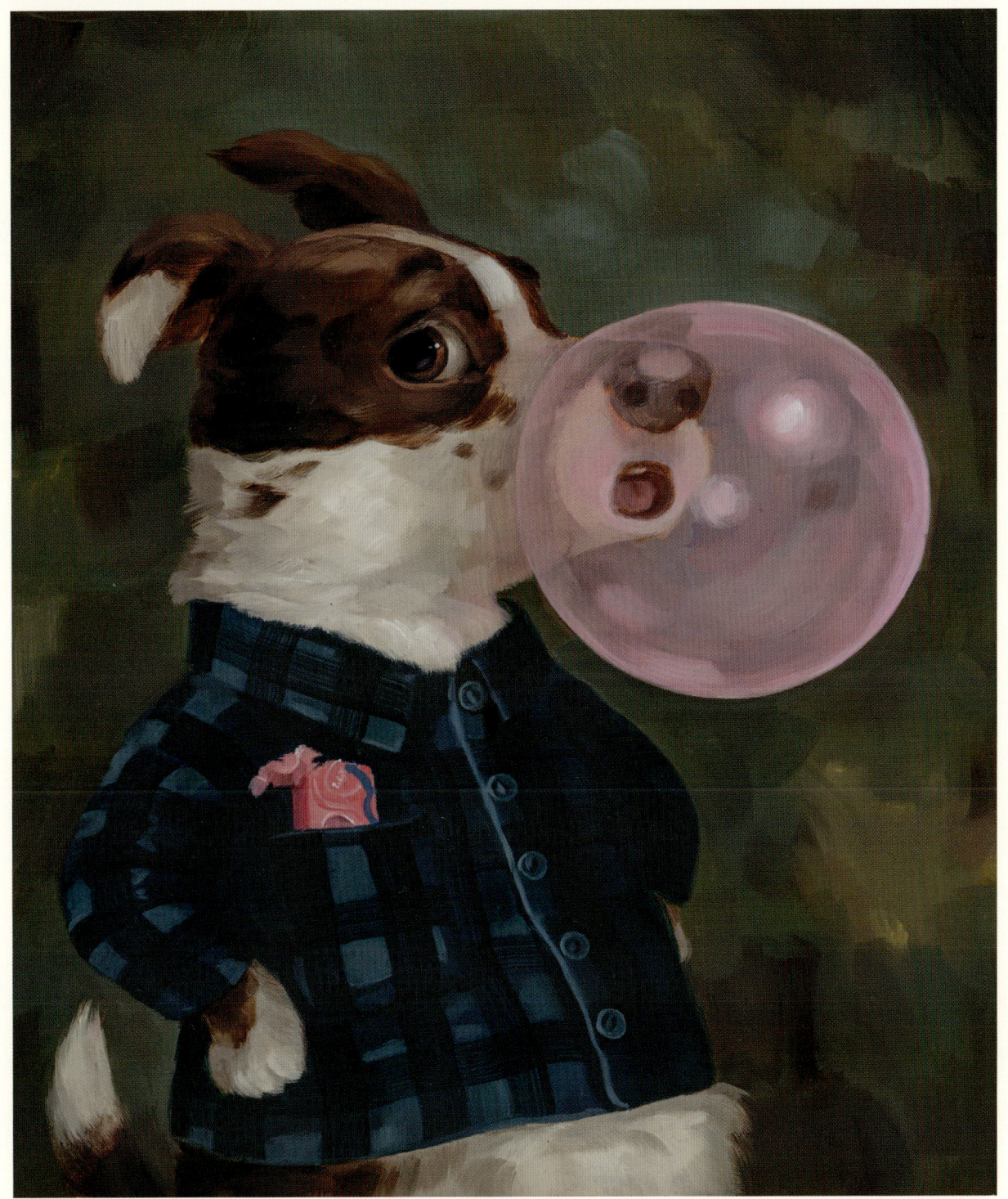

HUBBA BUBBA BUDDY | He was good and he knew it

EAT SLEEP RUN REPEAT |
That's just collie life

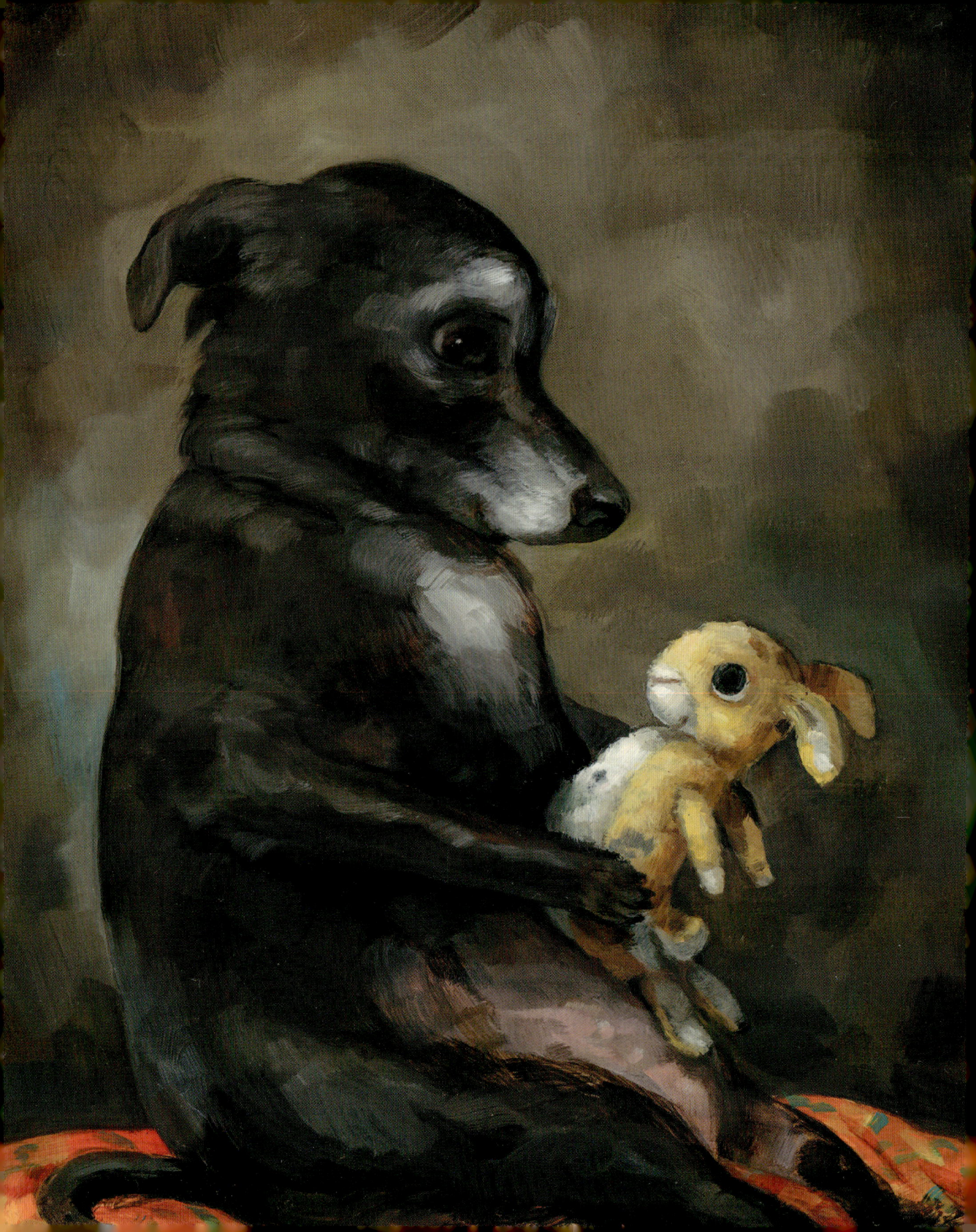

WELL LOVED

Yellow Bunny has always been there.

From the very first day this little dog came home.

Yellow Bunny has never complained at being tossed in
the air, having her legs nibbled, or being drooled on.
She's been up for it all with a smile on her face.

She's always ready for hide-and-seek or a snooze on
her favourite chair—napping is a favourite thing for this
sweet pup to do these days.

Although her colour has faded, Yellow Bunny's spirit
is still bright, the same as it ever was, and she smells
better and better as the years go by.

ACKNOWLEDGEMENTS

I've always dreamed of publishing a book of my work, and in this case, it's a book full of dogs. Each character I paint comes with a little story, and this book is my way of sharing both the animals and the stories that unfold in my imagination. So I hope you'll notice the titles and tales, as they're a big part of what makes this book a true labour of love.

When Artisan reached out, I was over the moon. Publishing a book is no small feat—it takes a group of talented, patient, sharp-eyed people to get everything just right. I had the pleasure of working with a lovely team: professional, passionate, and full of fun, which made the process a joy from start to finish.

A heartfelt thank-you to Zach and Lia for seeing the potential in my paintings and helping bring this beautiful book to life. To the entire team, thank you for your input, edits, and creative fingerprints. Abby, you're a true people-wrangler, and with artists involved, that's practically a superpower. Nancy, thank you for your wise eyes and calm expertise. I'm so grateful you worked on this book before your retirement, and I'll never forget how meeting you led us to a New York City dog park—which turned out to be one of the highlights of the trip. Jane, thank you for your patience and thoughtful design guidance throughout each phase. The collaboration of ideas made this book better than I ever imagined.

A special thanks to my 007 agent, Alina, and to Chessy. Working with you both is the best—the last couple of years have been a whirlwind and so much fun. What a great all-girl team we are! Who knows what's next?

Finally, at home in England, a huge thank-you to my son, Cal, and my partner, Jen.

Cal, you live among all these half-painted characters every day in our tiny apartment, eating your breakfast every morning before school with all those eyes on you. I love our chats and little brainstorming sessions. Your opinion *always* matters to me. As you set off on your own life adventures very soon, I hope you remember the chaos fondly. Love you!

To Jen, my partner in life, partner in paint, and constant cheerleader. Your love and support mean everything. The dedication and hard work you devote to your own art life are constant inspirations to me. I hope all your family know they are getting a book for Christmas!

———

And with that, I can hear the music playing . . . time to wrap it up.

Thank you!

I'll get my coat!